D1796595

Dissertation Discovery Company and University of Florida are dedicated to making scholarly works more discoverable and accessible throughout the world.

This dissertation, "The Structural and Cultural Construction of Race in the Handline Fishing Industry on South Africa's Western Cape Coast" by James F. Gates, was obtained from University of Florida and is being sold with permission from the author. The content of this dissertation has not been altered in any way. We have altered the formatting in order to facilitate the ease of printing and reading of the dissertation.

Cover Image Credit/Copyright Attribution: IIIerlok_Xolms/Shutterstock

For Heather—I wish she were here to share this with us.

ACKNOWLEDGMENTS

I have many to thank and none to blame but myself for the pages that follow. This dissertation would not have been possible without the assistance and support of many great people. First and foremost I am deeply indebted to the fishers in this study for their trust, their patience and their time. I can only pray that I have done their stories justice. Their indulgence was rivaled only by their hospitality. Special thanks go to Jonathan and Gerry for their willingness to tie me into the network of handline ski-boat skippers and the long hours of incessant questioning they endured. My gratitude also goes out to Andy Johnstone for his depth and breadth of knowledge and experience among artisanal fishers. I have the historian Dr. Lance van Sittert, then at the University of Cape Town, to thank for inspiration early in my fieldwork. I also have Dr. Marc Griffiths and the researchers at Marine and Coastal Management to thank for supporting data and their unique perspective on the fishing industry as a whole. Special thanks to Dr. John Sharp, then chair of anthropology at the University of Stellenbosch, for providing support and an exciting academic community.

I owe the greatest debt for any success I may have in the writing of this dissertation to Michelle, my wife. I am humbled by her love, support and careful attention to detail. Editor, lover and friend, she cleared my often fuzzy thoughts, created space in our life for me to write and put bread on the table for most of my graduate career. I could not have done this without my parents, Chuck and Judy Gates; they have been waiting a long time for me to finally get my first "real" job.

I owe my deepest personal and professional gratitude to my advisor, professor Brian M. du Toit. He provided an unequalled depth of experience as an anthropologist and, as a South

African, added significant personal knowledge to my subject. He took far more than a professional interest in my work, nudging carefully when I strayed down fruitless paths and pushing even harder when needed. Even though he never did let me beat him on the tennis court, he went far above the call of duty and took a strong personal interest in me and my family. My heartfelt thanks go out to the other members of my doctoral committee—professors R. Hunt Davis, Anthony Oliver-Smith and Suzanna Smith—for their patience and wisdom in guiding my interests and my writing. My gratitude also belongs to professors Christopher McCarty and H. Russel Bernard without whom much of the network analysis would not have been possible. Professor Charles R. Gailey at Nazarene Theological Seminary deserves my heartfelt thanks for getting me interested in anthropology and for his love and support along the way.

I am deeply indebted to the Pew Charitable Trust and the Pew Younger Scholar's Fellowship committee for their financial and moral support for the research that led to this dissertation. My gratitude also goes out to the University of Florida's Department of Anthropology for their support.

Finally, I thank Charisa and Anthony, my children, for their patience with me during my years of research and writing; I pray that what has been written here will one day help them to understand their world better and inspire them to make it a better place to live.

TABLE OF CONTENTS

LIST OF TABLES

LIST OF FIGURES

Abstract of Dissertation Presented to the Graduate School
of the University of Florida in Partial Fulfillment of the
Requirements for the Degree of Doctor of Philosophy

THE STRUCTURAL AND CULTURAL CONSTRUCTION OF RACE IN
THE HANDLINE FISHING INDUSTRY ON SOUTH AFRICA'S WESTERN CAPE COAST

By

James F. Gates

May 2001

Chair: Professor Brian M. du Toit
Major Department: Anthropology

The primary aim of this dissertation is to describe how race relations are socially constructed and historically situated through an analysis of the relationships between coloured and white fishers in South Africa's handline fishing industry. In-depth interviews with 102 handline ski-boat skippers on the Western Cape coast serve as the core data for this analysis. My primary aim was achieved by interpreting the images skippers use to describe themselves and others, and analyzing of the skippers' perceived social networks. This dissertation moves beyond common political and macro-economic analyses of race relations to in-depth exploration of the ways individuals structure social relations by race in a historically specific context. I show how fishing is embedded in a host of social and informal economic relations. Socioeconomic relations off the boat directly impact social relations on the boat.

"Race" and "ethnicity" are historically specific and socially constructed categories of group differentiation. "Race" and "ethnicity" are compared as analytical tools in the methodological tool chest of social analysts. Specific attention is paid to the role that anthropology played and continues to play in the use of these concepts as analytical categories. I argue that in the South African context, both past and present, race remains the most potent construct of social categorization. Specifically, I sketch the history of the ideology and politics involved in the development of "coloured" as an identifiable group in South Africa. Descriptions of the structural development of this category are balanced by the role of human agency. I review the historical roots of those categorized as coloured, the common stereotypes associated with being coloured, the challenging issue of race mixing, the role that intra-racial politics played and the role that language played in the debate over coloured identity.

Anthropology as a discipline is in danger of being rent in two by the tensions between those who practice it as a scientific enterprise designed to explain human variation and those who practice it as an experience designed to be shared and interpreted. I explore the possibility of a *via media* between the extremes of positivist nomothetic theorizing and the interpretive solipsism of postmodern deconstruction. The verbal images and metaphors skippers use to describe themselves and others reveal deeply rooted racial stereotypes and prejudices. An analysis of these skippers' perceived social networks reveals to what extent these racial stereotypes and prejudices structure perceived interaction.

CHAPTER 1
INTRODUCTION

Reflexive Reflections: A Day in the Life of an Anthropologist

Two-thirty in the morning and I was wide-awake, sitting in my bakkie, waiting for the

men to arrive. It wasn't supposed to be that cold in late January, but I didn't even notice it, much.

I felt conspicuous walking into the little petrol station convenience store dressed like I was. I

looked like the stereotypical "skollie." But who was going to care at that time of the morning? I

remember wondering if the shop attendant and the security guard were suspicious of why I was

there, since they kept looking in my direction while they continued their conversation. I was

dressed in a pair of dirty tekkies, some old sweatpants, two shirts and a warm jersey. They told

me to wear layers. I thought the wool knit cap I borrowed from my neighbor was probably a little

much, but I wanted to at least look the part. I later learned just how much I would need that cap.

I looked over at the white gumboots that were two sizes too big for me and hoped that I wouldn't

be too clumsy in them. The oilskins I borrowed from the same neighbor who lent me the wool

cap were a little snug, but they would have to do. I checked the LCD clock on my dashboard as it

slowly changed shape, letting me know that only one more minute had inched by. It was very

difficult getting up at a time when I normally had not yet gone to bed, but it was time to begin the

most important phase of what I had been preparing for the previous three years, maybe the

previous eight. I had it all planned out, written out, hypothesized, theorized and historicized. I

had attended lectures, helped to organize conferences, presented papers, passed my exams,

begged for funding, defended my ideas and made the long trip to get over there. I spent the

previous couple of months in the libraries, interviewing government officials and academicians,

driving to communities separated by more than 400 km at the extremes, spreading my name

1

around to those who needed to know, driving around with people I knew could introduce me to the right people, making the contacts necessary to get the information I needed. But somehow, as I sat in my bakkie with the engine running, trying not to become impatient, I felt totally unprepared for what I was about to face.

Jonathan told me to meet him sometime around 2:15–2:30 AM at the Engine Garage on the northern edge of the city. He knew that it would be another hour and a half or so to drive the 80 km up the West Coast road to get to Yzerfontein, and he wanted to be one of the first ones in the queue. He said that Charles and Mailie would be riding up with him from the southern suburbs, but that Balie, Talliep and Albert would be finding their own way to the Garage. He wasn't sure if Albert was coming. Albert had only been with him for two weeks, and he mentioned that he didn't know if he was reliable or not. I had wondered the day before why they wouldn't just all ride up there together. I didn't know at the time that the crew lived spread out across so many different parts of the city. Jonathan told me the day before that Albert had to make it there all the way from Khayelitsha, known as the poorest black suburb in Cape Town. He thought we might have to wait on him. As it turned out, Albert stayed overnight with a friend much closer, in Jo Slovo Park. Although I didn't recognize him until Jonathan later introduced us, Albert was the first to arrive. Charles, or "Boertjie," as they called him, lived down south of the City in Muizenberg, a mostly white, middle-class suburb of Cape Town. He rode up with Jonathan and Mailie because he lived close to both of them, and they had arranged to meet down there ahead of time. Balie and Talliep arrived together; they both made their way up from a large, sprawling complex of historically coloured suburbs usually lumped together and identified as Mitchell's Plain.

It was 3 in the morning and still no white bakkie pulling a six-meter ski-boat behind it. I had my cell phone on me, and I knew that Jonathan would be carrying his, as most handline ski-boat skippers did. But I didn't want to call just in case I had gotten the time wrong. After all, we had just spoken the night before. But when 3:30 AM rolled around, my impatience outgrew my sense of tact. I called Jonathan only to find out that some of the guys, he wouldn't say who, had overslept and that he was on his way. If he wanted to go to sea for the day with a full crew, more often than not he had to rouse them.

Jonathan was the skipper. He was the only one among the group that really spoke English at home and with any regularity. Balie, Talliep and Mailie all spoke a variant of Afrikaans that they referred to as "Kaapse Afrikaans." Albert spoke more Afrikaans than English, but neither were one of the three other languages he spoke at home. The rudimentary Zulu I had learned as a kid didn't get me very far, and Albert and I spent the rest of the time speaking in a language that was native to neither of us. I had spent the previous couple of months brushing up on the Afrikaans I had learned while living for most of the 1980s in what was formerly known as the Transvaal. I learned quickly that I spoke what the fishermen termed "suiwer" Afrikaans; they could tell I had learned my Afrikaans in the heart of white, conservative Afrikaans country. No one really minded explaining the colloquialisms that this Yankee didn't understand; after all, most were amazed that someone from the United States could speak Afrikaans at all, let alone with a "boere" accent. They knew that I was the student there to learn from them.

The diversity of Jonathan's crew and the cordial relations between them made me want to believe what I was being told about race relations time and again by skippers in the handline industry. They insisted that there is not, nor has there ever been, any racism at sea. Coloured and white skippers alike would argue that the sea was the great equalizer, that the environment and the hard worked leveled the playing field and created a meritocracy like none experienced elsewhere in South Africa. "A fisherman is a fisherman," they repeated as if recited when they earned their skipper's ticket. But this was my first day to go to sea, and I wasn't quite ready to wrap up my conclusions from what I had heard thus far.

Four o'clock rolled around and everyone had finally arrived. I learned on the ride up the West Coast road that it wasn't unusual to schedule a meeting time with the expectation that no one would really be there until at least forty-five minutes later than scheduled. Fortunately this time, at least, I wasn't on my way to somebody's house for dinner, somebody who expected the same courteous "tardiness." I think my impatience was far more a sign of my excitement than my commitment to punctuality. After all, I was about to go on my first trip out on the ocean to interact with the very people I wanted to get to know over the coming months. I had finally identified a group of fishers that I wanted to interview for my research, and I was on my way to sea with one of them. I was nervous about the uncertainty of it all. I was nervous about how well I would be accepted. I was nervous about how well I would be able to communicate. I was nervous about asking the right questions, about making a good impression, about not sounding as ignorant as I felt. So I decided to be honest with them about my ignorance. After all, they were now my teachers.

We closed the canopy window as four of us crammed into the back of the bakkie with seven pairs of boots, oilskins, lunch bags and fishing tackle baskets. I learned a lot more about the men I was about to fish with on the way to Yzerfontein than I did the rest of the day. I had planned to talk to the guys as much as I could throughout the day. I used the time we had on the ride up to the harbor to share who I was, what I was doing and to get to know some background information about each of them. Little did I know that I would not have much of an opportunity to talk to any of them in any more detail the rest of the day. Much of our personal conversations ceased once we reached the queue of boats at the harbor.

When we arrived at the harbor, I was disoriented. I had never been there in the dark, and there were so many boats and people around that I didn't recognize it. I was initially overwhelmed by the chaos. It was five-thirty in the morning, and it looked like we were at an open-air bazaar. My first instinct was to marvel at how representative the racial demographics of the crowd at the harbor were compared to the country as a whole. I learned later that the power relations as they relate to race were also representative of the country as a whole, but the country of not so long ago.

I was unaware of it at the time, but there was an important reason I was left alone as soon as we arrived at the harbor. Each of the six crewmembers quietly got themselves dressed in clothes very similar to the ones I had borrowed from my neighbor. As soon as they were done getting their raingear on, they dispersed. I didn't see most of them again until we were all getting on the boat when it was our turn to launch from the slipway. I saw Jonathan talking to some of the other skippers but did not realize the importance of those conversations at the time. He called me over and introduced me to some of the other skippers. Come to find out, these were some of the skippers that Jonathan trusted the most and who trusted Jonathan the most. They were sharing information about where they had found fish the day before and what direction they were planning to head for the day. In the last couple of years the skippers had begun to rely on cell phones to make these connections, but this morning Jonathan was using the oldest medium available for this type of communication, a face-to-face conversation. The skippers were able to share exactly where they had found fish the day before; even if they weren't well familiar with the waters around Dassen Island, most of the commercial skippers had invested in a global positioning system (GPS) in the past five years.

The thick fog that had slowed our traveling speed up the West Coast road hung on the water until well after 11 o'clock in the morning. Those boats that had not invested in a GPS had to follow someone who had. Jonathan told me there were plenty of skippers who routinely relied on other boats to show them where the fish were biting. The better skippers called them "holhangers" (lit. those that hang on my ass). If you were dependent on someone else to find your fish, you weren't a very good skipper. I was told that the skippers who regularly worked on the water had strategies for throwing the "holhangers" off their trail. Some would call out coordinates or location on the public Very High Frequency radio (VHF) and then contact their closer colleagues over the cell phone. Some of the skippers admitted to installing scramblers and decoders on their VHF radio prior to the introduction of the cell phones. Catching shoaling fish on the open ocean was a competitive environment, and the right information from the right person gave the skipper the competitive edge.

On the ride out to sea from the slipway I quickly found out why that wool cap was so important and why I was told to bring the extra clothing. The wind on the open sea cut through every piece of clothing I was wearing. I wasn't told this, but I think there was another important reason for the layers of clothing. The ride to and from the island was so rough, so bumpy that any extra padding was more than welcome. As we bounced our way out to the island I gripped onto the wood edging that lined the different "laaitjies" in the boat. Each commercial handline boat was partitioned into cubicles, two for each man who fished on the boat. One of the laaitjies was for standing in, the other for loading fish. It was important that each man have his own laaitjie so as to keep track of each man's catch for the day. As they were all paid on the share system, i.e., for 50% of what they caught for the day, each crewmember wanted to make sure the skipper could verify his particular totals.

The division of labor on the boat started even before we left the Engine Garage back in Cape Town. Jonathan and Boertjie fueled the bakkies and the boat and planned their strategy for the day while the others loaded the bait and the gear onto the boat. This was the first time I was acutely aware of race relations on the boat. I was to find out later that Albert was one of the exceptions among handline crew. Very few of the crew were identified as black. Most were identified as either white or coloured. I wondered why the only white guy on the boat seemed to be the skipper's right hand man. I was later to find out that it is quite odd for any white fishermen to crew for a coloured skipper, particularly a coloured skipper that owned his own boat. Boertjie was Jonathan's right-hand man and had been fishing with him for almost two years. He was twenty-five years-old at the time, had a high school diploma and recently got out of the Navy. Boertjie said he was fishing because he couldn't find work, an ironic statement given his sheer physical output at the time. He claimed that he couldn't find a "real job" because he was now disadvantaged by affirmative action in the new South Africa. Earlier one of the coloured crewmembers from another boat jokingly jabbed at his white colleagues: "Ja, nou's julle die kaffers, en ons die baase" ("Yeah, now you're the Kaffirs, and we're the bosses").

I was constantly aware of my own race and my status as a foreigner and wondered how that would impact how people acted around me or responded to me. I found out later that I had been very fortunate to be introduced to the network of skippers by Jonathan. Jonathan turned out to be my closest and most reliable contact in the network. Jonathan was one of the most well-respected and well-known skippers in the fraternity. He was well connected because he was connected to a number of key persons from each of the main regional subgroups in the network. Jonathan learned early on that I was very interested in asking tough questions about race and its impact on the fishing industry. The fact that Jonathan trusted me meant that I had access to his trusted network. Since he was well connected between both coloured and white skippers, he was able to introduce me to subgroups that would otherwise have been difficult to contact.

The fact that I am white most likely influenced the kind and degree of responses I received from each of the skippers I interviewed. More than a few times the racialized language of the white skippers was so matter-of-fact that it was as if they assumed I understood the way it worked, as if I should understand, as if it was common sense. I'm not sure if the white skippers would have been so unguarded in their racialized language had I not been white and had I not spoken Afrikaans in such a "suiwer" way. I noticed a similar assumption of familiarity when any of the skippers, white or coloured, spoke of the women in their lives. Because I am a man, it was assumed that I understood. Often when I asked them to explain what they meant or how things work, a certain level of impatience was not uncommon. A number of times I was sharply reminded of my race when a coloured skipper would politely pause for a caveat apology after talking about "those whites."

When we finally laid anchor after what seemed like an eternity of pounding on the hull of the boat, I had no idea we were only three soccer fields away from Dassen Island. The fog still masked the area we were fishing. As we laid anchor the men baited their hooks quickly with the sardines from the boxes they opened. Jonathan brought some of the "good stuff" along, the pike, but they wouldn't use it unless the fish weren't biting well. Each of the guys took out the spool with the thickness of gut that they felt would be most appropriate for how the fish were biting that day. Before preparing their lines, each fisher put neoprene tubes, called finger "lappies," over their fingers for protection against cuts from the lines. They each threaded hooks for bait onto two lines, and what they called a "lood" or a stainless steel spinner on a third line. For the rest of the day's fishing each man would tend three lines, baiting and throwing them back as fast as they reeled them in. Jonathan let them know, from the information on his electronic fish-finder, approximately how deep the fish were swimming and each man measured out his own estimation of the fathom depth. Each fisher "guesstimated" a fathom as the length of his own wingspan.

Everyone was quiet on the boat as we were heading out to sea. The noise from the twin 85 h.p. Yamaha outboard motors and the crashing hull made conversation impossible. Of course, feeling the need to hold on for dear life did little to encourage intimate sharing. In fact, the conversation on the boat for the rest of the day shifted away from the personal type of conversation I was able to have on the ride to the harbor. The atmosphere on the boat shifted into a high energy, jovial gear. Balie, the crew who stood closest to me once we started fishing, began singing a risqué song about a woman he longed to be with. Much of the language on the boat was what the skippers would later describe as "inappropriate for female company." Many of them called it "vissermanstaal" (lit. fisherman's language) or simply "vloektaal" (lit. profane language). It was understood that men could talk like that when they were on the water, since rarely did anyone see a woman out on the sea. The language was particularly aggressive when any boat passed within a few boat-lengths of another. Crews took offense when another skipper "charged down" on their fish.

On the way out Jonathan had me stand with him by the console. When we anchored he had me stand in the foremost laaitjie that he said no one else was using. Come to find out I had taken the potential place of another crewmember for the day. Had I not come along for the day,

Jonathan would have picked up an extra crew from the many that were waiting for a "site" on the harbor. At Yzerfontein, in contrast to the slipway at the Cape Town powerboat club, there tended to be a surplus of "paloepas" available for skippers who needed crew. A guy was a "paloepa" when he was seeking a site. A crew that bounced around too often from boat to boat received a bad reputation as a guy with "rubber boots" and would reportedly be less likely to get a site in the long run.

By taking one crew member's spot on the boat I not only took away the income for one of the potential crew on the harbor but I reduced Jonathan's profits in the loss of the absent crew's share. Between the constant activity on the boat, the lack of privacy in the context of a boat full of listeners, the economic cost of an extra, non-fishing body, it turned out that the boat was not the most appropriate place for doing interviews with each of the skippers. After about an hour of taking notes and attempting conversation I decided to try handlining for snoek. I was given a couple of "vingerlappies" and warned against the razor-sharp teeth for which the snoek are famous. Balie, my teacher, would not let me take the first ten snoek off the hook for fear that I would get all cut up. They could tell by my hands that I was not a fisher—that and the fact that I probably left more behind in the water than I took out of it, both in terms of bait and the food that I tried to eat all morning.

I was told you can tell when you are in an area of high snoek concentration when you're being bothered by the seals. The fishermen were constantly cussing at the seals on that day. We remained anchored the whole morning, a decision that turned out to be the right one for that day. By the time we headed back to the harbor we had over 400 snoek on the boat. I had caught 15. The four main schools of snoek that swam under our boat caused a frenzy of activity. Lines got tangled, tempers flared, but never were the hooks out of the water for more than a few seconds. We could see other boats drifting in and out of our range of vision through the fog; they were also catching. It was when the fog lifted sometime soon after 11 AM that I realized just how close we were to the island and how many ski-boats were out chasing a living. We were some 300–400 yards away from the island, and it seemed like you could walk from one boat to the next to reach the shore. I checked the slipway records later on and found out that there were 84 boats that launched from Yzerfontein's single slipway that day. Yzerfontein's record for a single day during the 1999–2000 season was 143 combined recreational and commercial ski-boats.

The ride back to the harbor was smoother than the ride out. We were loaded down with a ton of fish and were plowing our way back to the slipway. We passed a group of penguins, a pair of dolphins and a whale in the distance on our trip back. I was too tired at the time to get excited. Little did I know, but we had a full two hours of work ahead of us.

As Boertjie pulled the boat out of the water, Jonathan polled those on the docks for the going price down at the fish market. By knowing the going price he could make sure he was not underbid. At Yzerfontein the private powerboat club grounds are used for selling the fish and cleaning the boats. Informal hawkers and fish shop owners come from as far as the southernmost suburbs of Cape Town, tipped off by some of the skippers that there has been a good catch of snoek for the day. Fish are sold to the highest bidder willing to take the entire load for that day. Jonathan did the bidding; sometimes the skipper designates one of the crew for that task. Once the fish are sold and offloaded, the crew cleans the boat and the equipment while the skipper finalizes the transaction. We weren't finished cleaning the boat until close to 3 PM.

I arrived home more exhausted than I think I had ever been. I was impressed that these guys would travel all that distance, return home, just to do the same thing the next morning. The fish were biting, and they knew they had to take advantage. There were plenty of times when the fish weren't biting, and they would have to make do. The work was physically demanding. The hours were long and often monotonous. I was determined to explore the relationships that kept these guys going. More than ever I wanted to understand how relationships in the handline fishing industry were structured and constructed. I wanted to understand why race seemed to be so central to the social networks of these roaming handline ski-boat skippers.

Summary of Chapters

Following the Introduction, Chapter 2 outlines the theoretical and disciplinary context for the analysis that follows. "Race" and "ethnicity" are defined as historically specific and socially constructed categories of group differentiation. "Race" and "ethnicity" are compared as analytical tools in the methodological tool chest of social analysts. Specific attention is paid to the role that anthropology as a developing discipline played in the use of these concepts as analytical categories. As an example of the power that these categories have to influence society, I proceed with a discussion of the difference between Competitive and Paternalistic Race Relations. Chapter 2 continues by placing this study in the context of economic anthropology. I particularly focus on the role that anthropology has played in the understanding of economic activity as embedded in social context. The chapter ends with a review of the recent literature on social relations in maritime communities.

Chapter 3 discusses the methodological concerns at the heart of this dissertation, beginning with a discussion of the historical development of methodology in anthropology. This chapter explores the possibility of a *via media* between the extremes of positivist nomothetic theorizing and the interpretive solipsism of postmodern deconstruction. I analyze the strengths and weaknesses inherent in various approaches and make a case for selective use of methods from various camps. The chapter continues by outlining the major research questions to be explored and hypotheses to be tested. Specific detail is given on social network analysis and its use in understanding the construction of race among commercial handline fishers in South Africa. Informant selection, data collection and the structured interview used are discussed in detail.

Chapter 4 is an historical analysis of the ideology and politics involved in the development of coloured as an identifiable group in South Africa. Descriptions of the structural development of this category are balanced by the role of human agency. I specifically focus on the development of racial identity in the context of political oppression. I review the historical roots of those categorized as coloured, the common stereotypes associated with being coloured, the challenging issue of race mixing, and the role that internal politics played in the construction of modern coloured identity. The chapter concludes with a look at Afrikaans as a central part of the debate over coloured identity.

Chapter 5 builds on the foundational assumption that race, class and gender are socially constructed categories that influence thought and behavior in historically and culturally specific ways. This chapter explores how the issues of race, class and gender merge in the construction of the "Cape Coloured fisherman." The influence of race and class in South Africa's fishing industry provides the socioeconomic and political context for this construction. An analysis of how handline fishermen construct the "true fisherman" and the "myth of the colour-blind fisher" show how race, class and gender are woven into the fabric of human experience. An ethnographic description of a fishers' protest march on parliament provides a transition to the important discussion of the construction of gender in South Africa's handline fishing industry. A general discussion on gender relations in fishing precedes an analysis of gender in the patterning of the social networks and perceptions of skippers on the handline ski-boats.

Chapter 6 provides the historical and socio-economic context for handline fishing. After a brief introduction to the modern South African fishing industry, I trace a selected history of events important to understanding the modern handline industry. This historical sketch begins with what is known of fishing in South Africa prior to 1652, proceeds through its lack of development during Dutch settlement, the easing of restrictions on fishing with British colonization and the birth of the modern industrial fisheries in the early decades of the twentieth century. The sketch continues with post-World War II developments and the beginnings of the apartheid era as they marked the significant beginnings of the ski-boat industry. An analysis of recent developments in the management of South African fisheries provides the political context in which handline fishers operate. The chapter ends with a discussion of the limitations of the historical sources available for the handline fishing industry.

Chapter 7 is an ethnographic description of the roaming commercial handline ski-boat fishers on South Africa's Western Cape coast. Following a brief introduction, an analysis of their personal histories provides a sense of who these skippers are and what brought them to the handline industry. The mobility of the roaming handline ski-boat fishermen is discussed with a focus on how this mobility influences the skipper's sense of place. The second half of the chapter deals with handline fishing as embedded in informal economic relations. Variations in the technology of handline fishing and the fish sought after are described in socioeconomic context. The chapter continues with an analysis of the important socioeconomic relations off the boat that directly affect social relations on the boat. The chapter concludes with a description of the influence that government fisheries management has on the linefishers.

Chapter 8 deals with the impact of race on the social networks of handline fishing skippers. The theory behind social network analysis as structural analysis is applied to the case of the roaming handline ski-boat skippers. Both global and ego-network representations are explored. Specific attention is given to the cliques that emerged and reasons for the centrality of particular individuals in the group. The chapter concludes with an analysis of race and the structure of ego networks. Chapter 9 consists of concluding remarks that point to the future potential of this research.

CHAPTER 2
THEORETICAL EXPLORATIONS

Race and Ethnicity as Tools for Constructing the Other

Anthropology and the Construction of Race and Ethnicity

Prior to the twentieth century many terms for the categorical variation among humans were conflated. Race, ethnic group, nation, culture and people were commonly used interchangeably as meta-categorical labels on human difference. Even though the term ethnic has been traced at least back to Victorian England, the term ethnicity did not make it into English dictionaries until the 1950s (Hutchinson and Smith 1996). Well into the twenty-first century, race and ethnicity have often been used as synonymous labels to distinguish between the broadest possible categories of human variation. A historical glimpse of how race and ethnicity came to label these categories provides the broadest base possible from which to understand race and ethnicity as tools in the construction of reality. Understanding the historical variations in the use of the concept helps to understand the many permutations of the concept read in contemporary literature. As Karl Mannheim said (1936), all ideas have an address. Knowing the address of concepts as broad and diversely used as "race" and "ethnicity" helps provide a roadmap for their future use.

While ancient conceptions of human difference were not labeled "race" or "ethnicity," the sense of kinship, group solidarity and common culture that these terms refer to is older than the written record. Historians place the development of ethnicity in the context of urbanization, nomadic conquest and enslavement, long-distance trade, endemic disease and the need to replenish urban labor forces. Long distance trade, for example, led to permanent communities of aliens in major urban centers. "These trade and skill diasporas, like ancient slavery, attained legal definition from very early times, as the rights of merchants prescribed by the laws of Hammurabi show" (McNeill 1996:107).

The rise of universal religions also played a homogenizing role in macro-group formation.

> Beginning about 500 B.C., the rise of portable and universal religions—i.e., Buddhism, Judaism, Christianity, and Islam together with some less successful faiths like Manicheanism—provided an effective cultural carapace for trade diasporas, insulating them from their surroundings in matters of faith and family as never before. Portable and universal faiths, in fact, permitted followers of a religion that differed from that prevailing in the environing society to maintain a corporate identity indefinitely, generation after generation. (McNeill 1996:107–108)

Territory, religion and language heavily influenced group identity further away from the Middle Eastern center of Western civilization. In the far east, for example, the development of relatively homogeneous people groups varied. While the relative homogeneity of Japanese ethnic identity tended to be established from the beginning of the written record, China did not exhibit a similar isolation. Except for the ancient gulf between the Ainu and other residents of the Islands of the Rising Sun, "whatever ethnic diversity initially existed among those ancestors disappeared before the historic records begin" (McNeill 1996:108). While there was a sense in which Chinese civilization maintained a greater cohesion than was true of European, western Asian and Indian civilizations, the imperial aspiration of the Han dynasty, for example, ensured contact with groups that are familiar to Westerners as Turks, Tibetans, Mongols, Manchus and Koreans.

Modern notions of ethnicity have their most immediate roots in the rise of the nation state. John Armstrong emphasized the essential distinction between sharp identities maintained for centuries and those that have developed as a result of the more recent diffusion of nationalist ideology (Armstrong 1996). He highlighted the development of ethnic diasporas. Jews and Armenians are particularly well-known examples of relatively homogenous communities who have settled in trading enclaves after being forced to leave their homelands for economic or political reasons. Decentralized religious organizations, sacral language, myths, texts and liturgies played an important part in socialization for these groups. "The intensity of identity produced by older sacral myths—based on but not always coextensive with distinctive religions—has never been exceeded by modern secular myths" (Armstrong 1996:121).

The term "*ethnos*" comes from the ancient Greek term for distinguishing separate people groups, particularly those who were not Hellenic. At the time Herodotus was writing, while the Greek peninsula and the islands surrounding it were solidly Greek in identity, there were small communities tied deeply to that identity scattered throughout Asia minor, Sicily and the alien worlds of geographically proximate foreign powers. Except when forced to do otherwise by foreign powers, each of these scattered communities had their own government, coinage, calendar and laws, and its own temples and cult, most often tied to the traditions of the Hellenic state. Greeks living in the heartland or in the periphery had a common label for all other peoples: *barbaroi*. Calling other groups barbarians "was a clear signal of the qualitative differentiation, commonly but not always with a pejorative implication" (Finley 1996:112). *Ethnos* was a term used to distinguish between the various politically organized *barbaroi*.

Through the Middle Ages right down to the late eighteenth century, educated Europeans accepted without question that the universe was organized as a Great Chain of Being. This meant that everything in the universe, including people groups, was organized into an immense number of hierarchical links, beginning with the most insignificant and rising to divine perfection itself. The notion of the Great Chain of Being shines through in Dante's <u>Divine Comedy</u> as a general moral hierarchy and was applied to all aspects of life, including the classification of nations. Belief in the Great Chain of Being lead in part to the hierarchical and paternalistic world of the Elizabethan England as revealed in Shakespeare's <u>MacBeth</u>. It was only the power of the scientific revolution in the methodology and discoveries of Bacon, Galileo and Newton and the dualistic and/or materialistic philosophies of Descartes, Locke and Hobbes that brought about the eventual collapse of this hierarchical metaphysical outlook

Corrosion in the concept of the Great Chain of Being did not necessarily lead to the evaporation of hierarchical thinking. New ways to conceptualize difference were developed in modernity that looked strangely like the old, except this time it was the canons of science rather than the canons of the church that dictated reality. With the new scientific paradigm,[1] conceptions of human difference in language and customs were tied to the idea of human progress. People groups would still be ranked with European cultures as the ideal.

With the rise of the social sciences and other sub-categories of the academy in the nineteenth century, classification systems and nomenclature became more specific, more precise. But the early ancestors of anthropology themselves did not make a careful distinction between race and ethnicity when describing general categories of human variation. We see, for example, in L. H. Morgan's Ancient Society (1871) a ranking of human cultures (with his own at the top, of course) but no explicit discussion of the relationship between race and ethnicity. Herbert Spencer's social evolutionary approach in the late nineteenth century conflated biological and cultural variation, applying Darwin's models of biological selection to cultural variation. Early physical anthropologists like Hrdlicke promoted the classification and ranking of people groups based on phenotypic differences. At the beginning of the twentieth century, social anthropologists studying South Africa were categorizing and ranking groups based on physical types. The San, for example, were ranked low on the evolutionary scale because of their "pedomorphic" facial features and protruding "steatopygia" (see Saul Dubow's Illicit Union: Scientific Racism in South Africa (1995)).

The earliest discussions about the relationship between race and ethnicity centered around the relationship between the cultural and the biological aspects of human variation. In the early part of the twentieth century, Boas challenged the association between biology and culture, pointing to the need to understand individual cultures in their respective historical contexts. One of Boas' main concerns was to address the overt racism inherent in much of the social analysis of his contemporaries. Although he was largely successful in pulling the anthropological community in his direction, he, too, did not carefully distinguish between ethnicity and race as analytical categories. This is particularly surprising as one of his contemporaries, whom he heard lecture and whose writing can be seen reflected in Boas' own, was perhaps the most explicit about race as the central marker of difference. In 1903 W.E.B. Du Bois prophetically claimed that the color line would be the problem of the twentieth century. A phrase like "color line" clearly expresses an understanding that phenotype is somehow involved as the major marker of difference, but it does not tell us how nor to what extent.

At the end of the second World War the analysis of race had escalated as a politically charged issue. The horrors resulting from the racial categorization of the Nazi eugenicists convinced social scientists to shy away from racial theorization. In 1941 a prominent Harvard anthropologist, Ashley Montagu, published a work that later typified anthropological dogma for more than half a century. In Race: Man's Most Dangerous Myth (1974) Montagu successfully argues against the necessary link between the biological and the cultural, with specific critique directed against biological determinism. It was his leadership that led to a post-war UNESCO statement arguing for the use of "ethnic group" as a concept more heuristic for analysis than race. For the researchers of the time, ethnic group carried less historical baggage and could be used to discuss cultural variation without specific reference to phenotype.

For political conservatives, as Manning Marable has pointed out in his discussions of affirmative action, a shift toward the language of ethnicity and, consequently, the removal of the language of race as a key component in understanding social inequity allowed for the conversation to shift away from the historical connection between race and oppression (1996). He believes that this shift was in part responsible for the current attack on race-based affirmative action in the US because of how it shifted the focus from compensation for historical wrongs to an emphasis on diversity for diversity's sake. Many more groups could now be the beneficiaries of a set of programs originally intended to primarily benefit racially oppressed groups. William Darity's work clearly shows that, even with the affirmative action programs of the last thirty years in the US, African-Americans in general have still not been given a level playing field. South Africans have only just begun to struggle with the need to address reparations and the appropriate mechanisms to carry out such justice.

Anthropologists who did not want to see discussions of biological variation pushed to the margins of anthropological discourse began using the fluid concepts of genetic variation, preferring to speak of clines and probability estimates rather than static categories. They were beginning to build on work done by the human biologists that confirmed that there was more variation within than between generally defined "racial" groups.

In her Annual Review of Anthropology article on the status of race as a category of analysis in anthropology, Faye Harrison (1995) argues that most anthropologists from the mid-twentieth century on moved to a "no-race" policy. This was effectively, a "no discussion of race" policy. What was helpful in this period was the growth of the sophistication of research on the social construction of human categories of variation under the auspices of "ethnic studies." What was not helpful, as confirmed by Mukhopadhyay and Moses (1997) and the authors in the February 1999 issue of the *American Anthropologist*, is that the singular focus on ethnicity-based principles of classification and organization could not adequately explain the persistent power of racism and its impact on those affected by it. Their work gives evidence of the dangerous decline in the usage of race as a valuable concept in anthropological textbooks and other works. To ignore race as an important marker of social difference is to deny the experience of those most oppressed by it.

Many current works have moved beyond the identification of race with biological or phenotypic types to a social-constructionist perspective. Gregory and Sanjek's (1994) work explores race as a socially constructed and contested domain. Gert Oostindie and colleagues built on Harry Hoetink's concept of racial distance in describing racial and ethnic relations in the Caribbean, describing a continuum of racial experiences (Oostindie and Hoetink 1996). Kevin Yelvington (1993; 1998) shows the complex relationship between race, class and gender, particularly for working women in Trinidad. Edmund Gordon (1998) shows how confusing the analytical differences between race and ethnicity can become, using the Creoles of Nicaragua as examples. The evidence from each of these works shows that to ignore race, to ignore blackness, for example, or even shades of blackness, is to ignore the core identity for the groups studied. To ignore race is to ignore the historical experiences of those most affected by race as an organizing principle.

As David Roediger (1991), Noel Ignatiev (1995), Karen Brodkin (1998) and Ruth Frankenberg (1993) have shown us recently, it is just as important to historicize the construction of what it means to be white. If George Fredrickson (1981, 1995) is correct, and I think he is, South Africa's current racial categories must be understood in the politicized light of the struggle between white supremacy and black liberation. In discussing coloured identity in South Africa it is then that much more important to understand the categories against which colouredness is being contrasted.

In describing the racial and ethnic relations in Colombia, Peter Wade tells us of the pressure for *blanquemiento* (whitening) in a culture that promotes itself as a country of *mestizos* (mixed race) (1995). Wade's work also shows the danger of excluding race in our understanding of social differance. In this case the dominant acceptance of mixed race as the ideal has marginalized those stereotyped as the bottom of the scale, i.e., black Colombians. He shows that, while there is variation in the experiences of black Columbians of different classes, the ladder of social mobility is more difficult to climb because of their race.

In her study of Cape Verdean immigrants to the US, Marilyn Halter shows just how complex the relationship between race and ethnicity can get. She chooses the term racial-ethnic group to describe a people who do not fit neatly into the prevailing definitions. In Between Race and Ethnicity (1993) she shows how difficult it has been for some Cape Verdean immigrants to be incorporated into the dichotomous black-white category of US racial thinking. Unfortunately, her new term leaves us with no less opaque a concept for analytical purposes.

In exploring systems and structures of social inequality in South Africa, the dominant contemporary tendency is to substitute the language of ethnicity for any discussion of race. Racial rhetoric is so politically sensitive in South Africa that most have simply avoided its use. In a recent study done on the identity of those historically called Coloured, Brigit Pickel (1997)[2] avoided any discussion whatsoever of race in either her historical or theoretical analysis. However, she implicitly incorporates apartheid racial (not ethnic) categories in her questionnaires and analysis. While the language of ethnicity may be more politically acceptable, it is less than historically accurate. The dominant categories of human variation in South Africa remain predominantly racially constructed.

Currently, there is much debate over the use of the term coloured as a designation for any particular group of people in South Africa (Adhikari 1994, Pickel 1997, Morris 1992, James and Caliguire 1996, Du Pre 1994). The well-known anthropologist Micheal Whisson (1971) was arguing in the early 1970s that coloureds do not even constitute a group but a residual category of persons whose sole common feature is negatively defined. Despite the analytical and political problems with this category, its common use in government statistics, the press, television, radio and private conversations reveals its persistence as a marker of difference. With this in mind, I have chosen to retained the term "coloured" as a referent to a heterogeneous and ill-defined group of South Africans whose experiences differ significantly from other South Africans. Even though there may be more intra-category than inter-category variation, to say that all citizens should simply be called South Africans is to deny the historically peculiar situations people of various sub-groups have experienced and continue to experience. Particularly in the rural fishing communities of the Western Cape coast, the ascription of coloured identity, both by self and other, is common. Not only is it common, but for many it is assumed to be natural. I use coloured here with a lower case "c" to distance myself from the politically ascriptive use of "Coloured" under apartheid[3]. I retain the South African spelling to distinguish between this group in South Africa and a large body of literature on the "people of color" in the US and other parts of the world. In short, I see coloured as primarily a racial referent with ethnic subdivisions.

Broad categories of human variation, like race, ethnicity, class and gender function best when understood as historically conditioned, culturally contextualized categories. As descriptive categories they are always open to change, dependent on the historical variation of the groups under discussion. For those who want to use these categories for describing the causes of present or past behavior or as prescriptive tools for predicting future behavior, they must consider the variations in all of the dimensions that these broad categories encompass. Given that diversity exists and that named groups exist, the focus should shift beyond a debate over the labeling of such difference to exploring the content of such difference. To such an end, any useful definition of race as a marker of social difference should be broken down into at least the following dimensions: 1) what is the historical depth under consideration, 2) what is the spatial scope of the distinctions, 3) how discrete need the variables be before we can consider one group different from another, 4) for how long does a group have to exist before it can legitimately be called a racial, 5) how much movement is there of people between the categories, 6) is it possible to avoid evaluating one group as superior or inferior if such a classification is made, 7) what are the relations of power implied by the distinctions being made and 8) is there more variation between or within the defined categories?

Competitive Versus Paternalistic Race Relations

"Race" has always been used as a characteristic in the competition between "us" and "them." Although Du Bois is correct in prophetically stating in 1903 that the color line is *the* problem of the twentieth century, the color line has divided societies since the beginning of recorded history. St. Claire Drake's work has shown how race has been an organizing principle for societies throughout history, from the Babylonian, Syrian, Persian and Egyptian empires, through the Greek and Roman empires into the middle ages and beyond (1987). A keen example of how race was used to justify oppression in the Middle Ages is found with the Christian Crusades at the turn of the first millennium. Although popularly justified as acts of religious conversion, the history records have shown that political and economic dominance was at the core of what motivated the crusades (Latourette 1975). Racial ideology was an integral part of the crusader's rallying cry: "Death to the Moors," a common battle cry. The conception of difference was specifically associated with phenotypic distinctions.

Pierre van den Berghe (1978) has spoken of a transition between what he calls paternalistic systems of race relations to competitive systems of race relations. A system of paternalistic race relations exists when one socially defined racial group positions themselves as somehow superior to other socially defined racial groups. The group that perceives themselves as superior uses race as a primary characteristic to define who the "other" group is. Attitudes do not become a system until they have been fleshed out in ideological and material constructs in defense of prevailing racial attitudes. While race was an integral part of the way people constructed the world prior to the middle ages, the best example we have where race relations were paternalistically systematized is the advent of European colonialism.

The transition van den Berghe refers to between paternalistic and competitive systems is a relatively recent transition. It is not until the twentieth century that race relations have been, in the majority of cases, anything but paternalistic. Paternalism, the way van den Berghe and other contemporary writers use the term, intensifies and is systematized in context of European modernization and expansionist rhetoric. A paternalistic system of race relations grew out of the combination of Western confidence in the idea of progress and the imperial (colonial) expansion into new worlds. If Cartesian doubt can be credited with starting the era of modern scientific thought, then Newtonian physics must be credited with providing the impetus for an ideology of progress that is still with us. The Enlightenment brought with it a confidence in human evolution, both personal and social. With the industrial revolution, confidence ran high that Western civilization was more advanced than other societies have ever been. Technological sophistication took on a universalizing evaluative quality. People groups were classified and ranked according to European notions of the ideal.

Some of the earliest modern social analysis shows how race was swept along the growing stream of modernization theories. In the eighteenth century the social theorist Jean-Jacques Rousseau argued for a ranking of the races and, while implicitly assuming his culture to be the ideal, made a case for the admirability of other cultures, the "noble savage." The evidence for the paternalistic categorization of the races was perhaps nowhere better on display than at the 1893 World Fair, that international celebration of Western civilization and technology. Here the "savages" were put on display with the same glamour as the latest technology.

It was not until well into the nineteenth century that writers were starting to distinguish between race and culture or ethnic group or nation or people group in general. The paternalism of Western nations is evident from much of the literature on nineteenth and twentieth century Colonialism. Crawford Young (1994) and Mahmood Mamdani (1996) show the surviving effects of European colonialism on modern Africa. Africans were not effective in throwing off the shackles of paternalistic colonial systems until well into the twentieth century.

To state the obvious, competitive race relations can only exist when there is the possibility for competition. One group cannot so dominate the other that there is no room for competition. When one group retains material and ideological hegemony over another (see Godelier 1986), there is little possibility for competitive race relations. Competition is squelched by the same state apparatus that supports the inequitable distribution of resources.

In From Savage to Negro (1998) Lee D. Baker echoes the transition to which van den Berghe refers. Here the author traces the role Anthropology played through the 1950s in the construction of Western conceptions of the "other" or, more specifically, those of African ancestry. Part of what allows for competitive relations to emerge is the valuation of the life and experiences of those defined as "other," where the other is no longer outside the dominant conversation of what is to be valued. Conversation here refers to more than ideological or verbal communication. Making the "other" part of the conversation also means that institutions are put in place (or removed) in order to effectively ensure the possibility for competition. In the case of European colonialism in Africa, the adoption of independent African governments was the first major political step in creating the context for competitive relations to exist.

It is much easier to provide examples of paternalistic race relations than competitive race relations. However, a few examples of relatively competitive race relations can be raised. Consider, for example, the way in which racial categories have been institutionalized in the census categories of countries like the United States, Brazil and South Africa. As Anthony Marx shows (1998), these three countries have relatively recently provided the institutional infrastructure that makes race-based competition for resources possible. Robert Price (1997) argues that South Africa has virtually guaranteed a continued focus on the racial categories of the past by instituting redistribution programs that are intended to compensate via the same hardened categories. Increased competition is guaranteed by the hardening of these categories. Kevin Yelvington (1995) gives a good example of how the competitive nature of race relations in Trinidad is further complicated by variations in class and gender among those defined in each racial category.

If we follow Timothy Keegan's work on the effect of colonial expansion on South Africa's racial paradigms, van den Berghe's schema fits. Keegan (1996) shows how the racial paradigm developed over the course of Dutch and British (and later Afrikaner) colonial expansion. He argues that some of the harsher racial categorization and paternalistic systems of racial relations came from the British, not the Boers. The prevailing thought of mid-twentieth century historians of South Africa was that the Cape Liberal tradition provided room for competitive race relations to develop. Since the Cape Liberal tradition espoused equal rights for all true citizens, it was theoretically possible for any person in the Cape to gain access to political power. After all, the constitution of 1853 did not exclude *de jure* non-whites from voting. However, there were property requirements attached to the franchise, requirements that made it extremely unlikely that too many Khoi, San, Xhosa or any other non-white could participate. By the 1870s the property requirements were strengthened and by the 1890s race became an exclusionary qualification. Wilmot James and Mary Simmons (1991) also outline how race became paternalistically institutionalized during the history of the western Cape.

But there is little doubt that, when the National Party came to power in 1948 and the whole apartheid edifice was erected, any possibility for competitive race relations was virtually wiped out. An entire political and economic infrastructure ensured that the transition to competitive race relations would not happen. The most restrictive of these actions had to have been the series of Acts that were passed around 1950 that formed the foundation for the apartheid system: the Population Registration Act, the Group Areas Act, the Immorality and Indecency clause and later, the Prohibition of Mixed Marriages Act.

It was not until the late 1980s that the true possibility for competitive race relations in South Africa became a reality. This is not to say that many or even most South Africans did not carve competitive space for themselves in an extremely restrictive environment, but the infrastructure for true mass competition was not there. In the late 1980s the structures of apartheid were collapsing, the unions that fought so hard in the previous decades had made significant strides and the educational institutions were opening their doors to begin making true competition possible.

It is difficult to make a judgement regarding the applicability of van den Berghe's analysis to South Africa's history outside of the context of European expansion. If we consider some of the new work being done on the Zulu expansion (Gump 1994), it is difficult to argue for its applicability, although for different reasons. Senzagakona certainly developed hegemony over a vast area of South Africa via his impi army, but I am not sure we can describe the rhetoric that must have been used as racial, if our category by definition includes a phenotypic dimension.

An interesting example of how restricted the competitive nature of race relations could be for at least one black South African sharecropper throughout the first eight decades of this century is found in Charles van Onselen's work (1996). Van Onselen shows how Kas Maine negotiates a space for himself and his family in the midst of a century of changing race relations. He never fully surrendered his right to compete with the white farmers. This was expressed in the central metaphor of the book: The plow may be his, the oxen and the shares may be his, and the seed may be his, but the land is not.

There is no doubt that South Africa is now transitioning to a more competitive system of race relations. A major part of making this transition a reality will be the attention given to the redistribution of resources though programs like the Reconstruction and Development Programme and other affirmative action initiatives. While the ties that bind its citizens to the paternalistic system of race relations are far from severed, it is slowly but surely being transformed. What remains to be seen, however, is if the news ways of constructing social relations in South Africa will continue to rely on old systems of classification. To date, these old systems of classification remain socially, economically and politically significant.

The Anthropology of Fishing

Economic Anthropology and Its Application to Fishing

According to Stuart Plattner, economic anthropology is the study of economic institutions and behavior done in anthropological places in an ethnographic style (1989:1). "Anthropological places" is a concept increasingly difficult to define. Historically, anthropology has left the study of technologically advanced state societies to their sister sociologists. A discipline born the child of imperialism and colonial expansion, anthropology's great quest has been to understand how lifestyles of the remotest "other" relate to what is more commonly known and done in our own society. Ultimately, the anthropologist is interested in comparing the range of human experience over the course of human history, making anthropology perhaps the most ambitious discipline. What makes anthropology specifically ethnographic is the focus on research methods (like participant observation and in-depth personal interviews) that target individual levels of thought and experience, while at the same time attempting to connect these thoughts and experiences to the broadest possible categories of human experience.

Anthropology was once in the salvage business, attempting to save primitive societies before they were destroyed by the advancing waves of modern, Western thought and technology. "The ethnographer arrives on the scene of a world on the wane and salvages it in texts before it is lost to modernization" (Marcus 1994:45). Consider the primary subject matter of economic anthropology: Hunters and Gatherers, Horticulturalists, Trade and Markets in Precapitalist States, Peasants, non-Western Markets and Marketplaces, the Impact of Industrial Agriculture, the Informal Economy, Women and economic institutions, to name the more prominent themes. But the salvage business was in a sense a step away from the paternalism of the anthropologist as culture broker, interpreting the world of the primitive, the conquered, to the outside world.

Anthropologists were once relatively unconcerned with the impact of history and macro-social forces on their subjects. Ethnographies often were written in the "ethnographic present," assuming that societies were static, integrated, self-sustaining systems. An attempt was made to describe "primitive" or "peasant" cultures, before Western contact changed them, as timeless cultural constructs untouched, pristine and isolated. "Anthropologists could believe in the static 'ethnographic present' only when we were unaware of the extent to which local cultures are products of world history" (Kottak and Colson 1994:398).

We were once interested in native rationality, in describing the seeming bizarre "other" as sensible and intelligent once the local context is understood. Assuming the psychic unity of humankind, we debated whether the categories of economics as understood in the West could be applied as pan-human categories. "Formalists" analyzed choice as the product of rational decisions in the context of limited means. "The crux of the [formalist] approach is the assumption that individuals in every culture exercise rational choice in a means-ends, constraints, and opportunities framework" (Plattner 1989:13). The formalists, lead by Raymond Firth (1970) saw all relationships as exchange relationships, as utilities to be maximized.

The "substantivists," lead by Karl Polanyi (1957) and George Dalton (1961), argued that non-western societies were qualitatively unique and that the application of Western meta-theories to these societies unjustly distorted their reality. Substantivists saw the use of the classical economic paradigm as ethnocentric; such theorizing was either wrong or too simplistic and irrelevant. They argued that scarcity is not a necessary condition of human society but a historically derived condition. Scarcity of options grows out of the scarcity of wealth, which is a direct result of the extractive penetration of Western capitalism. The rational choice paradigm cannot be universalized because the differences between cultures are too great. With no labor market and no money, reciprocity and redistribution were considered analytical tools far more important than market exchange. Instead of focusing on monetary value, anthropologists focused on the value of production for use rather than production for exchange. Substantivists argued that "interest," "capital," and "credit" are inappropriate categories for describing band and tribal societies.

Evidence that this debate was never resolved lies in the fact that both of these strains of thought survive in anthropology today. Critique of nomothetic theorizing lies at the heart of a good deal of current feminist, Marxist and postmodern anthropology, while stalwarts of cultural materialism and sociobiology continue the search for appropriate macro-theories. Rational-choice theorists in anthropology, however, continue to be committed to the neo-classical model of economics as derived from Smith (1905) and Keynes (1936). Rational choice theorists focus on prescriptive theories specifying how people should act if they want to make efficient economic decisions. The fundamental assumption here is that people know what they want and should maximize their energy to get it (Schneider 1974). People are assumed to be calculating beings who understand their own values and act with forethought. People are also assumed to have the necessary knowledge concerning costs, income and yield with respect to their options. It is also assumed that people have the ability to calculate the maximal choice. So, rational-choice theorists will speak of opportunity costs or the loss of alternatives due to choices we make. Or they will refer to diminishing marginal value, where the quantity of input eventually outweighs quantity of output. Employer-employee relationships are described in purely economic terms. With confidence in free market capitalism, it is assumed that self-interest will eventually make the world a better place for all (Friedman 1953).

A strong reaction to the confidence in theories of Western capitalism came from those committed to the historical materialism of Marx. Anthropologists who borrow from Marx focus on how history and ideology operate to determine the distribution of wealth and power in a society. The central focus is on the control over the means of production and the various stakeholders that are affected by this control. Anthropologists influenced by Marx analyze class conflict and face head on the contradiction between the ideal that all should be equal and the reality that society is stratified. Following the work of Maurice Godelier (1986), an important trend has been the analysis ideology that upholds special interests while appearing to benefit general concerns. The focus on hegemony shifted the focus in anthropology to issues of politics, power, hierarchy and inequity.

Godelier's notion of hegemony has allowed social relations to become the center of economic analysis but not without its critics. Immanuel Wallerstein (1974; 1979) criticized Godelier and the Marxists for their lack of grounding in history. He argues that individual economies and cultures are not disconnected from others and that, in many cases, there are direct and dependent relationships directly responsible for the welfare (or its opposite) of the other. Eric Wolf showed that power relationships have a face, that specific historically significant people and institutions are responsible for the underdevelopment of many other parts of the world (1982). With its focus on the micro and the local, anthropology was spiraling into the self-referential chaos of historical particularism. For those who were caught in this trap, Wolf and Wallerstein helped raise the scope of the anthropological lens to view the global interconnectedness of culture and economics.

Nowhere is the importance of this global perspective in anthropology more obvious than in the study of fishing communities. And nowhere is anthropology's role in interdisciplinary conversations more clear. The anthropological analysis of fishers and their communities embodies the tensions in the history of economic anthropology itself. The smallest of the traditional fishing communities are by trade dependent on a globally significant resource. Fishing is often romanticized as a primitive, local trade, yet even the most remote fishing communities are bound to the consequences of global fishing efforts. Fishing is often atomized as work, and the embeddedness of this work in the host culture is often ignored.

Anthropologists have become central participants in discussions about how to manage public natural resources. Researchers committed to understanding the connection between ecology and culture have developed an interdisciplinary field around the issues involved in the local and global control over natural resources. James Acheson (1981, 1987, 1989, 1990, 1994), Eleanor Ostrom (1990) and Bonnie McCay (1987) have lead the way in focusing anthropology's lens on an issue that forces us to be dependent on multiple disciplines with strands of evidence. The central theoretical issue in what has come to be known as Common Property Resource Management stems from Garret Hardin's "Tragedy of the Commons" argument (1968). The argument stems in part from the Malthusian assertion that unconstrained freedom to produce children will result in a population disaster for the world. Hardin used the parable of a pasture held in common property by a community of herders to show that coercion is necessary to prevent the destruction of the resource. He tried to show that the need for each person to maximize the personal gain necessarily leads to the destruction of the common grazing area. Hardin argued that coercion can be mutually agreed upon but need not be just. Arguing that injustice is preferable to total ruin, Hardin advocated the use of draconian state intervention into local affairs.

The Tragedy of the Commons theory assumes that the users of common property resources are individualistic profit maximizers driven by economic goals to overexploit the resources on which their livelihood depends, despite the best interests of the society as a whole (McCay and Acheson 1987). It assumes that the users of these resources have the technical capacity to exceed the biological maximum renewal rate of the resource. It also assumes that those using common property resources and the local communities they live in cannot or will not erect effective institutions to protect the resources they live on. Naming it the Free-rider problem, theorists challenged the presumption that people would act for the collective if it was known that such action could bring collective benefit (Olson 1965). Finally, theorists committed to the Tragedy of the Commons model deduced that the exploitation of collectively owned resources can be halted only by instituting private property or by the government taking action. Private property was thought to result in a more efficient use and conservation of resources and greater increases in wealth than do less exclusive forms of property (Ostrom 1990).

Economic anthropologists have important challenges to make to the assumptions of the Tragedy of the Commons model. Ostrom argues that what makes these models so powerful is that they fit many situations around the world. What makes them dangerous is when they are used as proscriptives, where the huge assumptions are taken on faith as being fixed (Ostrom 1990). Anthropologists have shown that there are institutions that effectively limit exploitation. Assets are rarely open-access (Berkes 1985). Communally owned property (as opposed to open-access property) is not automatically subject to overexploitation. This is common in many parts of Africa where grazing lands are owned by the community, clan or tribe. In many fishing communities, ownership rights are established formally or informally over "fishing space." The case of the lobster fishers of Maine has proven how communally "owned" property resulted in less exploitation and greater economic benefit for those involved; access is far more controlled in *perimeter-defended* fishing areas than in *nucleated* fishing areas (Acheson 1988). Durrenberger and Palsson's study of Icelandic fishers (1985) show how state and local level resource management can operate together effectively. The Tragedy of the Commons focuses too narrowly on property rights. Problems associated with open-access property rights are more closely related to political economy (issues of population growth, industrialization and the expansion of the capitalist system and markets). As is the case in South Africa, poverty, underdevelopment and overpopulation push conservation priorities way down the list on the national agenda.

Maritime Anthropology: A Review of Recent Literature

In the past twenty-five years there have been three pivotal publications that deserve attention for any student of contemporary maritime anthropology. The first is M. Estellie Smith's edited volume: Those Who Live from the Sea (1977). Published in the late 1970s her work included a summary of key debates in the study of fishing communities from an anthropological perspective. The articles focused on themes such as the organization of life around occupation, the political economy of small commercial fishing communities, technological change and its impact on local fishers and the relationship between captain and crew in the context of changing fisheries and markets.

A second work of pivotal importance is Antonius Robben's Sons of the Sea Goddess (1986). This work is particularly important because it is one of the first works to clearly articulate the embedded nature of fishing. While Robben clearly focuses on the business of fishing in small communities in Brazil, he is more concerned with the social relations involved in the communities that fish. He shows the interdependence between producers and consumers, between various stakeholders in the industry and between the fishers and their families.

The third publication of pivotal importance in the history of maritime anthropology is the journal titled *Maritime Anthropology*. This journal was published out of the Netherlands and was discontinued in the early 1990s. It helped to draw together works from diverse perspectives that were each concerned with fishers, families of fishers and fishing communities. This journal was in part responsible for promoting a field some called Maritime Anthropology. It provided a good overview of the debates that dominated the literature in the seventies and eighties. Included among these debates were the analysis of captain-crew relations, debates over the validity of the "Tragedy of the Commons" model for commercial fishing, the impact of social change on commercial fishers and the lessons to be learned about commercial fishers from archeological sites.

More recent works that have become pivotal to our understanding about the organization of commercial fishing communities and/or have pointed in new directions include works by Matthiessen (1988), Acheson (1988), Acheson and McCay (1989), Eleanor Ostrom (1990) and Garrity-Blake (1994). Matthiessen (1988) showed implicitly how power relations are structured between men in the fishing industry. Although for the most part uncritical in his construction of gender, Matthiessen highlights the fishing industry as work that deeply resonates with traditional male roles and aspirations. He is particularly clear about how much male fishers value their independence and freedom. James Acheson (1988) has shown us how local fishers take control over the management of their territory and fishing rights. He tells us of a "limited entry" system developed by local lobstermen to limit competition, protecting the resource and their own livelihoods. Their limited entry system was reinforced by locally constituted "gangs" and backed up by threat of violence for violators.

Even more recently Barbara Garrity-Blake's analysis of the North Carolina/Virginia menhaden industry broadens the scope of analysis (1994). She focused her analytical lens on historical changes in the industry and the impact of these changes on social conditions. With a study spanning a hundred years she provided the depth of insight lacking from many earlier works. Her work also added a new twist in that it focused on the construction of race and the power relations associated with race. She showed how changing race relations were and were not reflected in the captain-crew relations in the industry.

Two final pivotal works to be mentioned are Acheson and McCay's edited volume The Question of the Commons (1989) and Eleanor Ostrom's Managing the Commons (1990). While both focus on theoretical issues beyond fishing, both are directly focused on the central debates

that have dominated the maritime anthropology literature in the last two and a half decades. Both

discuss the strengths and weaknesses of different approaches to what has come to be known as

Common Property Resource Management (CPR). The central concern of CPR is the ecological

health of a region that contains a resource available to anyone. CPR researchers have examined

fisheries, forests, grazing lands, water and air under their microscopes.

Much of the maritime anthropology literature has focused on fishing as a lifestyle,

something more than a job. No work represents this theme better than Antonius Robben's

(1984). His work shows the embeddedness of economic relations. Others have focused on the

culture of fishing in their search for recording the history and emphasizing the heritage of the

commercial fishing lifestyle (Ram 1991, Turner 1991, Smith 1993, Johnson 1995). As an

example, the story of Cortez, a central Florida fishing community, is told by Ben Green (1985).

Another central issue the maritime literature has recently explored is the "skipper effect."

Those interested in the skipper effect devise ways of testing whether the knowledge and skills of

the captain have a significant impact on their success as often defined by the size and frequency

of their catch, independent of other variables such as technology, weather, fishing region, etc.

Durrenberger has worked on this problem and, as with most of the literature so far on this topic,

has concluded that the answer to this problem lies in future research (1993).

Garrity-Blake's work (1994) provides a good example of an anthropological study that

includes an analysis of how technological change affects social relations in the industry. She

shows how the electric spool adopted after World War II not only increased production but

decreased the size of crew needed and the skill needed of those who were hired. This had a

particularly harsh impact on the African-Americans working in the industry. Work yet to be done

in the menhaden industry includes an analysis of the impact of spotter planes on the industry.

Anyone familiar with commercial fishing industries knows that it is an extremely

dangerous occupation. Popular literature and film has recently reminded us of the immediate dangers of an unpredictable ocean (Junger 1997; this book was also made into a motion picture). Some social scientists have used this context to gain understanding in how humans approach and cope with risk. Pollnac and Poggie's work (1995, 1998) on the Icelandic fisheries measures what people are willing to do, how much risk they are willing to take and how high the benefits have to be for the different levels of risk. An interesting observation in their findings is that the benefits from fishing for which people are willing to risk heavy stakes are not necessarily material. They include personal motivations like a sense of worth or purpose.

Some of the most recent work has focused on the gendered division of labor in the fishing industry. Works like Matthiessen's (1986) would lead us to believe that the fishing industry is dominated by men. Thompson (1985), Nadel-Klein and Davis (1988), Smith and Jepson (1993) and Smith, Jepson and Lee (1993) have shown us the complex division of labor common in commercial fishing families. They have shown that for women there is, in part, a complex blend of traditional gender roles (e.g. mother, teacher, nurturer, housekeeper) and non-traditional roles (marketing, sales, breadwinner, head-of-household, business manager). Further work needs to be done in this area to see how and why these roles vary, how they vary with different types of fisheries and how changes in the fisheries are reflected in changing gender roles in the home. But it is also important to study how each gender constructs expectations for the other.

Gaps in the knowledge base of maritime anthropology include the following issues:

- What are the boundaries of a fishing community?
    - Can this be determined by economic or industrial relations alone?
    - Can community be better defined by a less-geographically centered analysis?
    - What is the connection between the fishers and the local community?
    - How do fishers construct their own sense of community?
- How do race and ethnicity play a role in structuring relations among commercial fishers?
    - What impact do race relations play in structuring the networks of commercial fishers?
    - How do the small entrepreneurial businesses reflect the racial stereotyping and biases of the society in general and what effect does this have on access to the industry?
    - How is race/ethnicity used as a tool in the competition over fishing rights?
- What role does the construction of gender play in organizing social relations in the industry?
    - How and why do men construct fishing as a particularly male form of work?
    - What do gender relations in the fishing industry tell us about the classical distinction between the formal and informal economy?

One of my objectives is to address the latter two of these gaps in the maritime anthropology literature.

Very few anthropological or sociological studies have been done on the fishing communities in South Africa, and even fewer on the activity of fishing itself. Most studies in the 1990s developed out of the need to understand the redistribution of fisheries resources in light of the changing political landscape. The most notable study was De Wet Schutte's (1993) study of thirteen fishing communities on the Western Cape coast. Schutte was commissioned by the Department of Environmental Affairs, the Welfare Department and the African National Congress to collect baseline data with an eye towards improving pending community development projects. One of his most interesting findings was the diversity of the fishing communities on the Western Cape coast. He challenges the notion of "the West Coast fishing community," preferring instead to speak of "those in the fishing industry on the West Coast" or "those fishers who live in coastal communities" (1993:107). He found that the homogenized image of fishing communities did not accurately reflect the stark differences he found between different communities; each had a unique identity and unique day-to-day problems.

Another significant finding in Schutte's work relates to race relations in the coastal communities. He found that the further the communities along the coast were from Cape Town, the worse the relationship between local white and coloured residents. When making recommendations for the implementation of community development programs he recommended that the local political dynamics in each community be taken into account, including the racial dynamics as they differ from community to community.

In the last few years there have been some promising developments in research on fishers and their communities. Two notable master's theses, Isaacs (1998) and Lindsay (1999) analyzed how local fishers perceived and responded to their social, political and natural environment. Lindsay's qualitative study investigated and described the perceptions of the fishery resource held by commercial and recreational fishers in the town of Struisbaai. Though her research employed a range of methods, including informant interviewing, participant observation, and the use of secondary data, her findings were based primarily on a series of in-depth interviews with individual fishers in Struisbaai. Her paper described the ways in which commercial and recreational fishers in Struisbaai "perceive, conceptualize, and ultimately use the fishery resource" and explores "the fishers' perceptions of the resource as they are informed by Apartheid's psychological and social legacies" (1999:i).

Figure 1. Handline Fisherman Pulling Snoek into the Ski-Boat
source: Stibbe and Moss (1998)

Moeniba Isaacs' master's project (1998) took on the form of a report to the University of the Western Cape's School of Government. She highlighted the conflicts facing the fishing industry in South Africa exemplified in the fishing communities of Ocean View, Hout Bay and

Kalk Bay. In analyzing the various stakeholders such as the government, the fishing industry, organized interests (unions) and the unorganized interests (local communities), her research stressed the conflicts of maintaining stability versus redistribution (how to achieve empowerment), empowering fisher folk (share holding schemes versus local capacity building), and managing the marine resource (National fisheries management versus local community management). She specifically referred to theories of co-management and a historical overview of the fishing industry in South Africa that sketched the background to the processes leading to the White Paper up to the passing of the Marine Fisheries Bill (later to become the Marine Living Resource Act).

Aside from the political transformation of the fishing industry, the most publicized activity in the fishing industry during the late 1990s is the poaching of abalone and rock lobster. Significant work has been done on studying these activities and the impact of these activities on local coastal communities (Hauck 1999; Hauck and Hector 2000). Supported by the University of Cape Town's Institute of Criminology, Hauck and Hector have gone to considerable lengths to understand how local fishers conceptualize the management of marine species and their willingness to participate in such management. The strength of their research is in its ethnographic detail. They move the theoretical discussions of co-management and other fisheries management paradigms from the classroom to the communities where fishers live.

An important piece of research was funded by the government's Department of Marine and Coastal Management and involved a survey of subsistence fishers and fisheries all along the South African coast (Clark 2000). Although lacking in ethnographic detail, the scope of this project was impressive and provided conceptual tools useful for future research. Subsistence fishers all along the South African coast were surveyed about their socioeconomic status, resource harvesting techniques, activities and aspirations. The study was intended to provide MCM with a baseline to understand subsistence fisheries in order to know how to better implement subsistence fisheries management plans. A key finding in this research was an identification of the diversity of activities that can be defined as subsistence fishing. Researchers involved in this project found that there was too large of a conceptual gap between "subsistence fisher" and "commercial fisher" and recommended an intermediate category, the small-scale commercial fisher. It is the fishers in this intermediate category, the small-scale commercial handline fishers on the roaming ski-boats, who take center stage in the analysis that follows.

Notes

---

[1] See Thomas Kuhn's The Structure of Scientific Revolutions (1970) for a description of this transition in history.

[2] For a critique of this book, see Gates (1999).

[3] Throughout the dissertation I place categorical racial labels in the lower case, except where used as part of a title. Given my position that these categories are socially constructed and historically situated, the lower case indicates that these labels are neither proper nouns nor deserving of codified titular status.

CHAPTER 3
RESEARCH METHODOLOGY:
ANTHROPOLOGY AND THE STUDY OF DIFFERENCE

Understanding the Ethnographic "Other"

A Methodological Journey

Despite the ever-shifting boundaries and elusive meanings of "postmodernism," it is

possible to point out some of the more helpful and some of the more dangerous paths down which

influential "postmodernist" thinkers are moving and, more specifically, the value of this

movement for writing ethnography. In its recognition that all representations of the "other" are

inherently political and in its emphasis on the provisional nature of cultural interpretation,

postmodernism leads down a fruitful path. This journey down fruitful paths continues as

postmodernists bring to light, together with feminist influences in anthropology, the need for

reflexivity in writing ethnography. When postmodernists lead us down the road of subjectivist

epistemological obscurity and ill-defined moralism, the road gets all too rocky. In their denial of

relative objectivity as a goal for ethnographic description, postmodernists take us further down

the road to an analytical black hole. Postmodernism also leads down the rocky road of

narcissistic solipsism when the sole purpose, or even the dominant purpose, of the ethnography is

the reflexive examination of the author's own position in the research. By focusing on questions

raised by postmodern anthropologists, it is possible to show that the centripetal forces of

postmodernism and the centrifugal tendencies of the scientific enterprise have the potential for

complementary existence.

The anthropologist steps off the plane into the exotic land of the "other." Social

philosophers and researchers have long been concerned with understanding and communicating

41

the ideas and behaviors of people groups different (often radically) from their own. The history of cultural anthropology as an academic discipline is the history of research that helps the "other" become familiar. But as the world is made smaller through mass communication, rapidly advancing communication technology and the increasing ease of international transportation, the "other" is no longer so unfamiliar. The cultural diversity that the anthropologist once had to bring home in his briefcase is now an integral part of our own neighborhoods. The boundaries between the "we" that study and the "they" that are being studied are breaking down while, at the same time, new social categories are being formed. I believe it is with the analytical tools that cultural anthropology provides that we can best come to understand the dynamics of these changing social categories.

The typical product of the cultural anthropologist's research takes on the form of an ethnography. An ethnography is a text in which a portrait, sometimes even a masterpiece, of a particular group of people is painted. Alongside other functions, writing ethnography (as dissertation, professional articles or monograph) serves as a form of academic capital, a *rite du passage* to the scholarly world of anthropology, an expected entry on the *curriculum vitae* of the aspiring tenure track professor. As such, the ethnography becomes an intellectual product on the publishing assembly line.

Any discussion of methodology (epistemology) cannot be wrested from the academic context in which anthropologists are trained. Sally Cole notes that she "went about the task of producing an ethnography that would pass the examining board that would license [her] as a professional anthropologist" (1992:118). The anthropological dissertation, "typically a straightforward analytical and descriptive account from fieldwork, is the ethnography that most anthropologists must write. Since the granting of professional credentials has depended on its evaluation, it has tended to be a conservative exercise" (Marcus 1986:265).

Taking its cue from contemporary literary theory, cultural anthropologists have had to reexamine their discipline in light of critiques increasingly being labeled "postmodern." But for one in the process of deciding which methodologies prove to be most useful, questions raised by postmodernists are cause for examination, not reexamination. To discuss postmodernism is like taking a journey with no prescribed destination, no directions and a thousand back-seat drivers (pardon the hyperbole). No one knows quite where it is going, how one will get there or who is giving directions. The multiplicity of interpretations of postmodernism is evidence that it is a highly contested theoretical domain. Postmodernism is like an amoeba with flexible boundaries and often directionless movement. Those who claim to be postmodernists are often willing to ingest any theoretical or methodological tidbit that may advance their cause. However, despite the ever-shifting boundaries and elusive meanings of "postmodernism," it is possible to point out some of the more helpful and some of the more dangerous paths down which influential "postmodernist" thinkers are moving and, more importantly, the value of this movement for cultural anthropology.

Preparing for the Trip

As with any other academic discipline, cultural anthropology is involved in the production of knowledge, and the ethnographic text is our most common academic product. Anthropologists are in a continuing dialogue over the goals for the ethnographic representation of culture. Should ethnographic description aim at the interpretation of the individual's symbolic representations of her world, or should ethnographic description aim at providing valid generalizations about cultural phenomena? Are these two goals mutually exclusive? Furthermore, anthropologists are in disagreement over what the relationship should be between the researcher and the subjects studied. How explicit should the details of this relationship be made in the ethnography, and to what extent should the ethnography reflect the dialogue between the anthropologist and his informant(s)? These are questions of methodology (epistemology), i.e., questions regarding the assumptions behind the process of writing ethnography, questions that reveal how we know what we say we know.

Russ Bernard (1994) makes a broad distinction between two epistemologies dominant in cultural anthropology: interpretivist and positivist. He makes an important distinction between epistemology (methodology) and methods. "Positivists and interpretivists may disagree on matters of epistemology," Bernard says, "but when we talk about methods at the level of strategy and technique, methods belong to all of us" (1994:169). One's methodology consists of the body of assumptions that informs and directs the methods (strategies and techniques) we use in research. The primary questions that drive our research both inform and are informed by these assumptions. Although placing himself firmly within the logical positivist tradition, Bernard believes that

> all anthropologists need a thorough grounding in the various approaches to knowledge that have characterized our discipline. This means exposure of all students, whatever their initial predilections, to the philosophical foundations of structuralism, symbolism, interpretivism, hermeneutics, phenomenology, positivism and empiricism. (1994:174)

Although the dominant debate in the discipline throughout the last three decades of the twentieth century has been between positivists (e.g. Kuznar 1997) and interpretivists (e.g. Geertz 1973, 1988), the debate has escalated where the battle lines are drawn between those committed to a scientific, empiricist epistemology and those intent on deconstructing the foundations for the scientific enterprise itself, i.e., a postmodernist epistemology.

Michael Agar envisions the current debate in anthropology between the postmodernists and those committed to the scientific, empiricist method as a war in which there is, as with most wars, more destruction than anything else. In The Professional Stranger he notes that it is "high time for some peace negotiations" (1996:4), and I would have to agree. My work is not a comparison and contrast between scientific method and postmodernist critique. This chapter is not intended to give a full documentation of the scientific epistemology followed by a full articulation of the postmodernist critique. This sketch is less ambitious. Rather than facilitate the destructive polarization often reflected in such generalized comparisons, I will aim a more constructive lens at postmodernism.

Postmodernism includes a set of critical epistemological or methodological tools that direct the writer (and reader) to challenge established ways of representing, or writing, culture. More specifically, postmodernism emphasizes the radical heterogeneity of culture and the "decline of ideological hegemony in politics and social life" (Dickens and Fontana 1994:4). Regarding cultural anthropology, postmodernism aims its strongest critique at its most popular contribution to academic inquiry: the ethnography as a re-presentation and interpretation of culture, or more specifically, the ethnographer as re-presenter and interpreter of culture. Yet there are more helpful (fruitful) paths and more dangerous (rocky) roads down which postmodernism can lead cultural anthropology. For my own research, I will take the more fruitful paths and steer clear of the rocky roads.

I will discuss these fruitful paths and rocky roads in this essay. In its recognition that all representations of the "other" are inherently political, postmodernism leads down a fruitful path. The re-presentations of the ethnographer both contribute to and are affected by relations of power. The power relations that affect the writing of ethnography occur in the academic world of the anthropologist, in the socio-political world of those being studied and in the interchange brought about by the contact of these two worlds. In its emphasis on the contextualized nature of cultural interpretation, postmodernism leads down another fruitful path. When postmodernism leads down the road of subjectivist epistemological obscurity and ill-defined moralism, it leads down a dangerous road. The radical subjectivism of the deconstructionist agenda ultimately denies the potential for comparison among groups; in its attempt to highlight ambiguities, *differance* and discontinuity, postmodernism forgets that there are also regularities, patterns and discernable intracultural continuity.

Vehicle Inspection

As the Ecclesiastical philosophers recognized, there is nothing new under the sun (Ecclesiastes Chapter 1). This proverb also applies to anthropology as a discipline: "In anthropology we are continuously slaying paradigms, only to see them return to life, as if

discovered for the first time" (Wolf 1994:220). According to Roy Rappaport:

> Two traditions have proceeded in anthropology since its inception. One, objective in its aspirations and inspired by the biological sciences, seeks explanations and is concerned to discover causes, or even, in the view of the ambitious, laws. The other, influenced by philosophy, linguistics, and the humanities, and open to more subjectively derived knowledge, attempts interpretations and seeks to elucidate meanings. (1984:154)

Citing continental philosophers, social theorists and literary critics such as Paul Ricoeur (1971),

Jacques Derrida (1972, 1978), Michel Foucault (1980a, 1980b), Jean Baudrillard (1981), Jean-

Francois Lyotard (1984), Pierre Bourdieu (1987), and Jurgen Habermas (1987), postmodernists

reflect this second tradition. In postmodernism we hear the strong echoes of Robert Lowie's

famous statement that culture (civilization) is a "thing of shreds and patches" (1920:441).

Subjectivity is prized over objectivity. The particular is given primacy over the general.

Postmodernism "remains more a socio-cultural theory than a set of epistemological and

discursive principles" (Agger 1992:109). The distinctions between post-structuralism and

postmodernism are difficult to determine. "One would have to engage in purposely simplifying

taxonomy of names and their intellectual contributions in order to map the terrain of post-

structural and postmodern cultural studies adequately—and even then the map would blur some

crucial points of difference" (Agger 1992:109). Such a map is beyond the scope of this essay.

However, as Dickens and Fontana highlight, not all who consider themselves postmodernists (i.e.,

critics of modernism) would fully embrace Derrida's style of deconstructionism (Dickens and

Fontana 1994). Yet, in its emphasis on culture and, in fact, all of reality as text, deconstruction is

inseparable from the postmodernist agenda. Deconstruction involves:

> the attempt to take apart and expose the underlying meanings, biases and preconceptions that structure the way a text conceptualizes its relation to what it describes. This requires that traditional concepts, theory, and understanding surrounding a text be unraveled, including the assumption that an author's intentions and meanings can be easily determined. (Denzin 1994:184)

Deconstruction provides the critical tools for postmodernism to challenge representations of the

"other" in ethnographic texts.

Fruitful Paths and Rocky Roads

One helpful path down which postmodernism steers anthropology is the recognition that

all representations of the "other" (as the product of research) are inherently political, which in this

case is defined in the broadest sense as the power to influence decision making. Representations

of culture are inherently political because culture itself is a contested domain. We can no longer

speak of "the Nuer" or "the Andaman Islanders" without acknowledging the intracultural

variation, the diverse and often competing voices each claiming a stake in what it means to be

Nuer or Andaman. Deeply indebted to Foucault's notion that knowledge and power exist in a

dynamic, interactive relationship (1980b), postmodernism recognizes the need to deconstruct

hegemonic representations of culture that operate to effectively oppress certain portions of

society. These power relations are commonly divided along the lines of age, class, gender and

race, among others. The search for statistically significant patterns of thought and behavior (the

core agenda of positivist anthropology) has its limitations in that it focuses on dominant

representations, the most politically influential persons, hegemonic rather than subaltern forces,

the core rather than the periphery. If one is intent on deconstructing and redefining the core-

periphery debate, statistical probabilities can only take you so far. Postmodernism points to the

need to create a space for under-represented voices. And as Agar so insightfully recognizes,

> Ethnography is *populist* to the core, in this sense—skeptical of the distant institutions that
> control local people's lives; certain of the fact that the best society is built from the
> *participation* of its members in decisions that affect them; aggravated by injustices
> caused by distant institutions that force people to live in worlds not of their own making.
> (1996:27)

A second fruitful path down which postmodernism has redirected[1] cultural anthropology

is an emphasis on the provisional nature of cultural interpretation. As all culture is constantly

changing, representations rely on changing contexts. Both the ethnographer and the people who

are studied are influenced by historically (politically, socially, economically) situated

circumstances as, for example, Evans-Pritchard's research for writing The Nuer was influenced by the support he gained from the Sudanese government, or simply the fact that he was an upper-class, white male British researcher, or the reality of pending civil war in 1939. Postmodernism highlights the need to recognize the historical contingency of cultural interpretations. Postmodernism challenges the "definitiveness" of the ethnographer's representation and deconstructs the role the ethnographer in "writing culture" (Clifford and Marcus 1986).

In an attempt to practice what they preach, postmodernists promote reflexivity in ethnographic writing. The ethnographic "other" has been the under-represented voice in the classical ethnographies (e.g. Radcliffe-Brown's The Andaman Islanders (1922) or Evans-Pritchard's The Nuer (1940). Sally Cole believes that contemporary ethnography should be a "collaboration" between her and the group(s) with whom she is working. She is an advocate for a "contemporary ethnography wherein anthropologists self-consciously attempt to acknowledge their presence and integrate their personal experience or political consciousness in the writing of ethnography itself" (Cole 1992:115). This acknowledgment and integration is called "reflexivity." Explicit reflection on the observer-observed relationship is an integral part of a reflexive ethnography. The anthropologist not only places those studied in their historical (economic, political and social) context but analyzes their own historical context and how their position relates to the ones being studied. Reflexive ethnographers often include verbatim dialogue with particular informants in an attempt to place interpretive power in the hands of the informants. They are known for their use of the first person narrative in the life histories (individuals or groups) and for the personal narratives of anthropologists, where the anthropologist is studied as subject (Crapanzano 1980, Dwyer and Muhammad 1982, Behar 1993, McClaurin 1996).

Reflexivity can be taken to an extreme. Consider the soliloquized comments of Malcolm Ashmore, a sociologist being reflexive about reflexivity.

> In order not to be scientific, one must be outside science; but to study science or anything else from the outside is to be scientific. Therefore, in order to study science

unscientifically one must abandon objectivity and study it from the inside. But to be inside science means to be scientific. And therefore... (Ashmore 1989:109)

His point is not to destroy the goal of objectivity in science but to problematize it. He concludes not that we should throw out objectivity but that "in the study of science (and knowledge practices generally) the student *cannot avoid* being inside and outside at the same time" (Ashmore 1989:109). The danger of hyper-reflexivity is that we will be like the sixth century monastic Hesychasts, believing that navel-gazing will bring us closer to our goal. Consider one of the anthropologists representative of the postmodern ethnographers, James Clifford. "The other for Clifford is the anthropological representation of the other" (Rabinow 1986:242). Although it is essential to critique the way we represent others in our ethnographies and to acknowledge our own position in the ethnography, the ethnography is not an autobiography. I want my ethnography to say something important about someone else.

Another of the dangerous roads to which a postmodern perspective leads anthropology stems from postmodernism's marriage with Derrida's style of deconstruction. "A deconstructive cultural studies does not linger very long in the land of nomenclature, taxonomy, glossaries or conceptual refinements as if these events could somehow take place outside of the con-texts within which everything is subsumed under the rule of undecidability" (Agger 1992:110). Derrida built on de Saussure's insight that language consists of a system of relations among arbitrary signs whose meanings are defined by the differences that set them apart from one another. Derrida challenged all claims to knowledge that do not recognize the constantly shifting nature of representations of reality, since representations of reality are all that we can approximate (Dickens and Fontana 1994:1–24; 183–202).

Ben Agger (1992) explores the contributions of "poststructuralism" (deconstruction) and "postmodernism" to the emerging tradition of postmodernist cultural studies. A critique of this deconstruction, or postmodernism in general, is at one level futile given the self-proclaimed aversion to theoretical constructs and the distrust of authoritative definitions in postmodern cultural studies. As Agger notes, "Deconstructive cultural studies... is especially capable of theorizing its shifting, evolving nature, resisting fixed definitions at every turn" (1992:109). Yet, it is still possible to judge the internal consistency between various claims made by those promoting postmodern cultural studies. One question that needs to be asked of the postmodern agenda is this: are the methods of Derrida's deconstruction consistent with the political aims claimed central to a postmodern cultural interpretation?

In order to construct postmodern cultural studies as something more than deconstruction, Agger proposes a constructive political aim for postmodernism. Agger hopes to do more than highlight hidden assumptions and inconsistencies. He wants to shift "the cultural-political balance of power" (1992:101). The political agenda of Agger's postmodernism is clear: to destroy the authority of "positivist cultural empiricism" (1992:94) or "mainstream positivist sociologists of culture" (1992:97). But if Agger's aim is solely destructive, the end result would be nihilism. Agger attempts to posit a constructive aim for postmodernism, i.e., "restoring the value of marginalia" and non-hegemonic interpretations of culture. But is deconstruction consistent with this aim?

Cultural study "intervenes in the cultural field... as a subversion of unchallenged authorial privilege" (1992:97). But cultural study, as interpreted by Agger, cannot ultimately make use of deconstruction to meet its political aims. If, by exposing hidden forms of power, the critic is to provide voice and power for those left out of the "mainstream," they soon become part of the power center themselves. The center may have shifted, but hegemony itself continues. In attempting to "restore the value of marginalia" (1992:107), deconstructive cultural criticism creates a new center. This center may be formed of novel ideas and may empower persons formerly marginalized, but the marginalized soon become the hegemony. Consider the "gods" of postmodernism themselves. Although they would certainly deny the status of authority for themselves, persons like Derrida, Foucault, Bourdeau, De Saussaure and Adorno are consistently invoked in "postmodern" literature for their critical acumen (dare I say theoretical position?).

Although Agger states that "*poststructuralism and postmodernism oppose their methodologization*" (1992:94), he reflects a contradiction inherent to postmodernism when he states that "Derridian cultural studies... has devoted much more attention to the development of critical method than to the building of substantive social and cultural theory that functions politically" (1992:108). Deconstruction itself is methodological while claiming no methodology. It is theoretical while claiming an aversion to theory-building. It centers discussion on the continual process of analysis of text while claiming decentralization as its aim. Deconstruction leaves a "vacancy of meaning that needs to be filled" (1992:102) but leaves us not only without the tools to fill the vacancy but ultimately without the possibility of filling the vacancy. In trying to fill this vacancy with a constructive political aim, if Agger is not open to the criticisms of Derrida himself, then he contradicts the deconstructive methodology. The alternative is to remain in a continual process of deconstruction upon deconstruction upon deconstruction. The methods of Derridia's deconstruction are inconsistent with the political aims claimed central to a postmodern cultural interpretation.

Derrida's style of deconstruction extrapolates on the reality of historical conditioning, mentioned above as a fruitful enterprise, to the extreme of epistemological obscurity, a rocky road too dangerous to travel. Following the logic of deconstruction, since no knowledge or understanding of the "other" is possible, i.e., only interpretations upon interpretations, the best that ethnographers can do is to deconstruct the variables that influence (or bias) their own interpretation of reality and their interpretations of the "other." The tendency of this intense subjectivity is to degenerate the study of culture to the level of psychoanalysis, negating any real possibility for comparative research. While deconstructionists like Mark C. Taylor (1984) are enjoying the infinite wandering of exploring interpretation upon interpretation (a process he calls *trace*), the cultural anthropologist needs to move on to explore the differences and similarities between groups of people. "The new ethnography turns a blind eye courtesy of its own ideology here, I think. They're so committed to the complexity, ambiguity, subversion and relativity of any given moment that they lose sight of *patternized variation* that regularly occurs" (Agar 1996:10).

There is another dangerous road down which postmodernism leads the ethnographer. In their eagerness to emphasize the subjective nature of reality and to describe culture as a contested domain, postmodernists have lost sight of (and often attacked) objectivity as a goal for research (Clifford and Marcus 1986). The goal should not be to destroy the desire for validity and reliability in research (i.e., the two key components of scientific objectivity) but to reexamine who determines what is valid and reliable and for what purpose. Even those who most fervently preach the gospel of a positivist commitment to the scientific method do not claim access to absolute TRUTH but rather emphasize provisional truths. Striving for explanations, or interpretations, that others can agree upon does not negate the possibility for amplifying the voices of the marginalized.

Geertz believes that there is no substitute for local knowledge,

But maps and charts may still be useful, and tables, tales, pictures, and descriptions, even theories, if they attend to the actual, as well. The uses of ethnography are mainly ancillary, but they are nonetheless real; like the composing of dictionaries or the grinding of lenses, it is, or would be, an enabling discipline. And what it enables, when it does so, is a working contact with a variant subjectivity. It places particular we's among particular they's, and they's among we's; where all, as I have been saying, already are, however uneasily. (1994:463)

"Objectivity means becoming aware of one's biases, and transcending them, not the lack of any biases.... Striving for objectivity is important even if perfect objectivity is unobtainable" (Bernard 1994:172). In taking anthropology down the road of particularist, subjectivist descriptions, postmodernists may lead down a road they themselves wish to avoid. Ethnography can be the great enemy of ethnocentrism, "of confining people to cultural planets where the only ideas they need to conjure with are 'those around here,' not because it assumes people are all alike, but because it knows how profoundly they are not and how unable yet to disregard one another" (Geertz 1994:463).

A final rocky road to avoid when exploring the usefulness of postmodernism for cultural anthropology is its tendency to moralize without articulating clear moral principles. Postmodernism provides a moral agenda: to alleviate oppression. Yet the objects of oppression are not clearly identified; who is it that is oppressed and in what ways? As mentioned above, a strength of the postmodern perspective for cultural anthropology is its recognition of the need to deconstruct hegemonic representations of culture that operate to effectively oppress certain portions of society. Race, class and gender are invoked as core variables that contribute to this oppression (or hegemony). But postmodernism has the dangerous potential of becoming the very thing it critiques. It has the potential of becoming the arbiter of the hegemonic discourse, rather than the critic. When creating space for under-represented voices, what prevents the under-represented voices from becoming the hegemonic voices? Postmodernism provides critical tools to deconstruct the composition (definition) of power relations but has yet to define guidelines for reconstructing power relations in a manner that will ultimately result in a more even distribution of power. Moreover, it is not clear whether equity is even an important goal for postmodernists to pursue; for some the whole academic enterprise is nothing but an academic interpretive game.

Navigating Between Scylla and Charybdis

The discipline of cultural anthropology is in crisis over how to define its core product, the ethnography. As an attempt to apply the critiques brought to the writing of ethnography by postmodernism, consider this comparison of a classic ethnography, E.E. Evans-Pritchard's The Nuer, with one example of an ethnography influenced by postmodernism: Vincent Crapanzano's Tuhami. More specifically, attention is given to their differing approaches to the relationship between the general and the specific, between theory and text, between generalizations and the phenomena of experience. An argument is made for the necessarily interactive nature between both the theoretical poles (theory and text) and the relational poles (anthropologist and informant). This comparison is intended to neither oversimplify nor dichotomize differences among ethnographic approaches. A comparison and contrast between Evans-Pritchard's The Nuer (1940) and Crapanzano's Tuhami (1980) will reveal some of the fundamental issues with which current graduate students intent on ethnographic production must wrestle.

As mentioned above, cultural anthropology is involved in the production of knowledge, and the ethnographic text is our most common academic product. Anthropologists continue to dialogue over the goals for writing ethnography. Strong lines of preference are drawn around whether ethnographic description should aim at the interpretation of the individual's symbolic representations of her world or if ethnographic analysis should aim at providing valid generalizations about cultural phenomena. Furthermore, anthropologists are in disagreement over what the relationship should be between the researcher and the subjects studied. There is considerable debate over how explicit the details of this relationship should be made in writing ethnography, and to what extent the ethnography should reflect the dialogue between the anthropologist and his informant(s). A comparison of The Nuer and Tuhami should help illustrate these particular issues.

Doing his research in the 1930s, Evans-Pritchard was at the cutting edge of British social anthropology, following in the footsteps of his mentor, A.R. Radcliffe-Brown. Radcliffe-Brown, and consequently Evans-Pritchard, saw the goal of ethnographic research as the systematic analysis of the structures of society and how such structures functioned in the context of other such social structures. Radcliffe-Brown was famous for his analysis of kinship structures and how such structures could predict behavior. Reacting to what he perceived was an extreme particularism in the Boasians, Radcliffe-Brown sought comparative sociological laws that could explain similarities among cultures and account for differences. Evans-Pritchard believed in his mentor's approach and set out to prove the effectiveness of his theories through extensive field research. His goals are articulated in the introduction of The Nuer, "We first describe the interrelation of territorial segments within a territorial, or political, system and then the relation of other social systems to this system" (1940:4). Evans-Pritchard believed that social structures existed and sought to fill carefully reasoned structural-functional categories with the necessary ethnographic content, thereby adding validity and reliability to the theory. The goal of The Nuer was not only to describe "the ways in which a Nilotic people obtain their livelihood, and their political institutions" (1940:3) but also to provide research that supported a structural-functionalist theoretical paradigm. He was specifically intent on providing valid generalizations about cultural structures.

Evans-Pritchard's work was controlled by a deductive analysis of social situations. Intent on providing an understanding of Nuer culture, the specific was subsumed under the general, the individual understood only in the context of the group. Rather than describing the experiences of specific, identified individuals, Evans-Pritchard attempted to explain Nuer culture by defining, for example, the structure of kinship and providing examples to support the definitions. Although in the introduction he related some of the struggles he had in finding regular, consistent informants, Evans-Pritchard masked the voices of his informants in the omniscient ethnographic "we," relating information about the Nuer from an authoritative position. In order to obtain the kind of quality detail that he did, Evans-Pritchard had to have had numerous strong informants. But the identity of these informants remains beyond confirmation from the text provided.

Writing four decades later than Evans-Pritchard, Crapanzano reflects the influence of such anthropological icons as Clifford Geertz, Nancy Munn, James Clifford and George Marcus. Disillusioned with the attempt to fit cultural phenomena into preconceived theoretical constructs (constructed by academics), Crapanzano's mentors seek to deconstruct the relationship between anthropologist and informant in an attempt to provide a voice for the subjects of their research. These theorists are interested in highlighting the active role researchers play in the representation of the "other." The central goal of Crapanzano's ethnography is to examine the way in which the researcher and subject interact to produce a "negotiated reality" (1980:x). Taking an explicitly psychoanalytic approach,[23] Crapanzano examines in great detail the way in which Tuhami uses symbols in his creation of reality.[4]

The fulcrum of analysis for Crapanzano is the subjective experience of the individual. He attempts an inductive ethnography, starting from the phenomena of mutual experience between himself and Tuhami and building generalizations about Tuhami and his cultural context. In contrast to Evans-Pritchard, where details were provided in support of generalizations, Crapanzano attempts to show generalizations can be built from a particular life history (autobiography). He believes that Tuhami's tale "carries implicitly, if not explicitly, the Moroccan values, interpretational vectors, patterns of association, ontological presuppositions, spatiotemporal orientations, and etymological horizons that are embedded in his idiom" (1980:7). At times Crapanzano speaks with informative authority and at times allows the evocative voice of Tuhami to come through relatively uninterpreted (1980:14, 27–72, 91–130, 155–172).

The Nuer is a classic example (although a bit outdated) of the ethnography that attempts to make valid generalizations about cultural phenomena. The relationship between the ethnographer and the "informants" remains implicit. Evans-Pritchard chose to include neither lengthy quotations from informants nor direct dialogue with them in this ethnography. Tuhami is an example of an ethnography that is intent on interpreting the life of an individual as symbolic representations of reality. The relationship between the ethnographer and the individual studied is explicitly stated throughout the book.[5] The former ethnography moves from the general to understand the specific, from the theory to understanding the data, from generalizations about livelihood and political institutions to the details of Nuer existence The latter ethnography moves from the specific to the general, from one man's life to an understanding of life in Morocco, eschewing theoretical formulations.

Unfortunately, neither approach is entirely satisfactory. Evans-Pritchard's ability to present the dominant, patriarchal political and economic systems is admirable. However, his lack of attention to intra-cultural variation and to the representation of minority voices must be criticized, albeit as much a product of his generation of anthropology as a weakness in his method. In this work I get an understanding of how resources were controlled at the macro level yet remain unconvinced that the structures presented represent the majority of "the Nuer." Little attention is given to the structural roles for women or for those without access to political and economic resources. Evans-Pritchard falls into the trap of forcing the round pegs of Nuer experience into the square holes of structural analysis. And what I learn about the ethnographer from this work, I learn from reading between the lines (or the very short introduction). This approach can be improved upon by increased attention to under-represented forces and by making more explicit the relationship between the ethnographer and the ones being studied.

Tuhami: Portrait of a Moroccan is just that: an interpretation of one Moroccan's unique existence. One strength of this book is its ability to represent the multiple levels of reality from which Tuhami makes sense of his life in Morocco. From this I learn a little about a man named Tuhami and a little about an anthropologist named Crapanzano. The reflexivity of this work stands as not one of many agendas but perhaps the central agenda. I learn very little about Morocco or Moroccan culture and quite a lot about Crapanzano, the anthropologist. Cultural interpretation is reduced to the most subjective form of psychological inquiry: psychoanalysis. What generalizations are made are not done so by providing evidence but by reference to the conversation between the ethnographer and the individual. Other than such references, the reader must rely on the generalizations and interpretation given by Crapanzano himself. Crapanzano's attempt to place the ethnographic authority back in the hands of the "other" has collapsed in on itself.

A Case for Relative Objectivity

Objectivity, reliability and validity are laudable goals for the social researcher to target, even if they are ultimately unattainable. Kirk and Miller (1986) believe that systematic quantitative and qualitative social research can provide analytical tools that, while they are not to be taken as absolute criteria, are tools that get at greater approximations of truth in research. This provisional truth is ideally the kind of knowledge that is open to public scrutiny, testability and falsifiability. Objectivity "refers to taking an intellectual risk—the risk of being demonstrably wrong" (Kirk and Miller 1986:10). But if someone wants to prove the researcher wrong, he would have to do so on the terms as defined by the community of scholars. If validity and reliability are not absolute, someone must be responsible for defining the acceptable levels. If the community of scholars is responsible for setting the standards that data must meet, then the authority of valid and reliable (i.e., objective) research findings rests in the hands of the community of scholars, not simply some abstract methodology we call science.

One of the things that makes cultural anthropologists different from tourists is the attempt to collect information about people systematically. The social researcher wants to do more than observe and enjoy, although both observation and enjoyment are hopefully a part of the research process. Cultural anthropologists record their observations, interpret their observations in light of others who also study issues similar to those they have studied (i.e., a community of scholars) and attempt to communicate their findings in a language best understood by this community of scholars. Irrespective of other forms in which anthropologists want to communicate their findings (e.g. as reports to development agencies, political petitions for local community activists, screen plays, historical archival records, etc.), academic anthropologists need to communicate their findings in a form conducive to academic inquiry. This means in part that researchers need to agree on a common language. Researchers need a common language that contrasts data and noise, what is important and what is not important.

Kirk and Miller (1986) argue that the search for objective data is an essential component of a common research language for social scientists. By "objectivity" they do not mean some pure form of knowledge or absolute truth; they prefer to leave the search for this type of knowledge to philosophers and theologians. Objectivity is based on the assumption that there is a world out there that can be empirically known. But knowledge of this empirical world is always provisional, based on theoretical assumptions that the anthropologist must be able to articulate. "'Truth' (or what provisionally passes for truth at a particular time) is thus bounded both by the tolerance of empirical reality and by the consensus of the scholarly community" (Kirk and Miller 1986:12). This truth is always provisional because it must remain testable and falsifiable by those interested in studying the same issues.

The search for historically conditioned "objective" data necessarily involves the realization of as much validity and reliability as possible. "Reliability is the degree to which the finding is independent of accidental circumstances of the research, and validity is the degree to which the finding is interpreted in a correct way" (Kirk and Miller 1986:20). But to define what is truly "independent of accidental circumstances" and to determine when a finding is interpreted in a "correct" way remain open to debate. Alternative views are tested against the standards set by the intellectual community over time. Acknowledging the influence of a scholarly tradition allows for alternative views to challenge historically specific arguments in the contexts they were argued. As others join this community, they have the opportunity to change and reshape the definitions that form the foundation for quality research.

In the study of culture there should be a dialogical relationship between the general and the specific, between our understanding of the individual and the group(s) to which that individual belongs, between text and theory. Crapanzano joins the Boasians in his attempt to allow the historical particularity of Tuhami's experience to speak for itself, but one cannot understand individual experience void of historical and structural context. Interpretations of an individual's symbolic representations of the world must be placed in their social, political and economic context (con-text: literally that which goes "with the text"). This context necessarily involves a level of abstraction, a generalization from the individual to the social. The two are not mutually exclusive.

Furthermore, the relationship between the researcher and the subjects studied should be made explicit in the ethnography. It is important to know whose perspective of culture is re-presented in the ethnography and, if generalizations are made, on whose authority generalizations are made. While the relationship between the ethnographer and the informants should be made explicit, this relationship need not overwhelm the study. The reflexivity of the researcher can be taken to an extreme where all one sees is a portrait of the author and not the ones studied.

Like Odysseus on his perilous journey, the anthropologist must avoid the Scylla of sacrificing text to theory and the Charybdis of sacrificing theory to text. If the theoretical construct of the ethnographer does not take into account the complexity and dynamic nature of intracultural variation, the ethnography may be destroyed by the rocks of ethnographic validity. If all the ethnographer can offer is the uniqueness of individual experience, the ethnography will be sucked down by the whirlpool of nihilistic subjectivity.

Road Signs

Where postmodernism is helpful to cultural anthropology is first in its recognition that culture is a contested domain in both its construction and representation. Amplifying voices from the margins is important, if not central, to the writing of ethnography. Postmodernism is also helpful in emphasizing the historical contingency of ethnographic representations. Both the ethnographer and the people being studied are conditioned by historical (social, political and economic) motivations. Furthermore, as postmodernism encourages constructive reflection on the process of writing ethnography and on the relationship between the ethnographer and those studied, it takes us down another fruitful path.

If anthropologists are intent on answering comparative questions, they cannot buy wholesale into Derrida's style of deconstruction. On the one hand, deconstruction is a helpful methodological tool for analyzing the process of writing ethnography, for analyzing power relations between anthropologists and their "others" and for recognizing the contested nature of cultural interpretations. On the other hand, to follow all the way down the deconstructive road is to buy into a subjectivism that destroys any real chance of understanding anything other than the internal conversation with oneself, a solipsism dangerous to one's sanity. Postmodernism should aim its critical faculties at the construction of objectivity, at whom it is that defines the "objective" perspective and for what purpose. The goal of objectivity itself does not have to be destroyed in the process. Furthermore, anthropologists are not precluded from taking a moral stance (see Schepper-Hughes 1987, 1995), but writers must carefully articulate by what moral principles the ethnographer should operate.

Steering Clear

One way to picture the debate between postmodernists and those committed to the scientific exploration of the social world is by means of a metaphor from modern physics.[6] Postmodernism acts as a centrifugal force on anthropology, compelling us to take seriously the particular parts of our world in all their uniqueness and ambiguity. The scientific approach acts as a centripetal force, forcing us to take seriously the structures and patterns of culture that tie the world together. If either the centrifugal tendencies of postmodernism or the centripetal forces of science claim exclusive right to the driver's seat in cultural anthropology, it will destroy the dynamic character of anthropology itself.

By maintaining a dialogue between these opposing forces, checks and balances are provided that keep the discipline from either collapsing in on itself or exploding into chaos. If the anthropologist can only talk to and about herself, her solipsistic wanderings will be of no use to anyone else. If the anthropologist has no tools with which to organize the chaos, no one will listen.

Analyzing Race via Social Networks

Research Statement

Research over the past thirty years has shown that social networks are of crucial importance in understanding the procurement and retention of employment (Granovetter 1973, 1974, 1982; Lin and Dumin 1986; Zimmer and Aldrich 1987). A strong interest has also grown in the roles that race and ethnicity play in constructing and maintaining social networks, particularly as each relates to employment (Cobas et al. 1993, Cobas and DeOllos 1989, Light and Bonacich 1988, Du Toit 1998, Ooka and Wellman 1999). The role of inter- and intra-racial social networks has been shown to be particularly central in the procurement and retention of resources for entrepreneurs (Sanders and Nee 1996). While some have shown the importance of intra-racial ties for success in entrepreneurial development, little work has been done to study the importance of inter-racial ties on such success or lack of success (see Ooka and Wellman 1999 for an exception). This study provides insight into the structure and content of personal and professional networks of commercial fishing skippers and crew on South Africa's Western Cape coast. Particular emphasis is on the role that the construction of racial and ethnic identities plays in developing and maintaining these social networks. Special interest is taken in understanding the networks of those fishers classified as "Coloured" under apartheid and how new constructions of that racial and ethnic identity operate in everyday work life.

As much of cognitive anthropology and social psychology has shown, people develop implicit models of whom they know and respect in their heads (and how these people are connected), and these models in turn influence with whom they choose to associate. The choice of associates becomes particularly important in the context of employment, where the structure and content of personal relationships often determine the success in the development and maintenance of a livelihood (Granovetter 1973, 1974; Lin and Dumin 1986; Sanders and Nee 1996). In particular, small-scale entrepreneurial enterprises thrive and survive on the size and quality of social networks (Light and Bonacich 1988). These networks help to establish ties instrumental to the success of the enterprise, ties that minimize the uncertainty associated with limited institutional infrastructure. Add to this uncertainty the high-risk environment of commercial fishing, where captain and crew depend on each other not only for a living but for a safe return home, and social networks become crucial for personal and professional survival. Through quantitative and qualitative analysis of these social networks I explain: 1) what kinds of individuals are more likely to be involved in social networks of greater racial heterogeneity, 2) to what extent individuals use inter- as opposed to intra-racial ties for procuring and sustaining employment, and 3) what characteristics of the networks themselves lead to the greater likelihood of full-time employment (i.e., less dependence on other sources of income).

In understanding racial and ethnic relations in South Africa, little attention has been paid to the structure and content of social networks. With few exceptions (see De Jongh 1995) researchers have focused on social networks as metaphor, as a heuristic device, or predominantly in the context of formal kinship studies. But advances in methodological techniques for the systematic study of social networks have made it possible to move beyond an understanding of social networks as metaphor to an analysis of the structural properties of personal and professional relationships (Scott 1991, Wasserman and Faust 1994, Johnson 1994, Degene and Forse 1999). Yet social network analysis techniques can be even more powerful when combined with the analysis of cultural content (Emirbayer and Goodwin 1994). While social research in the past half century has tended to split into social structural and cultural analytical branches (among others), these branches are still part of the same tree. A narrow focus on social structure runs the danger of disguising human agency and obfuscating human creativity. A myopic focus on individual experience runs the danger of ignoring larger social processes that shape human thought and behavior. In an attempt to understand the effect of race and ethnicity on making a living in South Africa, this project navigates between the Scylla of structural determinism and the Charybdis of interpretive solipsism via a synthesis of social network analysis and what Clifford Geertz called "thick description" (1973). Theoretical synthesis will emerge out of methodological synthesis.

Constructing Race and Ethnicity

For decades Anthropologists have challenged static and naturalistic views of race and ethnicity (Sanjek 1971; Drake 1980, 1987; Brodkin 1989; Eller and Coughlan 1993; Gregory and

Sanjek 1994). Racial and ethnic identities are socially constructed in particular historical contexts, malleable, and often overlap with other kinds of social identity (Roosen 1989). In the right context, some people also have the ability to assume various racial or ethnic identities in different situations (Okamura 1981). Fredrik Barth's (1969) focus on ethnic boundaries was a necessary correction to primordial definitions of ethnicity but limited in its ability to describe ethnicity as a product of individual consciousness and social interaction. Recent debates over the salience of ethnicity as a social force have concentrated on how ethnic relations function at the communal level, e.g. the relationship between ethnic conflict and the modern state (Anderson 1993, Erickson 1993, Vail 1993). Most of the latter studies define ethnicity in instrumentalist terms (Cohen 1978). This approach is helpful to the degree that it emphasizes ethnicity as a social, political and cultural resource to be called upon when the opportunity presents itself. There are two main weaknesses in the instrumentalist literature: 1) the inability to describe how ethnicity functions as a flexible form of individual identity and 2) the limited ability to describe the structural constraints that racial and ethnic categories place on human interaction. Instrumentalists tend to be overly dependent on studies of the elite and over-confident in the power of rational choice (Hechter 1986).

It can be argued that much like ethnic categories, racial groupings are "imagined communities" (Anderson 1993) in the sense that they are social inventions not fabrications. But there are considerable differences in the styles in which different racial and ethnic groups are imagined. Classifying the "races of man" was the *raisonne d'etre* of early social science. Essentialized categories conflated biology and morality. The Boasians limited the definition of race to the biophysical and morphological characteristics and divorced it from the learned behavior of language and culture. But the Boasian anti-racism was based largely on assimilationist assumptions (Baker 1998). Recent works have moved beyond these assumptions and reinvigorated research on race in anthropology (Harrison 1995; Wade 1995; McClaurin 1996; Mukhopadhyay 1997). One of the strengths these works share is their ability to describe racial categorization as an historical process, deeply rooted in local culture and constructs of the "other."

The current study is expressly concerned with the structural and cultural meaning of race and ethnicity, concerned with how individuals conceptualize and utilize identity in relationship to others. With one eye on the historical development of "coloured" as a socio-economic and political category (Marais 1939; Venter 1974; Goldin 1987; Lewis 1987), the central focus of this dissertation is on how this racial and ethnic identity is socially constructed and made useful in the context of social networks. As we learn from the social psychological approach of Donald Horowitz (1985) and DeVos and Romanucci-Ross (1995), ethnic identity is grounded in individual experience and played out in social relationships. By careful observations of the language, the dominant idioms and the stereotypes perpetuated in the context of the social networks of commercial handline fishing captains, this study will help paint a picture of contemporary inter- and intra-ethnic relations in South Africa.

In April of 1996 *The Economist* reported that people in South Africa who were classified as coloured under apartheid feared being lost between the economic power of whites and political power of blacks. At a time when the nature of coloured identity itself is being questioned and redefined, those who have historically been known as coloured wonder about their place in the new South Africa. Where do those categorized as coloureds fit into attempts to create equal opportunity in employment for all South Africans? In the fishing industry, as with many other industries, management has been historically white and the labor historically non-white. In the small-scale handline industry, "non-white" specifically refers to those classified as coloured.

As a contribution to the sub-discipline of economic anthropology, this research explores the roles race and ethnicity play in the structuring of professional networks (Gladwin 1989). Economic activity is embedded in a complex web of social relations and institutions (Appadurai 1986). It has become a truism in anthropology that ethnic identity and racial stereotyping enable or restrict economic success (Gregory and Sanjek 1994; Lipuma and Meltzoff 1997). Yet neither the construction of racial or ethnic identity nor the development of economic activity can be divorced from the relational context in which both occur simultaneously. "We should expect that different social groups, situated in different objective conditions as to their capacity to earn a livelihood, will have distinct experiences giving different meanings to a cultural concept that at first might appear homogenous" (Narotsky 1997:222–223). Therefore, the use of systematic social network analysis tools, combined with the cultural detail gathered from in-depth interviews and participant observation, will serve to move the debate over employment discrimination beyond the rhetoric of individual experience. At the same time, the ethnographic nature of the other methods employed will add qualitative depth to research that, thus far, has concentrated predominantly on aggregate labor statistics (Jiobu 1990; Uchendu 1995; Lipuma and Meltzoff 1997).

As a study of the relations of production in the commercial fishing industry this project is forced to move beyond traditional understandings of employer-employee relations and typical employee-wage structures (Smith 1977; Robben 1986; Bailey 1991; Smith and Hanna 1993). The skippers and crew of small handline boats, i.e., the primary subjects in this study, do not fit neatly into predefined economic categories. The skippers, in most instances, are self-employed entrepreneurs. They are dependent on a wide variety of uncertainties such as the physical environment (weather, ocean currents, tides), the condition and availability of the resource (i.e., fish stocks), ever-changing government regulations, large fluctuations in market demand for the product and the health of up to twelve crewmembers. Captain-crew relations approximate traditional employer-employee relations but rarely contain any formalized contracts. Crewmembers are dependent on the same conditions as the captain but with the added variable that they do not control when they go fishing. They are dependent on the captain for initiating their workday.

Figure 2. Handline Fisher Bringing a Snoek into the Boat
source: Stibbe and Moss (1998)

As an analysis of social relations in the commercial fishing industry this study also

contributes to the expanding literature on the relations of productions among workers involved in

natural resource exploitation (Palsson 1991; Durrenberger 1992, 1993; Smith and Jepson 1993;

Garrity-Blake 1994). Particular themes from this literature that will be explored include: local

participation in fisheries management (Miller 1979; McCay 1987; Acheson 1990; Ostrom 1990;

Pollnac 1991; Smith and Jepson 1993), variations in the use of technology to exploit natural

resources (Bernard 1987, Zerner 1991), the risk and uncertainty involved in fishing for a living

(Pollnac, Poggie and Vandusen 1995; Pollnac, Poggie and Cabral 1998) and the question of

fishing as a marker of identity (i.e., a fishing culture, or "more than a job" (Smith and Jepson

1993; Eacker 1994, Garrity-Blake 1994).

Interpreting Social Structure

If there is to be a synthesis of structural and interpretive approaches to understanding

significant social constructions (such as race and ethnicity) and their impact on lived experiences

(such as job procurement and retention), then one way to begin that synthesis is by a synthesis of research methods. There should be an intimate connection between the answers sought in a research project and the types of questions raised. "If substance ("data," "findings," "facts") are products of the methods used, substance cannot be considered independently of method; *what* the ethnographer finds out is inherently connected with *how* she finds it out" (Emerson 1995:11). This project will proceed by combining research priorities from the interpretive literature and tools from social network analysis.

"Network analysis is a recent set of methods for the systematic study of social structures" (Degenne and Forse 1999). In describing the broad streams in the types of network approaches used in anthropology, Jeff Johnson notes that there is a major distinction in the literature between those who use the concept of social networks metaphorically (Walsh and Simonelli 1986; O'Conner 1990) and those who use social networks as a formal/analytical research tool (Johnson 1994). This study intends to move beyond understanding social networks as a heuristic concept to a more detailed and systematic approach to collecting and analyzing information about these networks. By following this analytical approach to understanding social networks this project stands with one foot in a tradition that can be traced back to the works of Durkheim (e.g. the concept of organic solidarity) and the mid-century structural-functionalism of A.R. Radcliffe-Brown. Network analysis owes a more immediate tribute to the works of John Barnes (1951; 1969; 1972), Clyde Mitchell (1969), Elizabeth Bott (1971) and Ron Burt (1982), to name a few. Network analysis is used as an inductive attempt to identify patterns of relationships and the behaviors or thoughts that correlate with those patterns. "Then it sorts out *a posteriori* and *identifies the concrete constraints of structure on behaviour at the same time as it uncovers constraints on structure from group interactions*" (Degenne and Forse 1999:2–3). The primary focus is not on the attributes of individuals but on the relationships between individuals.

Social network studies can be divided into two basic types: ego-centered (also called personal or partial networks) and whole network (also called global networks) approaches. Whole networks are an "abstraction of the overall, 'global' features of networks in relation to a particular aspect of social activity" (Scott 1991:31). For a review of anthropologists studying whole networks see Johnson (1994). The present study is concerned to a limited degree with whole networks. More centrally this study concentrates on the networks that are "anchored around a particular individual so as to generate 'ego-centered' networks of social relations of all kinds" (Scott 1991:31). Studying the entire network of handline skippers will allow for the analysis of group formation. While ego-network data cannot provide accurate descriptions of the overall social structure of a population, this approach "gives representative samples of the social environments surrounding particular elements and is compatible with conventional statistical methods of generalization to large populations" (Marsden 1990:438). It is my intention that the summary measures on the ego-network data and the interpretive ethnographic analysis will complement one another for a fuller explanation of the effect of race on social relations in the fishing industry.

One of the weaknesses in this study is its inability to measure how networks change over time. By nature of its cross-sectional design this study is forced to deal with the charge of static bias. Social structures such as personal networks change over time, but the description and prediction of such change is beyond the scope of this project. This project can serve as a baseline for future diachronic analysis. However, for analysis of how current conditions relate to conditions in the past I will rely on generalized comparisons with the historical literature on race relations in South Africa (James 1991; Bekker 1993, Vail 1993; Fredrickson 1995; Pickel 1997).

A sample of first order zone cognitive network ties served as a proxy for understanding the typical social relations in which commercial skippers were involved. "First order zone" refers to a person's direct contacts, someone they interact with personally (Barnes 1969). The specific focus will be on cognitive networks or the way people construct their social universe in their heads. The measurement of actual exchanges is beyond the scope of this project. Although key research has shown that informants are relatively inaccurate in detailed recall of their exact social interactions (for a summary see Bernard et al. 1984), the bias in informant inaccuracy is towards typical interaction (Freeman and Romney 1987, Freeman et al. 1987). In-depth interviews will make it possible to add historical detail to such typical interactions (e.g. how long an alter is known by an ego and in what capacity/ies).

Research Questions and Hypotheses

The following research questions and hypotheses structure the content for this dissertation.

1) What kinds of individuals are more likely to be involved in social networks of greater racial heterogeneity?

   H1: Education will have no significant effect on the racial heterogeneity of social networks.

   H2: Age will have no significant effect on the racial heterogeneity of social networks.

   H3: People with a racially heterogeneous friendship network will be more likely to also have a racially heterogeneous professional network.

   H4a: People categorized as historically disadvantaged will be more likely to have racially heterogeneous professional networks.

   H4b: People categorized as white/European will be less likely to have racially heterogeneous professional networks.

   H5: There will be no significant difference in the racial heterogeneity of friendship networks between different racial categories.

   The racial heterogeneity of a friendship network will be measured as the proportion of same-race ties as determined by the skippers' answers to the friendship name generators 1–3. If they categorize 40% or more of their close friends as racially different from themselves, their friendship network will be considered heterogeneous (which is slightly more liberal than Ooka and Wellman's use of 50%) (Ooka and Wellman 1999). A person's professional network will be considered racially diverse if 40% of the groups of professional contacts they have are diverse. Each group of contacts will be considered racially diverse if ego judges 40% or more of those in the group as racially different from themselves. Professional groups for skippers include: Factory Ownership (FO), Factory Management (FM), Factory Labour (FL), Boat Owner (BO1 & BO2*), Boat Skipper (BS1 &BS2*), Boat Crew (BC1 & BC2*), Administration Local (AL, ministry, staff), Administration National (AN, ministry, staff), Administration Research (AR), Other (O). The differentiation denoted by * is: 1=own boat, 2=other boat.

One of the strengths of the ego-centered approach to network analysis is the ability to combine the analysis of individual traits with analysis of the kinds of relations that exist between individuals. It is often assumed that education has a liberalizing effect on perceptions of difference and a consequent increase in inter-racial relationships. This assumption will be challenged by analyzing how education relates to the racial diversity of friendship and professional networks, proving that, for the range of education common among commercial fishers, education will not impact the racial heterogeneity of social networks.

Works on the ethnic solidarity of migrants have shown older migrants are more likely to build densely knit, tightly bounded social networks (Light and Bonacich 1988). But following Portes (1995) it will be argued here that age itself will not be a significant determinant of the racial heterogeneity of social networks. It will also be argued that those whose friendship networks are racially heterogeneous will be more likely to have racially diverse professional networks. The reverse is not assumed to be true. Historically disadvantaged racial and ethnic groups in South Africa (e.g. black or coloured) still face systemic racism. Therefore, persons from these groups will be more likely to use diverse networks for their success. Conversely, persons from historically advantaged communities (i.e., white) will be more likely to use densely knit, tightly bounded social networks to maintain benefits they already have. I believe that friendship networks are more socially conservative than professional networks and will thus be more homogenous regardless of how ego classifies himself and others.

2) To what extent do individuals use inter- as opposed to intra-racial ties for procuring and sustaining employment?

   H6a: Members of historically low status racial groups will be more likely to use inter-racial ties than intra-racial ties for obtaining employment.

   H6b: Members of historically high status racial groups will be more likely to use inter-racial ties as opposed to intra-racial ties for obtaining employment.

H7: Tenure in the fishing industry will be positively associated with the use of inter-racial ties.

Building on the work done by Ooka and Wellman (1999), it is assumed that people make use of both inter- and intra-racial ties for finding (and keeping) jobs. "The advantages (or disadvantages) of working in an ethnic economy or ethnic niches depend on the resources that particular ethnic groups can mobilize through their co-ethnic networks" (Ooka and Wellman 1999:3). Inter-ethnic ties have been shown to be advantageous, particularly for developing entrepreneurs (Cobas et al. 1993). But job seekers and entrepreneurs can also increase their opportunities by making use of important ties outside "co-ethnic networks," particularly with persons of higher status ethnic groups.

Informant Selection

Network analysis name generators and interpreters formed a major part of an in-depth interview schedule administered to 102 commercial handline skippers that live and travel from Struisbaai (south east of Cape Town) to Lambert's Bay (north west of Cape Town), a geographic range determined by the residence of those in the network. Each captain was interviewed at the place of their choosing, most often in their homes. Where possible, private time was reserved for the lengthy interview with the skipper alone. The interviews with the skippers lasted a minimum of one hour and more often than not ran longer than three hours. Consent was verbally requested from each skipper prior to the formal interview (see Appendix D).

The method of subject selection for the study is drawn from the social network analysis literature. The research design is cross-sectional where "data are collected at one point in time from a sample selected to describe some larger population at that time" (Babbie 1990:56). This design will be used to provide for in-depth description of current social relations. It will also allow for the determination of the relationship between individual demographic characteristics and the racial composition of social networks and for the determination of the degree to which certain types of individuals use inter- as opposed to intra-racial ties for procuring and sustaining employment. Analysis of how these conditions relate to conditions in the past will rely on more generalized comparisons with the historical literature on race relations in South Africa (James 1991; Bekker 1993, Vail 1993; Fredrickson 1995; Pickel 1997).

The sampling frame used for the study is a subset of a list of all fishing boats registered on South Africa's Western Cape Coast. Significant data collection and analysis on the commercial fishing industry are published annually by the editors of the Fishing Industry Handbook: South Africa, Namibia and Mozambique (Warman 1999) in cooperation with the national fisheries regulation body, Marine and Coastal Management (formerly Sea Fisheries). Information in this data set includes the boat names, owner names and contact details, length of the boats (among other detail), number of crew on each boat and an independently researched category for the type of fishing done on the boat. Information from this list proved helpful in making initial contacts, but personal confirmation of the information from these sources highlighted the inaccuracies in the national database. The lists could not distinguish between full-time and part-time commercial fishers, nor did it carefully distinguish between those operating mobile ski-boats and those operating the less mobile "chakkies". Using the government information as a starting point, informants were selected by snowball sampling from confirmed cases. Those finally selected were all full-time, commercial handline ski-boat skippers that traveled the coast following the fish and were actively fishing between September 1999 and August 2000. Skippers of the more traditional handline chakkies were omitted due to the profound difference that geographical range makes on social networks. Chakkies remain moored in their port of origin and are not transported from harbor to harbor in search of fish. From preliminary interviews, subsequently confirmed by the ski-boat skippers interviewed, the social networks of skippers on the chakkies and those on the ski-boats do not display much overlap.

The networks and experiences of active commercial skippers of handline vessels served as the fulcrum of analysis for this study. The type of boat and fishing is held constant so as to control for variations associated with the type of fishing done. The range of the boat length and number of crew will also be limited to increase the likelihood of comparable units. As expected, crew size correlates with boat length (86% for the west coast boats). The study was limited to skippers of handline boats with twelve crew or less. These skippers serve as the primary units of analysis. As will become evident, part of the analysis relies on the skipper and crew as a unit. Handline boats tend to be relatively small, independently owned operations dependent on informal social and economic ties for their success. This lack of formal restrictions on a skipper's choice of associates increases the likelihood that the associations are voluntary.

The initial cut in the data for selection of a sampling frame involves limiting the geographical range. Subjects were selected by snowball sampling (Babbie 1990), beginning with preliminary interviews of the skippers on commercial fishing boats registered in the ports ranging from Lambert's Bay in the north to False Bay in the south (Warman 1999:243–284). The reasons for this first cut are both theoretical and practical. The commercial fishing industry of the western Cape coast serves as the regional and industrial context for this study in part because this industry has historically been dominated by coloured workers (Marais 1939; Venter 1974; van Sittert 1992; Stibbe and Moss 1998). As was evident from statistics gathered during the 1994 elections, over 50% of voters living in the Western Cape Province identified themselves as coloured (Pickel 1997). The effects of the changes in South African race relations are of pressing concern to these voters (James 1996). Relationships in the commercial fishing industry are highly likely to involve employees who identify themselves as coloured.

From preliminary personal interviews with key informants it seemed, and was later confirmed, that many of the commercial handline skippers who were registered in the ports of interest concentrated their range of fishing between Lambert's Bay and False Bay. This is a reasonable range for skippers at the geographical extremes to travel in search of prime fishing (approximately two hours of drive time from Cape Town in either direction along the coast). This range also makes sense in light of the need for proximity to the lucrative Cape Town markets and the putative heavier concentrations of snoek[7], the primary species for commercial handliners on the western coast (Van der Elst 1981, Griffiths 2000).

Harbor masters, factory owners and managers, national local Marine and Coastal Management officials and other key informants were used to confirm the identities of the appropriate skippers in each region. Over the course of the first five months of initial research, from September 1999 through January 2000, I identified approximately 155 skippers of what were identified as "full-time commercials" or active handline ski-boats in the study area. I continued to add to this list when one of the skippers mentioned full time handline ski-boats not already on the list. It became my intention to interview the skippers from each of these 155 ski-boats. After sorting through some errors in informant recall, boats that had been sold or were no longer in service, and skippers who had moved, 118 active full-time commercial handline skipper remained. Of these, 102 were interviewed, four declined when asked to participate, and twelve could not be reached for logistical reasons. I confirmed the status of each of the 102 interviewees as full-time commercial handline ski-boat skippers with at least three independent persons, at least two of which were other skippers. As there were significant tensions between full-time and part-time/recreational fishers, skippers quickly categorized others in one of the two camps. Where there was uncertainty, I gained confirmation from the skipper himself.

Data Collection

The typical procedure for collecting ego-centric network data is to elicit alters (persons tied to ego) via one or more name generators. Name generators are specific questions designed to elicit a list of individuals with whom the respondent has direct ties of a specific kind. Additional information about the alters is then generated through name interpreters. Marsden categorizes three types of name interpreters: "(a) reports on attributes of persons or alters enumerated (e.g. age, education, race/ethnicity); (b) reports on properties of the tie between respondent and alter (e.g. frequency of contact, duration of acquaintance, intensity); and (c) reports on the intensity of ties between pairs of alters" (1990:441). Research has shown that the demographic characteristics of alters can be reported with substantially greater accuracy than the attitudes of alters (Bernard et al. 1985). Projection plays a part in responses to questions asking for proxy reports on attitudes, particularly for more distant ties (e.g. friends as opposed to spouses) (Wilcox and Udry 1986). Therefore, respondents were not asked to divulge what they thought any of their alters thought or believed.

The name generators used in this study were designed to elicit the perceived characteristics of alters. They also focused on the perceived strength of ties between ego and alters. In terms of the properties of ties between ego and alter (e.g. frequency of contact, duration of acquaintance, intensity), respondent reports are generally in concordance with alter reports, particularly for close ties and reasonably general types of interaction (esp. frequency of contact, duration, kinship and intensity of relationship) (Hammer 1984). A combination of the intensity, frequency and duration of ties between pairs of alters has been shown to be the strongest indicator of tie strength (Marsden and Campbell 1984).

Name Generators

1) From time to time, most people discuss important matters with other people, people they trust. The range of important matters varies from person to person across work, leisure, family, politics, whatever. The range of relations varies across work, family, friends and advisors. **If you look back over the last six months, who are the four or five people with whom you discussed matters important to you?**

2) Consider the people with whom you like to spend your free time. **Over the last six months, who are the three or four people you have been with most often for informal social activities such as having a potjie or braai together, having drinks together, going to films, visiting one another's homes, and so on?**

3) **Who would you say are your closest three or four friends?** This may or may not be the people you spend the most time with.

4) **Of all the people working in the commercial fishing industry on the western Cape coast, who are the five or six people who have contributed most to your success in fishing—i.e., your most valuable work contacts?**

5) **Suppose you had a friend who wanted to do what you are for a living. Who are the most important people (that you know personally) you would introduce them to who would give them the best information and advice?** Who do they really need to get to know?

6) **Are there any individuals you regard as a mentor, someone who has taken a strong interest in how well you do as a fisherman and has provided you with the opportunity or means to do better?**

7) **Of all the people you know in the industry, who has made things most difficult for you to do well in what you do?** Remember that all names are coded and kept confidential and will not be released from my research except as combined statistics.

8) **If you decided to find a job in the commercial fishing industry, who are the two or three people with whom you would most likely discuss and evaluate your job options?** These could be people who work with you now, or people from other than where you work now such as friends, family, people who work on other boats or other people in the fishing industry.

9) When it comes to information you need that will enable you to catch more fish or get higher prices for your fish, **who are the skippers that you contact for important information** (e.g. where the fish are biting, what prices hawkers are paying on the open market, recommendations for new crew members, etc.)?

10) **If you wanted to have a friendly but business related sit down chat with the head of Marine and Coastal Management, who would be the people you contacted to set it up for you?**

11) Look over this list of names. **Can you name anyone else whom you would consider as important to you as the people you see on this list?**

The preceding name generators have been adapted for this study from the works of Fisher (1982), Burt (1984, 1985, 1997), Rook (1984), Leffler, Krannich and Gillespie (1986), Kochen (1989), Wegener (1991), Podolny and Baron (1997). One of the influences in developing these name generators is the finding that multiple name generators from multiple categories of relations elicit a broader social network (Burt 1997). By asking about personal and professional ties I was able to look for evidence of the overlap between the two types of networks. If social capital, for example, is a product of network ties, then "the strongest evidence of social capital occurs when personal and corporate relations together define the network used to measure social capital" (Burt 1997:371).

Name generators one through three are focused on the individual's personal network, irrespective of the social context. Name generators four through ten focus attention more specifically on contacts related to employment. The first of these name generators is taken directly from Podolny and Baron's adaptation of the network name generator on the 1985 General Social Survey (GSS) (Burt 1984, 1985; Podolny and Baron 1997) and is designed to sample ego's discussion network. The generators that follow are designed to elicit ego's #2) socializing network (Burt 1997:359), #3) intimate friendship network (Fisher 1982), #4) most valued work contacts (Burt 1997:359), #5) general employment info and advice (Podolny and Baron 1997:691), and #6) mentorship networks (Podolny and Baron 1997:692). The seventh generator is included to elicit conflictive ties, since some studies of social support suggest that the absence of non-supportive ties is more crucial than the presence of supportive ties (see Rook 1984; Leffler, Krannich and Gillespie 1986). Name generator eight is designed to elicit contacts for ego's alternative options in the industry. Name generator nine is to elicit ties that provide specific strategic information for ego's success as a skipper from other skippers in their category. It is designed specifically to tap co-worker networks, people in similar positions. Name generator ten is designed following the first step in a small world experiment. It is designed specifically to measure ego's proximity to the most important decision makers in the regulation of their industry (see the contributions in Kochen 1989). Name generator eleven was created because of Burt's findings that his respondents, having reviewed their name lists, added names to the end of their list but did not place these names in any of the generator categories (1997:359). Name generator twelve was generated to delve into the skipper's knowledge and perspective of his crew.

Name Interpreters (see Appendix B):

sex =	male (0); female (1)
age =	actual age in years
race =	ego's perception of what they would have been categorized under apartheid
reside =	the town/neighborhood they live in (smallest geographical unit known)
lang1 =	primary language spoken at home:
lang2 =	secondary language spoken at home

(*f*) =	How often do you communicate with this person: 1) Daily; 2) Weekly; 3) Monthly; 4) Less than Monthly
duration =	How long have you had a relationship with this person?
role =	What does this person do in the fishing industry, if any? Factory Ownership (FO); Factory Management (FM); Factory Labour (FL); Boat Owner (BO1 & BO2*); Boat Skipper (BS1 &BS2*); Boat Crew (BC1 & BC2*); Administration Local (AL; ministry; staff); Administration National (AN; ministry; staff); Administration Research (AR) Other (O) <* - 1=own boat; 2=other boat>
family =	How is this person related to you, if at all? (spouse, mchild, fchild, hmparent, hfparent, wmparent, wfparent, hsibling, wsibling,, hmparentsib, hfparentsib, wmparentsib, wfparentsib, hgrandparent, wgrandparent, other adult, other child)? (m=male; f=female; h=husband; w=wife; child=under19)
intimacy =	How close do you consider this person to you? 1) Distant (avoid contact unless it is necessary) ; 2) Less close (Ok to work with, no desire to develop friendship); 3) Close (close, but not one of the closest contacts); 4) Especially close (one of your closest contacts)
religion =	Do any of the members on your list attend the same religious congregation you do?
job =	Rank which of these people were most responsible for you getting the job as skipper? (top three)

In addition to important demographic characteristics such as sex, age, putative race, area of residence, marriage status and language preference, each skipper was asked to name characteristics of their relationship to the alters they name. Frequency, duration and intimacy are all indicators of tie strength (Marsden 1990). Role and family are included as traditional structural categories to be correlated with tie strength indicators. These are often found to be strong predictors of tie strength (Marsden and Campbell 1984; Marsden 1990). Religion is included as a measure of socialization.

The Structured Interview

The central tool for primary data collection in the project was a detailed interview schedule consistently applied across all interviewees (see Appendix A). The structured interview included both closed and open-ended questions, tables, Likert scales and important follow-up probes. At no time was the interviewee asked to fill out information for himself. The questions were organized into the following categories: Demographic and Personal History, Household, On the Job, Networks, Women in Fishing, Gear, Annual Round, Crew, Regulations/Licensing, Future of Fishing, Job Attachment and Job Satisfaction.

Demographic and Personal History questions were designed to elicit general sociological information for comparison within group and to other populations. Question four was particularly central to the research project as it asked the interviewee to identify under which race or ethnic classification he was identified during apartheid. Due to the contested nature of racial and ethnic identity in South Africa, particularly for those once classified as coloured, I asked directly about this categorization on two different occasions. Later in the interview, question thirteen, I asked the interviewee to explain what the classification they were once assigned meant to them in the present.

Questions about the household were primarily targeted at the contribution that fishing makes to the household income. After a few preliminary interviews and advice from others who had interviewed in the fishing industry I decided not to ask for gross or net income figures. With the informal nature of these businesses, skippers were constantly wary of direct financial questions. The government was in the process of formalizing their sector of the fishing industry. Despite the consent protocol that clearly identified who I was, what my intentions were and how they were protected, I was constantly queried as to whether I was representing either Marine and Coastal Management or the tax auditor.

I followed questions about the household with questions designed to elicit details about their experiences on the job. One of the more important questions in this section was the first; it asked skippers to describe the typical fisherman. This question was designed to elicit the attributes that fishers have of themselves and others like them. It was also designed to give the interviewees an opportunity to project their own cognitive models of who is who in the industry. This section included questions about their history in the fishing industry.

The network questions formed the middle third of the interview schedule, and approximately a third of the interview time was spent on these questions. The questions are discussed in detail above. Names were first generated on the Name Table (see Appendix), numbered by the name generator used. If names were repeated, they were written again, preceded by the corresponding name generator. No strict limit was given on the number of alters each skipper could mention in relation to any of the name generators. After names were generated from all twelve generators, the interviewer and interviewee went back over the list together to answer the name interpreter questions for each of the alters mentioned. Interpreter information was filled out for the first time the alter's name appeared on the list.

In preliminary interviews handline fishing was constantly described by men and women alike as "a man's world," "not a place for a woman." Women were clearly involved in the handline fishing industry in bookkeeping, marketing, sales, household management, running errands, preparing food, and often providing a consistent income and benefits with formal employment, but the network analysis design of this study precluded an in-depth analysis of women's perspective on or input into handline fishing as a business. The questions about women in fishing were designed to explore these skippers' stereotypes of women with an eye toward understanding how and why men construct fishing as gendered work. If women's voices are muted in this study, it is because these voices are muted in the conversations of the all-male skipper network.

The size and technological sophistication of the gear used for fishing is a good indicator of the capital each owner has available to invest in their handline ski-boat business. I assumed there would be much more variation in technology than what I actually found. Questions in the Annual Round section were designed specifically to inquire about the type of fishing engaged, the formal or informal seasonal patterns of fishing, and the geographical movement of this highly mobile class of fishermen.

Open-ended questions about a skipper's perspective of his crew were designed to allow interviewees to project their own categories of class and race onto those who work for them. As most were quick to make a categorical distinction between skippers and crew, these questions became important in determining how skippers viewed relations of power, specifically with relation to class and race.

Local and national political struggles over the access to fishing licenses and quotas were on the top of everyone's agenda for discussion. I intentionally left questions about the government management system until near the end of the interview so as not to allow such topics to dominate the entire interview. Responses to these questions tended to be long and passionate. With the passage of the new Marine Living Resources Act just two years prior and the implications of that act for handline fishers still not legislated, quotas and the boat licensing system were pressing concerns.

I ended the interview by having skippers assess where they had come from and what future they saw in fishing. Optimism for the future, job attachment and job satisfaction all contribute to mental health. Questions here were designed to explore what skippers thought of the future of the fishing industry and their place in it. I also wanted to know how attached they felt to the kind of work they were doing and whether they had searched out other options. Finally, I was concerned with how satisfied these skippers were with important aspects of what they did for a living.

With the time-intensive nature of the detailed interview schedule and the geographical scope of the social network, it became necessary to hire research assistants to increase coverage of the network. Three research assistants were hired from June through August 2000. Each assistant was trained in interview techniques and the specific issues important to the project. Each of the three assistants was an experienced interviewer in fishing communities. They were referred to my project by the coordinators of the Subsistence Fisheries Task Group (2000), a research project completed in February 2000. After listening to samples of completed interviews, I held three follow-up sessions with the assistants to discuss their progress and to clarify interpretation of the questions. See the Research Assistant contract (Appendix C) for details of our agreement.

Notes

[1] I use the term "re-directed" to acknowledge postmodernism's debt to earlier methodologies such as what Harris calls the Historical Particularists or the Boasians (Harris 1968).

[2] "The reader will recognize too, especially in my questions, a psychoanalytic orientation that I have found impossible to eliminate, so embedded is this orientation in contemporary Western thought" (Crapanzano 1980:10).

[3] See, for example, Crapanzano's interpretation of Tuhami's psychological servitude to the female spirit "A'isha Qandisha" (1980:71–72).

[4] An example of an ethnography where this reflexivity is taken to an extreme is Ruth Behar's Translated Woman (1993).

[5] As a metaphor, the picture drawn here should appeal to the postmodernist. As an analogy from modern physics, the picture drawn here should appeal to the scientist.

[7] I am indebted to Marc Griffiths of the Sea Fisheries Research Institute in South Africa for all of the information on this important southern African species. He generously provided a pre-publication copy of his latest work entitled: Life history of South African snoek *Thyrsites atun* (Pisces: Gempylidae): a pelagic predator of the Benguela Ecosystem (Griffiths 2000). Specific information on snoek throughout this dissertation has been taken from this paper.

CHAPTER 4
THE "SO-CALLED" PEOPLE:
COLOURED IDENTITY IN THE NEW SOUTH AFRICA

Identity in the Context of Oppression

In order to do justice to the complexity of issues surrounding coloured identity, it is

important to clarify the language used. Language is an integral part of culture, of cultural change,

of ethnic identity and of identity politics. The words we choose both reflect and affect our

perceptions and attitudes. Language colors our understanding. Our words often reflect the power

relations in society. The same term can be used for directly opposing purposes. This is

particularly true of terms used to distinguish one people group from another. The term

"coloured," as used at present when referring to a particular people group in South Africa, is, on

the one hand, saddled with the static baggage of South Africa's apartheid past and, on the other

hand, is a category fluid enough to include a host of new identities in a rapidly changing social

landscape. The ambiguity of the issues surrounding coloured identity has lead many academics,

journalists and popular writers to euphemistically refer to this group of people as the "so-called

coloured," invariably with "coloured" in quotation marks.

Race and ethnicity are both historically conditioned, socially constructed attempts to

distinguish one group of people from another by reference to each group's unique interaction

between ideological commitments and material conditions. Self-identification with an ethnic or

racial group involves an ever-changing process of identity formation in which certain individual

psychological and material needs are met (e.g. sense of belonging, inheritance of land) and

whereby collective (social) mobilization can take place to further a common interest. Persons of

the same ethnic or racial group may identify themselves (or have been identified by someone

84

else) with particular physical characteristics. Inclusion in a particular ethnic or racial group usually involves a shared sense of history or identification with a common past. The survival of the group depends on a commitment to preserving a certain level of distinctiveness of the group.

Primarily due to its use as a tool of oppression and domination, many South Africans have rejected the label "coloured." Those who have been classified as coloured by successive South African governments have a history of diverse origins, lack of social, economic or phenotypic homogeneity and an increasing heterogeneity of residence, religion and political affiliation. Legislative definitions, as exemplified in the Nationalist's Population Registration Act, relied on arbitrary and subjective definitions of physical appearance. The two major government commissions of inquiry into the "Coloured Question," the Wilcox Commission in 1938 and the Theron Commission in 1976, failed to agree on a substantial definition (Goldin 1987; Lewis 1987). Some will argue that there is a separate coloured culture. Some will argue that "coloured" is solely a term used by the white-supremacist state to preserve racial purity in support of its social evolutionary ideals. I will make the argument that the history of coloured identity in South Africa involves a very complex set of variables, a complex interplay between exclusion and cooptation, between collaboration and resistance, between centripetal and centrifugal forces from within and without. In the rural fishing communities on the Western Cape coast, and in most of the suburbs of Cape Town, questioning "coloured" as a viable category of identity is purely an academic exercise.

Ian Goldin expressly focused on the political mobilization of coloured identity, i.e., the "articulation and representation of coloured identity in organizations and institutions" (1987:xv). Although he acknowledged that a full understanding of coloured identity would require a larger study that would include studies of "religion, culture, language and other complex psychological manifestations of identity" (1987:xv), his work reflected the dominant stream of literature, placing ethnic identity primarily in its political and macro-economic context. Goldin noted that he was not interested in exploring "the "lower levels" of coloured identity, which relate to often inarticulate and hidden expressions of identity" (1987:xv). Although political and macro-economic factors cannot be ignored, few attempts have been made to connect the political and economic implications of ethnicity to these "lower levels." This dissertation is one such attempt.

Stereotypes

Richard van der Ross, a self-identified coloured, founder of the Labour Party and scholar of South African history, defended the use of the term "Coloured" as a word distinguishing a particular South African social group. However, it is with strong reservations that such self-identification was made. He believed that "Coloured People" was the least objectionable term and the one least likely to lead to confusion as it dominated the historic literature. To him the terms were not as important as the meaning behind the terms. Van der Ross attempted to flush out some of the destructive and erroneous meanings associated with coloured:

1. All Coloured people have the same origin.
2. Coloured people are easily recognizable.
3. Coloured people have their own culture.
4. All Coloured people are "the same," so that they "belong together."
5. Coloured people prefer to be together.
6. Even if they do not prefer to be together, it is better that they are together so that the "better class" can uplift the others.
7. Their own identity must be protected at all costs. Intermarriage and improper contact with other population groups should be avoided and forbidden.
8. Coloured people are a separate nation, or a nation in process of becoming (*nasie-in-wording*).
9. The natural consequence of their being (or becoming) a nation is that they should have their own "homeland."
10. Coloured people must be "protected" against any tendency to pass for White, or to marry or cohabit with Blacks.
11. It is right and good that Coloured people should have their own identity.
12. Unless this identity is accepted, protected and developed, Coloured people will not be fully developed or gain their rightful place in South Africa.
13. The alternative to the theory of Coloured identity is integration with either Whites or Blacks, and both these alternatives are unacceptable.
14. For economic purposes it is absolutely essential that Coloured people accept the concept of their own identity, or they will suffer economic ruin due to labour competition from Blacks, and the entrepreneurial superiority of Whites and Asians. (Van der Ross 1979)

Van der Ross' primary purpose in writing Myths and Attitudes was to expose the misconceptions surrounding the "myth of Coloured identity" (1979).

Marais reported that the Khoi were readily conscripted into the labor force of the settlers, readily traded their cattle for copper, beads and tobacco and were particularly vulnerable to the "tot system." The tot system was an attempt by land owners to "encourage" their laborers by supplying them with wine, or preferably brandy. Marais then traced this practice to perceptions of the coloured people of the late 1930's: "The habit of drinking to excess, implanted from generation to generation, is still one of the besetting sins of the coloured People" (1939:3). Vernon February was concerned with highlighting and challenging the stereotypes of coloured identity found in South African literature. He noted in particular how the definition of "coloured" was most often expressed in the negative, i.e., by what it did not mean. "The stereotype of the present-day 'coloured' draws, I venture to say, on a fairly continuous tradition starting with the depictions of Khoi in literature" (February 1981:23). February examined one of the first dramatic works to be written in Dutch-Afrikaans: *De Temeperantisten* written in 1832 by E. Boniface. February argued that in Afrikaner culture the stereotypes placed on the "Hottentot" were often automatically transferred to the coloured. "In general, then, writers portray the 'Hottentot' characters as care-free, comical, witty, loud-mouthed, fond of liquor, and prone to fighting easily" (February 1981:26). It is difficult to tell, however, which has been more damaging to coloured people and their identity: the liquor or the stereotype.

Stereotypes were also appropriated by coloured people themselves. The struggle over coloured identity created complex internal social relations. For some who came to accept the coloured identity as their own, the boundaries of coloured identity often became less fluid. They saw those who were trying to "pass themselves off as whites" and called them "play-whites." February refers to the practice of "venstertjies kyk" (literally: looking in the windows), which refers to what happened when coloured friends or relatives see the "play-whites" approaching. They pretend to be window-shopping in order not to embarrass the person or relative in question

(February 1981:198). Fredrickson argued that, at the end of the nineteenth century, this tendency to "pass" hindered the efforts of those who wished to politically mobilize coloureds. "It was so easy for successful and relatively light-skinned people with nonwhite ancestry to pass over into the European population that it was difficult for group-conscious leaders to emerge" (Fredrickson 1995:46). Yet early in the twentieth century such a consciousness did emerge, institutionalized by the founding of the African Political Organization (APO) in 1902.

Race Mixing

The controversial issue of miscegenation (race mixing) cannot be ignored as a factor in the development of coloured identity. The terms 'mixed race' and 'mulatto,' employed often by American media and academics, are often considered offensive by South Africans because these terms imply miscegenation (Morris 1992). The myth of a pure "race" has always marginalized people of mixed heritage. Although primarily a biological category, miscegenation has historically been associated with illegitimacy. The struggle for coloured identity is a struggle for legitimacy; it is the struggle for a self-affirmation of legitimacy, a struggle for legitimacy in the eyes of all South Africans and in the eyes of the world. Yet the history of coloured identity reflects, to some extent, the development of all cultures. The development of coloured identity and its complex history challenge static notion of culture and point toward the radical interconnectedness of all people, despite phenotypic distinctions.

Comparative historians have argued that a general strategy for managing race mixture usually develops early in a multi-racial society. As George Fredrickson put it, "The anarchic nature of the human libido has always created serious problems for guardians of ethnic boundaries and privileges" (1981:94). The earliest legislation passed in both the United States and South Africa that discriminated based on ancestry included laws restricting inter-racial sex or marriage. Legislators then had to deal with complex decisions over what should be done with the offspring of inter-racial unions. The United States tended to develop a binary, polarized system

whereby descendents of mixed unions were classified with their black progenitors, often
monitored by an arbitrary assumption of biological impurity referred to as the "one-drop rule." In
other parts of the world, other post-colonial, post-slavery nations developed more complex
categories. It is difficult to prove that Brazil's well-known struggle over how to classify mulattos
has resulted in a polarized system of racial classification (Harris 1964, 1993). Although the
difference in socioeconomic status between mulattos and blacks in Brazil is insignificant in
comparison with the relative privilege of whites, gradations of racial discrimination remain
evident (Marx 1998).

The South African case does not fit neatly into a typology of nations that include bi-polar,
tri-polar or graded-scale racial orders. As in the United States, race mixing in South Africa was a
problem that required a solution. The solution ultimately came in the form of government
proclamations that varied over time and eventually never explicitly defined who was coloured
and who was not. For a time, white South Africans bolstered their political numbers with
coloured allies partially out of fear of being outnumbered. But eventually the threat of being
outnumbered was overcome with draconian laws protecting white privilege. Apartheid
eventually destroyed even the marginal advantages that coloureds had gained under the promise
of citizenship.

Origins

One of the difficulties in determining the history of ethnic identity of the coloured is that
very few history books were written by those who would consider themselves coloured. If our
perceptions and understanding are influenced by the language we use, then history itself is
colored by the limited perspectives of the historians. Even if historians attempted to be as
"objective" as possible, they necessarily rely on documents that themselves have been written
mostly by non-coloureds. Although the standard histories of the past may not intentionally
contain false information, without significant input from coloured voices the histories remain

incomplete. Having said this, the challenge remains to find sources that reflect, or at least approximate, the perspectives of coloured people throughout their own histories. The term "histories" is more appropriate here than "history," for the stories of the coloured people are as diverse as the people themselves

February (1981) attributes the origins of the coloured to a history of miscegenation over a period of more than three hundred years. He traces the racial roots of coloured people to the Khoisan, imported slaves from Madagascar, Angola and Mozambique, and Dutch, German and French settlers. He notes several instances of sexual liaisons between European settlers, soldiers and sailors and slave women. The history of coloured people is a history of cultural and ethnic mixing. Marais[1] (1939) traces the major historical streams of coloured history:

> The history of the Coloured People is the history of the contact of aboriginal Africans (and a few Orientals) with Europeans. ... The historian of the Cape Coloured is at every stage in their evolution brought face to face with the European—the missionary who sought to convert and civilise them, the trader who often debauched them, the government official who tried to fit them into their "proper" place in an ordered society, and the farmer-colonist who wanted their land and their labour. (1939:ix)

The history of the coloured people is a history of contact between people groups. Marais showed that coloured people descend from four main groups: Slaves, Hottentots (Khoi), Bushmen (San) and the Europeans.

In 1834, the year when slavery was abolished in the Cape Colony, there were in excess of 39,000 slaves (Marais 1939:2). During Jan van Riebeeck's time a few hundred slaves were imported from Western Africa. After that, slaves were mostly brought from Mozambique, Madagascar and from different parts of the East (India, Sri Lanka and "the Malay Archipelago"). Imported rapidly in number during the late seventeenth and early to mid-eighteenth centuries, the importation of slaves tapered off near the beginning of the nineteenth century.

The emancipation of the slaves is often cited as one of the major factors that contributed to the formation of coloured communities. Although legally free, ex-slaves remained economically dependent on white farmers and the colonial government. For four years after the emancipation declaration, slaves were to stay on with their owners as transitional "apprentices." Eventually many freed slaves joined friends and relatives in towns formed by the missionary societies. These settlements were the antecedents to what were later to become urban coloured settlements in the western and southern Cape. The eventual emancipation of slaves in 1838 did not necessarily improve the socio-economic or political position of non-Europeans. As an example, access to "European" schools was at first limited and eventually forbidden for the growing coloured population.

A second group reported as ancestors of coloured people were the Khoi. Early evidence exists which refers to the marriage of an explorer, van Meerhof, to a Khoi woman, Eva in the early years of settlement (1664). But this officially celebrated marriage was more the exception than the rule. In fact, marriages between Whites and slaves of "full colour" were prohibited by law in 1685 (Marais 1939:10). However, even though they were neither sanctioned by state nor church, unions between European explorers, farmers and other settlers were not uncommon.

It was through trade and exploration that the Dutch settlers first came into contact with groups of Khoi all along the coastal belt. No one can tell just how long the Khoi had occupied the southern tip of Africa, but what soon became clear is that their very existence was threatened by Bantu expansion from the northeast and European expansion from the south. As noted above, Marais claims that the Khoi were readily conscripted into the labor force of the settlers, readily traded their cattle for copper, beads and tobacco and were particularly vulnerable to the "tot system."

When the Cape was occupied by the time the British in 1795, the Khoi had already been socio-economically and politically maginalized; most were landless and many had become dependent on the European farmers for employment[2]. However, the colonial government was afraid of Khoi insurrection and alliances with their frontier enemies (e.g. the Xhosa). Between 1808 and 1819 a few feeble attempts were made to provide Khoi with land, but the primary tactic that was taken to suppress insurgency was by regulating the servant-master relationship. "Their efforts at regulating the relations between master and servant mark the beginning of ['free'] labour legislation in South Africa" (Marais 1939:115). These regulations included an imposed pass system, laws that regulated residence and mandatory apprenticeships for Khoi children. Land was given for Khoi settlement mostly in the form of missionary grants. Therefore, most Khoi settlements in the Cape by this time were dependent on either the London Missionary Society or the Moravians (Marais 1939:134–154).

Marais also argues that the history of the coloured people includes the miscegenation of slaves and Khoi. People from both groups were "employed" as laborers on settlers' farms, and it was assumed on the basis of the relative scarcity of women that these two groups intermarried. However, little official evidence is available to support this conclusion. There is some evidence to support the influence of San lineages on Coloured family trees. The history of contact between the European and the San was much more violent than Khoi contact with the European. But if the San were "shot down in their tens and twenties during the first half of the eighteenth century, during the next fifty years they perished in their hundreds. That was the period of maximum extermination and it effectually broke the back of Bushmen [sic] resistance" (Marais 1939:15). Women were often killed with their husbands, but the children were shared among the farmers as "apprentices," became part of the slave communities and eventually "entered the ranks of the Coloured population" (Marais 1939:25).

In eighteenth century the term "Baster" was used to designate those of mixed parentage. "By the second half of the eighteenth century the Bastards were becoming a people apart from both Boers and Hottentots" (Marais 1939:11). It is interesting to note that the "Bastárds" were often the first to provide the colony with contacts and settlements in new areas. Marais claims this group as the "pioneers of the north-western Cape" as they, together with the missionaries, helped to settle the land with official land title recognition from the Cape government (1939:74–108). Yet even these communities were politically and economically marginalized. "They formed a curious intermediate class between the Europeans and the mass of the Coloured People.

Very conscious of their kinship with the former, they clung pathetically [sic] to such European standards as they knew, without having any hope of being admitted into European society" (Marais 1939:107).

In the early nineteenth century a community of whites, Xhosa, Khoisan and "mixed race" people established themselves on the northern frontier of the Cape. This group, calling themselves Griquas, survived as an independent community until the closing of the frontier in the late nineteenth century.

> Although the Griqua option was not a viable one for the broad mass of the Coloured people, the Griqua showed how a community of heterogeneous origins, and one that remained open to white and African members, could use an invented identity to create a sense of common solidarity, and mobilise that solidarity in defense of the group's interests. For the Griqua the adoption of Griqua identity was a voluntary choice on the part of the individual, not a genetic predetermination, and served as a means of advancing and protecting group material interests, and of conferring a sense of self-pride and belonging. (Lewis 1987:9)

Still today there are those in South Africa who consider themselves of Griqua descent.

Other groups of mixed racial origins in the early colony were also in the process of community formation. The Cape Muslims (inaccurately called the Cape Malays in reference to the origin of the Islamic slaves of the Dutch East India Company) formed Islamic communities and were mostly concentrated in Cape Town. "Islam at the Cape offered not just religious consolidation but also an 'impressive network of social, educational and religious institutions. They gained an identity as well as a religion" (Lewis 1987:10). Although the Cape Muslims were among the first coloureds to combine at the polls in the mid-nineteenth century, their tendency to be a self-segregating group, accompanied by the fact that they were not Christian, would hinder their ability to establish and mobilize a general coloured identity.

Politicization of Identity[3]

One cannot understand the development of coloured ethnic identity without taking into account the socio-economic and political context behind its development. With the establishment of official apartheid policies after the 1948 elections, it became clear that the conscription of

coloured identity was integral to maintaining the Spencerian foundation of race-politics. The

concept of racial purity was central to the National Party's apartheid policies. It was widely

recognized that poor whites had for years resided in the same areas as coloureds, particularly in

District Six and other areas of Cape Town. "The assertion of distinct ethnic identities demanded

that [mixed] communities be destroyed and that legislation be enforced which would prevent

miscegenation and residential mixing of races" (Goldin 1987:81). Under the leadership of prime

ministers D.F. Malan and H.F. Verwoerd, the National Party remained firmly committed to the

development of a distinct coloured identity. It was believed that coloured identity would

eventually lead to a coloured nation and that the "nations" could develop separately and equally.

Goldin criticized early orthodox explanations that it was religion (the distinction between

Christian and Heathen) that formed the basis for social differentiation in the early colonial

societies. He argues that British scholars such as I.D. MacRone attempted to prove racism as a

development purely of the Boer republics, thereby failing to recognize the ethnic hierarchies that

were exhibited by the earliest settlers and colonialists. Although apartheid was explicitly

institutionalized in the post-World War II South African Government, there was not a colonial

government along the way that did not contribute to its development. "Already, within the first

two decades of colonial rule, there existed in the Cape a complex racial hierarchy in which people

who were later designated Coloured occupied an intermediate position" (Goldin 1987:5).

Although political rights were given to both Europeans and non-Europeans from very

early on, it was not necessarily "on an equal footing" (Thompson 1949:6). Take the case of the

1853 constitution that established representative government in the Cape. The same political

rights were granted to European men as to non-European men. Each could register as a voter.

There were, however, clear class distinctions regarding to which level of government one could

be elected. A man could:

> stand for election to the Lower House—the House of Assembly—if he earned £50 a year,

or if he earned £25 a year and was also supplied with board and lodging, or if he occupied a house and land with a combined value of £25. A man could stand for election to the Upper House—the Legislative Council—if he owned immoveable property worth £2,000 clear of mortgage or moveable and immovable property together worth £4,000 above all debts. (Thompson 1949:6)

In other words, election to the Legislative Council was the privilege of the privileged, most, if not all, of whom were European. The Parliamentary Registration Act of 1887 stiffened the economic conditions for voter registration, and the Franchise and Ballot Act of 1892, in addition to a further increase in economic requirements, added a simple literacy test where each voter needed to be able to write his (for all voters were men) name, address and occupation. Throughout the history of the Cape Parliament, "many Coloured men who were qualified did not register; and no Coloured man was ever nominated for election to Parliament" (Thompson 1949:7).

Thompson argues that the Voortrekkers transported the tradition of racism north of the Orange River and maintained a strict color bar after the South African War when the Transvaal (1906) and the Orange River Colony (1907) were granted responsible government.

Since the late eighteen hundreds, South African governments attempted to establish "influx controls" that regulated the movement of all non-whites to the more prosperous areas (the cities, in particular). During the years following the Great Depression (early 1930s) and before 1948, enforcement of these influx controls was strengthened. "The strict enforcement of influx controls over Africans served to extend the relative advantages of an assertion of Coloured identity and to deepen the structural division between African and Coloured men and women" (Goldin 1987:72).

J.C. Smuts, prime minister from 1919–1924, established the Coloured Affairs Department and the Coloured Affairs Council, which served to institutionalize coloured identity for the purposes of apartheid. However, coloured people posed a dilemma for the Nationalists.

They shared a common language (Afrikaans) and historical homeland (the rural areas of the Western Cape), and many—although this was never publicly admitted—shared a common ancestry. In addition, due to the close involvement of Coloureds in Cape

> politics and to the language bond, many Cape Nationalists were well disposed to Coloured intellectuals and considered to be "brown Afrikaners," "a part of Western civilization" and deserving of a closer association with the Whites. (Goldin 1987:79)

In 1950 passage of the Population Registration Act, Immorality Amendment Act (section 16) and the Group Areas Act served to further institutionalize apartheid and the role ascribed therein for coloured people. With the Prohibition of Mixed Marriages Act of 1950, marriage across statutory racial divides was declared illegal.

The term "Coloured" was not a term evenly applied throughout the history of South African public discourse.

> By 1904 a distinct Coloured identity had been established in the Western Cape which stood in marked contrast to that which had existed only 10 years previously. Whereas in 1894 the term Coloured in the census and in other published sources referred to all "non-European" people, by 1904 the term referred to an intermediate category of people. (Goldin 1987:26)

Goldin believes that the exclusion of Bantu-speaking people from the government's official coloured category marked the triumph of social-Darwinism in South Africa and the entrenchment of racial hierarchy. But there were also internal forces that helped to reinforce the strengthening of coloured identity. Coloured identity was in part reinforced by those who wanted to defend their position over against "Africans" and to increase their leverage for preferential treatment by the government.

> From the beginning, however, the commitment to a Coloured identity was at best ambiguous. The continued existence of an intermediate group, it was recognized, depended on the success of policies which sought to promote the interests of Coloured people relative to Africans whilst at the same time preventing the assimilation of Coloured and White people. (Goldin 1987:27)

It is important to note that the codification of racial boundaries in South Africa was the result of complex and interrelated processes. Goldin reminds us that policies of preference for people defined as coloured existed before 1920 and were not simply a product of National Party rule.

Analyses of the political commitments of those classified as "Coloured People" exposes the weakness of homogenous constructions of Coloured identity (Goldin 1987; Lewis 1987).

Coloured people reflect a wide range of attitudes, ranging from conservative to militant, from left to right and from racially motivated to nonracial. On the one hand, the conservative tendency coalesced around the issue of building a coloured, separatist identity which fit into the government's apartheid plans and, on the other, the more liberal and militant coloureds distanced themselves from whites, refusing to fit neatly into apartheid categories, allying themselves with blacks and rejecting the notion of a coloured identity (Freedberg 1987).

According to Rosemary Ridd (1987), the people of the once highly populated District Six area [of greater Cape Town] rejected the white-imposed 'coloured' identity and spoke of "one South African People." This latter voice eventually became "muted" by the dominant white perspective. Ridd showed how some former members of District Six sometimes described themselves derisively as coloured and also applied the term to their perceived inferiors. Race and religion were major determinants of social status for this group, and women in particular stressed "respectability" as a defense against being called coloured (Ridd 1987).

Towards the end of the nineteenth century a coloured elite emerged which attempted to act within the dominant political paradigm. Van der Ross is careful to point out the socio-economic heterogeneity of coloured people.

> There are class divisions within the Coloured people. Formerly, these class distinctions were based to a large extent on physical appearance. Those who approximated more to the Caucasoid characteristics were accorded higher status. As, especially in the urban areas, these characteristics tended to correspond with higher income, the skilled trades or even the professions, a higher premium came to be placed on the "White" physical qualities. (1979:103)

In time, distinctions based on phenotypic characteristics became less of a factor. Increasingly more weight was given to education level, ability to excel at a particular skill and one's economic standing. "The growth of trade unionism, the development of a category of professionals, the activity of certain churches, the emergence of a greater number of university graduates and a greater knowledge of the outside world through reading, the media and travel, have all contributed to this change of emphasis" (Van der Ross 1979:103).

Resistance to the government was itself divided along racial and ethnic lines. The earlier political associations for non-white South Africans made few attempts to challenge the growing barrier being erected between coloured and black people.

> The ANC pursued a path to liberation which excluded Coloureds. The Non-European Liberation League and NEUM [Non-European Unity Movement], although in theory non-racial, were in practice preoccupied with issues of immediate concern to Coloured but not African people. (Goldin 1987:72)

It was only among some of the workers unions that practical steps were taken to break down the partition between black and coloured. "The Food and Canning Workers' Union and the CTSDWU [Cape Town Stevedores and Dockers Workers' Union] combated racial divisions within the workers with some success" (Goldin 1987:72).

In 1965 the Labour Party was founded with Richard van der Ross as its president. "The party was unequivocally a Coloured one, with its membership and organizational objectives defined to coincide with racial categories" (Goldin 1987:156). The struggles over the leadership of the party reflected in part the internal struggles of coloured identity. Until 1972 the party leadership confined its activities exclusively to matters relating to coloureds. In that year the term "Coloured" was omitted from the Labour Party's constitution. It was argued by the leadership that this term was rejected as an externally imposed label that served to divide the black majority (Goldin 1987:158). After 1972 the Labour Party continued to struggle with its identity, and the major camps were divided between commitments to black consciousness on the one hand and the reification of a distinct coloured identity on the other.

In 1955 the Coloured Preference Policy was initiated by the National Party in an attempt to increase the divide between coloureds and blacks. Goldin concludes that, in the Western Cape, at least, the Coloured Preference Policy had failed to increase this divide. He notes that, between the years of 1956 and 1960, divisions between coloured and black workers actually narrowed. "Whereas Coloured workers had previously failed to support mass resistance campaigns, this support was given in 1961 when Coloured workers participated in the Congress stay-away"

(Goldin 1987:123). The policy intended to unite coloured identity had failed to do so; class divisions were reinforced by continued economic and social stratification in the coloured communities.

According to Mohamed Adhikari (1994), the politics behind the formation of the Teacher's League of South Africa (TLSA) reflect the politics of racial identity. Conservative historians wrote of "colouredness" as though it was an inherited trait. Revisionist historians, challenging this notion, have analyzed racial identity as wholly imposed by whites. Adhikari's analysis of the formation of the TLSA suggests that coloured elites chose to define themselves racially to carve a niche for themselves in the social hierarchy. The TLSA was an effort to improve the condition of coloured education at a time when socio-political developments were intensifying the repression of Coloured people. Deon van Tonder (1993) reports that white South Africans demanded the removal of blacks from the townships of Sophiatown, Martindale, the Western Native Township and Newclare. The National Party responded with the western areas removal scheme. Coloured residents allied with whites against the blacks to protect their own interests.

P.W. Botha charted a new course in the relationship between the National Party and the Coloured communities[4]. "Insisting that the Coloured people were the 'allies of the Whites in the struggle for South Africa' and that White South Africans must 'adapt or die,' Botha set out to incorporate the coloured political leadership" (Goldin 1987:189). In the September 1984 conference of the Cape National Party it was announced that the Coloured Preference Policy would be scrapped. This change did not necessarily reflect a change in attitude toward coloureds but an attempt to incorporate the coloured vote).

Although there is currently much dispute over past national censuses, Census 1996, a census conducted by the majority government, retains the apartheid racial categorization. Estimates divided South Africa's approximately 42 million inhabitants into the racial divisions as portrayed in Table 1 and Figure 3.

Table 1. Population Group by Province (Percentages)

% Population	Eastern Cape	Free State	Gauteng	Kwazulu-Natal	Mpuma-langa	Northern Cape	Northern Province	North West	Western Cape	South Africa
African/ Black	86.4	84.4	70.0	81.7	89.2	33.2	96.7	91.2	20.9	76.7
Coloured	7.4	3.0	3.8	1.4	0.7	51.8	0.2	1.4	54.2	8.9
Indian/ Asian	0.3	0.1	2.2	9.4	0.5	0.3	0.1	0.3	1.0	2.6
White	5.2	12.0	23.2	6.6	9.0	13.3	2.4	6.6	20.8	10.9
Unspecified/Other	0.6	0.4	0.8	0.8	0.6	1.5	0.7	0.5	3.1	0.9
Total	100.0	100.0	100.0	100.0	100.0	100.0	100.0	100.0	100.0	100.0

Source: Statistics Council, Minister of Finance (1996)

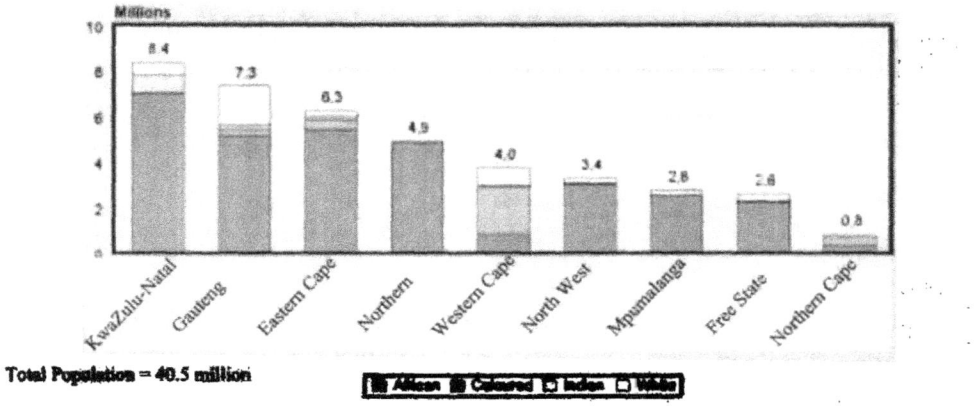

Figure 3. Population Group by Province (Millions)
Source: Statistics Council, Minister of Finance (1996)

Going by the categories in the 1996 census, the Western Cape has the highest Coloured

population in the country, constituting around 54% of the province's 3.9 million people. There are more women than men in the province, with 1.9 million males and 2 million females. The Western Cape has 21% African/Black people, 21% White people and 1% Indian/Asian people. This is a highly urbanised province, with 88.9% of its population living in urban areas. In this respect, it is second only to Gauteng. The Western Province leads the education ratings with a total of 10.6% of people aged 20 years and above having higher education qualifications. At 8.4%, Gauteng (including the Johannesburg area) is the second highest. Only 6.7% of people in the Western Cape province aged 20 years and above have had no schooling at all. At least 15% have had some primary education, whilst 19% have a matric (equivalent to the twelfth grade). The Western Cape has 39% of people with some secondary education (Census 1996).

Language, Race and Politics: Afrikaans and the Coloureds of South Africa

In the Republic of South Africa today the eleven officially recognized national languages include: Afrikaans, English, isiNdebele, Sesotho sa Lebowa, Sesotho, siSwati, XiTsonga, Setswana, Tshivenda, isiXhosa and isiZulu.

Coloureds and whites are known to socialize their children primarily into Afrikaans and English. The predominance of Afrikaans in the Western Cape province is primarily attributed to the high population of those who identified themselves as coloured.

The first official census of the Cape Colony was taken in 1865. Although its numbers must be heavily scrutinized, it is important to note the racial divisions made in the census. "The population was reported to comprise about 180,000 'Europeans,' 200,000 'Hottentots' and 'Others' (that is, Coloured People), and 100,000 'Kafirs'—people of African farming stock who were becoming the main labor force." (Thompson 1995:66). After South Africa was recognized as a British protectorate in the first decade of the nineteenth century, significant numbers of British settlers were beginning to settle in the Cape Colony. English started to compete with Dutch as the dominant language of European origin. The South Africa Act of 1909 established

Dutch and English as the official languages of South Africa. "By 1925, however, the Bible had been translated into Afrikaans, there was an Afrikaans dictionary, and there was a substantial literature in Afrikaans. In that year a constitutional amendment replaced Dutch with Afrikaans as an official language" (Thompson 1995:160).

Table 2. Percentage of South African National Languages Spoken by Province

	Eastern Cape	Free State	Gauteng	Kwazulu-Natal	Mpuma-langa	Northern Cape	Northern Province	North West	Western Cape	South Africa
IsiZulu	0.4	4.8	21.5	79.8	25.4	0.3	0.7	2.5	0.1	22.9
IsiXhosa	83.8	9.4	7.5	1.6	1.3	6.3	0.2	5.4	19.1	17.9
Afrikaans	9.6	14.5	16.7	1.6	8.3	69.3	2.2	7.5	59.2	14.4
Sepedi	0.0	0.2	9.5	0.0	10.5	0.0	52.7	4.0	0.0	9.2
English	3.7	1.3	13.0	15.8	2.0	2.4	0.4	1.0	20.3	8.6
Setswana	0.0	6.5	7.9	0.0	2.7	19.9	1.4	67.2	0.1	8.2
Sesotho	2.2	62.1	13.1	0.5	3.2	0.9	1.1	5.1	0.4	7.7
Xitsonga	0.0	0.5	5.3	0.0	3.5	0.0	22.6	4.7	0.0	4.4
SiSwati	0.0	0.1	1.3	0.1	30.0	0.0	1.2	0.5	0.0	2.5
Tshivenda	0.0	0.1	1.4	0.0	0.1	0.0	15.5	0.4	0.0	2.2
IsiNdebele	0.0	0.2	1.6	0.0	12.5	0.0	1.5	1.3	0.1	1.5

Source: Statistics Council, Minister of Finance (1996)

The fact that coloureds and whites shared a common language from at least the beginning of the nineteenth century did not preclude successive white governments from taking measures to socially and politically distance coloureds from whites. As Thompson points out, "In spite of the non-racial terminology of the 1853 constitution, the white rulers of the Cape Colony were treating the Coloured People as a distinct and inferior community, dependent on white employers"

(1995:66). The Smuts government of the 1930s established the Coloured Affairs Department and the Coloured Affairs Council, which served to institutionalize coloured identity for the purposes of apartheid.

The passage of the Population Registration Act, Immorality Amendment Act (section 16) and the Group Areas Act in 1950 served to further institutionalize race-based segregation and the role ascribed to coloureds in the Apartheid system. With the Prohibition of Mixed Marriages Act of 1950, marriage across statutory racial divides was declared illegal. Divisions were made primarily along racial and not linguistic lines.

While the common language between coloureds and whites did not prevent strong discrimination against coloureds throughout South Africa's history, this affinity facilitated the creation of an intermediate racial category for government classification purposes. Coloureds were accorded marginally better social and political status, until the National party policies of the mid-twentieth century. One of the ways white Afrikaners sought to maintain their social distance from non-white Afrikaners was by characterizing the Afrikaans spoken by coloureds of the Western Cape as an inferior dialect, as *kombuis taal* (kitchen language, or appropriate only for the uneducated working class). While the dialect of Afrikaans spoken in the predominantly coloured areas of the western Cape is markedly different from the standard Afrikaans of high school text books, the negative connotation placed on this difference was a function of maintaining social distance rather than any inherent qualitative difference.

In the early years of apartheid, politically conscious coloureds began to use English in public discourse as a means of disassociating themselves from white Afrikaners. Those who considered themselves pan-Africanist in orientation saw English as the language of international communication and were willing to settle for this European language as a means of communicating their plight to a wider audience. Yet for over a century Afrikaans (originally Dutch) was an integral part of coloured socialization. Although many coloured families of the latter half of the twentieth century, if not most, spoke both of South Africa's national languages,

most coloured children are raised speaking Afrikaans as their primary language. Some
considered Afrikaans important enough to coloured identity that they were willing to divorce the
language from its politically oppressive context.

Vernon February highlights the ambiguity of coloured identity in relation to Afrikaans
literature. In turning to coloured writers, February believed that only S.V. Petersen (1945), P.J.
Philander (1963; 1965; 1978) and Adam Small (1960; 1962; 1965; 1971) have earned places in
Afrikaans literary handbooks. February criticizes Petersen's work as socially conservative and
accommodationist. "Despite [his] historical legacy, one finds no such evidence of social realism
in Petersen's novel [As die Son Ondergaan]. Instead the story is a fairly straightforward account,
differing only slightly from the mainstream of Afrikaans literature" (1981:85).

Adam Small received the "brown Afrikaner" label from his politically active counterparts
for his willingness to accept a lectureship at one of the universities established especially for
coloureds. He was also one of the few coloured academics at the time who chose to write in
Afrikaans. Those coloureds who chose Afrikaans as a medium for their work were forced to face
the criticism of the coloured people who thought Afrikaans was to be avoided as the language of
the oppressors. While Smalls work may have made it into the corpus of Afrikaans classics, it was
largely ignored in the coloured schools. Small, in his earlier writings, represented a side of
coloured identity that chose not to make political ideology the central theme of his work.

> Ironically then, the Afrikaner who believes in apartheid, and the 'coloured' who rejects
> the system, will both be irritated by some of Small's poetry. And their irritation is rooted
> in their essential non-understanding of the function of humour as an instrument of play
> and unmasking in their society of ascribed roles. (February 1981:98)

Rather than fully identifying with the oppressive ideology of the dominant culture, Small saw
himself as a satirist, appropriating the tools of the dominant culture to expose the indignation of
his own people. His explicit intention was to disassociate the oppressive ideology from the very
language itself. Small refused to make Afrikaans synonymous with apartheid and baasskap
(domination).

Although Afrikaans is becoming an increasingly marginalized language in South Africa, I predict that it will not soon fade into history. With over eight million who speak Afrikaans fluently and arguably over three or four million who speak Afrikaans as their first language, even the recent changes in government priorities will not wipe out the influence of Afrikaans on South African society. As du Toit (1995) has shown for white Afrikaans speaking emigrants to Argentina, Afrikaans is a very resilient part of ethnic identity. What remains to be seen, however, is if those who have historically been called coloured will continue to raise their children speaking Afrikaans, continue writing in Afrikaans and continue valuing Afrikaans as their own.

Conclusion

There are many strands of history woven into the cloth of coloured identity. Even though under the apartheid regime it was assumed that these strands formed a coherent whole, there is little agreement in the literature as to whether this cloth has truly formed a piece of clothing. The major strands that have contributed to the debate over the existence of a coloured racial and ethnic identity should now be more visible to those who invested the time reading this chapter. The fall of apartheid and the movement in South Africa to majority rule will radically affect the continued development of this identity as all South Africans face radical challenges to their social identities. It remains to be seen if the new majority rule government will promote policies and preferences that support the making of a unique coloured pattern of cloth, or if they will attempt to sew the diverse patches of coloured identity onto a new, non-racialized South African garment.

Notes

[1] J. S. Marais has written what, for years, was a classic work, unequaled in scope, on the history of the South African Coloured. Any author interested in the history of the Coloured people must wrestle with Marais. Although his conclusions and inferences are clearly conditioned by his own historical context, he was considered progressive for his time. Taken in its historical context, The Cape Coloured People: 1652–1937 (1939) can provide valuable insight into the history of the Coloured people.

[2] Control over the Cape returned to the Dutch East India Company for a brief period following the initial British occupation, i.e., 1803–1806 (Thompson 1995).

[3] The phrase "politicization of identity" refers not only to the political institutions that were established to further Coloured political agendas but also to the process whereby Coloured identity became entrenched by its own institutionalization. In an attempt to gain political ground in the context of oppression, some South Africans chose to essentialize Coloured identity.

[4] D.F. Malan, H.F. Verwoerd and J.G. Strydom were all Transvaalers with limited personal knowledge of the Cape coloured population. The fact that P.W. Botha was from the Cape most likely contributed to this new relationship between the government and coloured people.

CHAPTER 5
RACE, CLASS, GENDER AND SOUTH AFRICAN FISHERS

Image-ining Race and Class

The Cultural Image of the 'Cape Coloured Fisherman'

In popular culture as well as in academic writing, the romantic image of the fisherman

has a long tradition. Fishermen have been venerated since the earliest of Western recorded

history. It is one of the most enduring forms of the oldest of human economic pursuits, hunting,

and it takes place in what many see as the most primitive of environments, the untamed ocean.

The historian Lance van Sittert explains it this way:

> The fact that fishing industrialized relatively late [in South Africa], and in many cases not
> at all, has made the fisherman a visible and seemingly enduring symbol of a bygone age
> when people interacted directly with nature free from the strictures of the capitalist work
> ethic in a perpetual struggle for survival. The fisherman—like the peasant—is envied
> this communion and supposed freedom accorded him by his work, the rewards of which
> are deemed all the richer for being so hard won! (Van Sittert 1992:vii)

Local tourism, amateur artists and coffee table book photographers are kept in business in the

Western Cape through their portrayals of the rugged, tattered men and their equally dilapidated

boats. Paintings, photographs, carvings, post cards, t-shirts and other curios color the romantic

image of the small scale local fisherman.

Van Sittert compared the romanticization of the fisherman to the mythologized image of

the primitive "Bushman" in Southern Africa. Both are painted as inextricably tied to nature and

free from the trappings of industrialization and modernization. For them, even time itself is

measured by the weather, by the seasons. Both are able to predict the weather, interpret and

anticipate the behavior of wildlife in their respective environments and find their way across vast, homogenous terrain without a compass. The fisherman is "a quiet, simple man who—although he has very little—wants for nothing save the company and community of others like himself, with whom he shares the happiness and peace-of-heart which only comes from daily communion with nature" (Van Sittert 1992:xiii).

Figure 4. A Somerset West Fisherman
source: SA Illustrated News 1884 (reprint)

Consider the reprint of the front page of an 1884 South African Illustrated News. These are sold to tourists at, among other places, curio shops in Hermanus, Fish Hoek, Hout Bay and the upscale Victoria and Alfred Waterfront in Cape Town. The picture is titled "A Somerset West

Fisherman." Sitting just offshore in a small rowboat, amidst other similar subsistence boats, the dark-skinned man in tattered clothes raises a club to finish off the wriggling *snoek* he has slung under his arm. His weather-beaten face, disheveled clothes and brutal manner have never truly been acceptable in "civilized society." It is an image that represents everything that modern society is not, yet in some way longs to be. He is an idealized image of the rugged, independent individualist that thumbs his nose at the modern rat race and the highly structured lives to which we are all bound. Even though he is everything that the modern individual is not, or maybe especially because of this fact, he is romanticized.

In the Western Cape the mythologized fisher is inevitably a man, he is inevitably a handline fisher, and he is inevitably coloured. Consider one of the descriptions in a popular coffee table book:

> The Cape Coloured fisherman is… a small man with a hardbitten face deep-etched by sea and sun and too often further ravaged by shoreside dissipations, with a mordant wit admirably expressed in the vivid 'Capey' dialect, and with a fish-wife who is a bold flaunting harridan-witch with a gift for invective enabling her to hold her own in any slanging match. (Franck and Robb 1975:65)

It is not uncommon to find fishers who have spent most of their working days at sea to have weather-beaten complexions, scarred arms and callused hands. The body takes a pounding at sea. For fishers who use their hands to reel in sharp-toothed game fish like *snoek*, sometimes over a hundred a day, the telltale physical signs are obvious to even the most casual observer. But most stereotypes of Cape fishers go on to interpret the weathered body as a sign of a hardened life. He is commonly described as morally suspect, prone to alcohol and drugs. "Shoreside dissipations" is a loose reference to the fisherman's puted tendency toward licentious behavior, toward a lack of moderation in life, toward addictions common to his station in life.

Many may be willing to make allowances for his excesses because of the difficult life he has led. In fact, the lighthearted way in which he is able to shrug off his troubles in life with a joke and a smile is seen as a virtuous attempt to rise above pitiful circumstances. It is a good sense of humor in the midst of one tough season after another that keeps the "Cape Coloured fisherman" sane. This paradoxical sanity is further confirmed by his ability to stand back and laugh at life with his "mordant wit." His humor contains a hint of the sarcastic, a caustic critique of the life he's been handed.

"Vivid Capey dialect" identifies a version of Afrikaans that is pejoratively contrasted with the "suiwer" (lit. pure) Afrikaans learned through formal education (see Chapter 3). In some Afrikaans literature and more commonly in conversations around the sizzling boerewors at a backyard braai you will hear the "Capey dialect" referred to pejoratively as *kombuis Afrikaans* (lit. "kitchen Afrikaans"). Ironically, in the development of what only in the early part of the twentieth century became known as Afrikaans, it was not uncommon for the Netherlanders to refer to what they saw as the bastardization of their language as *kombuis-Hollands*.

The archetypal fisher is inevitably a fisherMAN. The image of the fisherman as man is consistent with a popular Victorian perspective on gender identity and gender roles, particularly in the rural communities of the Western Cape. This gendered image embodies the idealized male, the primitive hunter. He has the physical strength to wrestle snoek from the sea and the bold ruthlessness to put them out of their misery by clubbing them over the head. He has the mental stamina to endure long hours on the rough ocean and the patience to painstakingly stalk his elusive prey. He has an innate courage and lust for adventure, the "call of the blood" that he cannot deny. And, of course, he is the breadwinner, the provider, bringing food for his dependent wife and children. While this "fish-wife" is often portrayed as dutiful in her support and quite capable of holding her own, she is written in as but a minor prop on the stage where her husband is the lead actor.

The archetypal fisherman is inevitably a handline fisher. As a handline fisher, the image revealed is of a man independent of all but the most basic of modern technology. With only the use of a line, a hook and some bait, this fisher is a prime example of the romanticized primitive. This simplicity underscores not only the fisherman's independence from modern technology but also his dependence on personal skill and ingenuity, his unique knowledge and timing and his hard earned yet mysterious good fortune (luck). As casual labor the typical handline fisher is bound to no one by contract or convention. He works for himself, for his family, but not for a boss. The weather is his only timecard. He is the happy-go-lucky day laborer that works when there are pressing needs for himself or his family but otherwise would be just as content to "skinner" (gossip) about the sea's secrets as he would be to explore them. Because his needs and desires are so few and so basic, he is not one for the moderation and frugality of the capitalist work ethic. What he earns today he spends today; "for tomorrow will take care of itself." And when the earnings from the fish are few, he'd be just as happy to receive a "tot" (alcohol) for his efforts.

Not only is the traditional fisher portrayed as the archetypal primitive man-hunter, but he is invariably portrayed as a coloured man. The association between the fishermen of the Western Cape and those historically categorized as coloured has a long history, and the correlation of "coloured" and "primitive" is not accidental. The association of coloured and fisher reveals some of the complexities involved in understanding the current construction of coloured identity. More often than not it is impossible to disaggregate the negative stereotypes attributed to the handline fisher from the stereotypes commonly ascribed to what are perceived as low class coloureds in general. The mixed ancestry of those classified as coloured has itself been used as proof of the illegitimacy of those so classified. Pejorative attitudes inherited from nineteenth century Social Darwinist descriptions of miscegenated "half-castes" weigh heavy on those interested in affirming "coloured" as a valuable social category. The best example of where the stereotypes of fisher and coloured intersect is in the assumption that both are prone to excess drink.

The ancestors of those classified today as coloured reportedly hail from diverse parts of the globe, including South Africa, Malaysia, Madagascar, the Philippines, and Europe. The typical list of ancestors attributed to coloureds includes indigenous Khoi and San, Malay ex-slaves and Europeans. More recently many of the fishing families in, for example, the famous Kalk Bay fishing community have been shown to have deep roots in the Philippines (Carse 1960).

Middens found close to Cape Agulhas, the southern most tip of Africa, include shells and Khoi fishing tools. Ten-thousand year old 'fish fyvers' (human-made tidal pools for catching fish) can still be seen along the coastline (Hutton and Lamberth 1997).

Malay ancestry has had a particularly strong association with fishing. By the middle of the nineteenth century whites were referring to Muslims, regardless of their origins, as Malays. "White ethnicity was likely to have been strengthened among those workers in Cape Town whose perceptions of the different physical appearances, origins or culture of other Capetonians was under-scored by divisions of labour or occupational specialisation" (Bickford-Smith 1995:34). Malays, for example, were seen by many whites to be a kind of aristocracy among 'non-Whites' in Cape Town. "Malays were in a comparably advantageous position to migrants from rural areas as White artisans, recently arrived from Europe, were to them. This was a result of skills acquired by Malays in, and passed on from, the period of slavery" (Bickford-Smith 1995:34). One of the more well-known of these acquired skills was fishing.

Descendents of the slaves brought by the Dutch from the Malay archipelago were thought to have inherited their ancestors' predilection for the sea, many of whom were thought to be fishermen in the islands of Malaysia. The first group of Malay slaves had arrived at the Cape in 1667. As one historian put it:

> For centuries, they had fished the inshore waters of the Malayan peninsula with seine nets and they could not for long be kept from Cape seas. Instinctive fishermen, their diet was largely based on what they caught. ... Later, freed slaves took up the trade: the Malays became regular fishermen of Cape Town and formed fishing communities round the Peninsula, supplying town and carrying their fish to the farms to barter for fruit and produce. (Lees 1969:8)

By the mid-nineteenth century Malay identity was being subsumed under the more general category of coloured. In the 1870s the most common synonym used by whites for 'Other than White' was 'Coloured,' but it would be incorrect to say that before the end of the century 'Coloured' *always* referred to all 'non-Whites.' History text books and civil records from this time "would have included those categorised in the 1875 census as 'Malays' or 'Mixed and

Others,' but not 'Kaffirs' or 'Bechuanas'" (Bickford-Smith 1995:31). At this stage, the

overwhelming majority of Muslims were coloured. An important distinction between the

stereotypes of coloureds in general and Malays in particular was that most people knew that

Muslims were not prone to drink.

So at least by the end of the nineteenth century the term 'Coloured' was used to refer to

the descendents of mixed marriages or liaisons between Europeans, local Khoi and slaves.

Although property ownership was not uncommon among those designated as 'Coloured' at this

time, most 'Coloureds' were locked into what one can see as structural poverty. "In White

minds, to be Coloured was to be associated with a socially disadvantaged lower class within the

Western Cape" (Bickford-Smith 1995:31). Their employment was characterized by a

proportionally high level of casual and seasonal labor.

Race, Class and South Africa's Fishing Industry

The racial composition of the modern fishing industry in the Western Cape is changing

but perhaps slower than some other sectors of society. Ownership at all levels of the fishing

industry is predominantly white. According to Hersoug, the situation facing the fisher folk of

South Africa can be viewed as a double form of discrimination (1998). He argues that the

combined debilitating effects of hundreds of years of colonial discrimination and over forty years

of the apartheid political system left the fishing sphere with the following distinctive

characteristics:

- An extremely uneven distribution of resources between whites and blacks (defined to include Indians, Coloureds and Africans);
- A skewed distribution of small-scale and large-scale operators;
- A totally uneven regional distribution;
- A fisheries administration dominated by white politicians and white administrators with little legitimacy among the predominantly black coastal communities (Hersoug 1998:2).

This uneven distribution was carried into the year of South Africa's first general democratic elections. The 1994 total South African quota amounted to 512,437 tons within the eight species that are regulated by Total Allowable Catches (TACs): hake, sole, pilchard, anchovy, horse mackerel, South and West Coast lobster and abalone. Of these quotas, less than one percent was allocated to non-white companies. Of the 2,700 registered commercial fishing boats, 7% are owned by non-whites (mostly coloured), whilst of the 4,000 fishing licenses issued, only 6% were issued to non-whites (including coloured people) (Hersoug 1998).

The conflicts in the fishing industry appear to be between the fishing communities, which are predominantly rural, relatively poor, coloured and white on the one side, and the government, organized labour and big business, which are urban, relatively wealthy, white and black on the other side. The Marine Living Resource Act's view on redistribution, empowerment and management comes from a 'top down' approach. Fisheries management in South Africa is by no means equitable in terms of addressing the needs of the local fishers and their communities. It has been more than six years since a democratic government came into power in South Africa, yet black empowerment in the South African fishing industry is at best symbolized by what Moeniba Isaacs calls an "*Irish coffee* syndrome."

> A few black bits of chocolate sprinkled on the top that represents the changes within the industry, the layer of cream that represents the white domination, and the black body of coffee that represents the majority of the workers in processing and on the boats within the industry. There is a clear indication that the present policy favours organised business, which is left with their own devices on how to deal with empowerment of their workers and the communities that they represent. (Isaacs 1998:98)

By generalizing the metaphor to all non-whites under the term black, as is the case in Hersoug's use of "black," Isaac's flavorful description blends together very diverse experiences, a blending that offends the discerning palate.

Historically the fishing industry in the Western Cape has been white-owned and coloured-operated (Lees 1969). With the possible exceptions of fish factory labour and deep-sea fishing crews, which are positions increasingly filled by black Southern Africans, this remains the case. The coastal communities of the Western Cape, from Waenhuiskrans/Arniston in the south

to Port Nolloth in the northwest, are to this day predominantly made up of Afrikaans speaking

coloured and white families. These coastal communities remain largely unaffected by the

relatively high migration rates of black South Africans from the Eastern Cape into the Cape Town

metropolitan area.

A particular conundrum for those committed to the equitable redistribution of resources

in South Africa is the role that coloured people will play in the redistributive process. Given the

realities of apartheid's Coloured Labour Preference Policy, the Western Cape is a particularly

difficult area to deal with in terms of redistributive programs. For decades policy limited many

coloured people and even more black South Africans education, training and job opportunities.

Also, "poverty has a strong employment dimension in South Africa: unemployment among the

poor stands at fifty percent and Africans suffer unemployment rates that are nearly twice those of

coloureds (38 percent and 21 percent respectively), and nearly 10 times the rate among whites

(four percent nationally)" (Ramphele 1996:85). These inequities cannot be ignored.

While the majority of those who suffered most under apartheid were black, the

advantages coloureds enjoyed over blacks were few and increasingly marginal during the

apartheid years. Yet even though coloured individuals and families benefited only marginally

from the apartheid system, many fear that any redistributive action that the government

encourages will exclude coloured people. An article in an April 1996 issue of *The Economist*

relayed the fears of coloured South Africans who complained that even after apartheid they

remain caught in the middle, only this time it is between the economic dominance of whites and

the political dominance of blacks. In an address to a meeting of the Institute for Democracy in

South Africa focused on addressing the plight of coloured communities in the new South Africa,

President Mandela addressed this fear head on: "It is necessary therefore to repeat categorically

that anyone who says affirmative action reserves jobs and opportunities for Africans only is

grossly distorting the policy of the government and the African National Congress" (Mandela

1996:7). The president also defended the projects of the Reconstruction and Development Programme (RDP), the ANC's first set of policy goals and initiatives to address redistribution of South Africa's resources. He claimed that the RDP projects at the time brought direct and indirect benefits to the coloured communities of the Western Cape. But in 1995, these words were more rhetoric than reality. Just how the RDP would benefit coloured people remained to be seen.

The fishing industry is one area where Mandela's 1995 rhetoric of coloured participation in the benefits of the RDP remains, for the most part, an unfulfilled promise. The structure of power relations in the fishing industry thus far make it unlikely that coloured families, particularly those living in the rural coastal fishing communities, will benefit from the redistribution of fishing resources in anything more than symbolic ways. The commitment to a redistribution of access to marine resources for historically disadvantaged persons is written into the provisions of the law:

> The Minister and any organ of the state shall in exercising any power under this Act have regard to the following objectives and principles: (h) the need to achieve to the extent practicable a broad and accountable participation in the decision-making process provided for in this Act; [and] (j) the need to restructure the fishing industry to address historical imbalances and to achieve equity within all branches of the fishing industry. (Living Marine Resources Act, Chapter 1, Section 2; Department of Environmental Affairs and Tourism 1998)

But the law leaves vague the specific identification of who is and who is not to benefit from this redistribution of resources. The Department of Marine and Coastal Management stated its intention to empower the poor by committing itself to the following long-term vision for a democratic South Africa (following the Macro-Economic Strategy as presented by the Department of Finance): "a competitive, fast-growing economy which creates sufficient jobs for all work-seekers; *a redistribution of income and opportunities in favour of the poor*; a society in which sound health, education and other services are available to all; an environment in which homes are secure and places of work are productive" (Department of Environmental Affairs and Tourism 1998:6; italics mine). The Marine Living Resources Act does not single out those historically connected to fishing activity as deserving of special consideration. "Historically

disadvantaged" and "poor" describe most South Africans.

Handline Fishermen Construct the "True Fisherman"

Handline ski-boat skippers have a vested interest in who is acknowledged as a true fisher,

in defining the categories for their own existence. Not only does their internalized sense of

identity depend in part on this construction, but they suspect that pending changes to government

fisheries allocations may in part be based on fitting some agreed upon definition of a "true

fisher." Regulators required proof of a history of involvement in commercial fishing on the latest

round of applications for fishing boat licenses (Department of Marine and Coastal Management

1999).

When asked to describe the typical or true fisherman, most skippers (regardless of race)

either implicitly or explicitly distinguished between themselves as skippers and the typical crew.

They made qualitative categorical distinctions that did more than detail the manager-employee

relationship. In their descriptions of the typical fisherman, skippers set social and moral distance

between themselves and their crew. As almost half of the skippers had some level of

employment in the trades, a manager-employee relation would be a very familiar relational

category. But the distinctions made between skipper and crew go beyond the functional and the

remunerative. When describing the crew in particular, many of the themes represented in the

words of these skippers are consistent with the more general construction of the "Cape coloured

fisherman" as described in Chapter 1.

Many skippers believe that the true fisherman is born that way. It is the "call of the

blood" that gives the true fisher his love for the ocean and the predisposition to learn its secrets.

One young coloured skipper with a decade of experience in handline fishing said, "A lot of the

fisher people come out of little fishing towns. You can say that they do. It's in the blood. Like

we say, the sea water must be in your veins, in your blood." An older white skipper with the same years of dependence on handline fishing was slightly more fatalistic: "I've wanted to stop fishing a long time ago. Honestly. But it's in a person's blood, so you just carry on, and on, and on." When one skipper was asked why he had decided to get into fishing instead of some other type of employment, he replied:

> It's in my family's blood. My mom's dad had a fishing fleet in Port Elizabeth. So fishing started from my mom's side of the family. I fished as a kid, on ski-boats and the rock and surf in Natal, in East London on holidays. When I retired, other work was hard to find. It's still hard to find today. Fishing is an easy option for me, something I enjoy. I just made up my mind that I was going to fish for a living.

Another coloured skipper spoke of his father as mentor in the industry: "I was born a fisherman. The sea is something that gets in your blood. My dad is now 77. He still works on the sea. He runs his own ski-boat. We've got the same [kind of] ski-boat. He's had his a long time, and he's worked it all along." While the general cultural image of the fisher tends to portray the "call of the blood" as primordial, as mysteriously or genetically inherited, handline skippers make room for the influence of the social environment on biology. One skipper noted: "I've always been in fishing. When you're a child, you go with your daddy to sea. I wanted to go. And now you start loving it. And that's basically how it gets into your blood. It gets into your veins."

Most of the skippers mentioned the value of experience and longevity in the industry as characteristics of the true fisherman. One of the fishermen from a small southern Cape coastal town characterized the true fisherman as follows:

> It's someone that makes his life from the sea, that's only dependent on the fish from the sea. The guy that retires here from the Cape, he's not a true fisherman. He's retired. He's finished working. For him it's almost like a by-catch. He's already taken out his quota. He'd have to fish for a number of years before I can say he's a true fisherman. I'd say plus/minus ten years before I could classify him as a fisherman.

This characterization emphasizes that the true fisherman is one who is not only dependent on the fishing industry but one who has been dependent on fishing for quite some time.

The image of the "romanticized primitive" is not so strong in skippers' discussions about the true fisherman. The valorization of the physical nature of fishing is common, but skippers on the ski-boats avoid portraying fishers as independent from the technology of the modern world. Some veneration of the physical nature of handline fishing is found in how skippers talk of their choice of crew. One of the first things a skipper does when deciding on a new crewmember is to judge his physical appearance. A good crew needs to look like he knows how to catch fish. One skipper in his early thirties, who himself had been a crew member as long as he had been skippering, said that the process was simple: "You look at his gear and his hands. His gear needs to be 'agtermekaar' (lit. neat and complete). His hands should be weather beaten and cut up." This criterion owes less to some romanticized image of the primitive hunter than it does to the role that experience plays as a criterion for selection. Skippers assume that the hands of a potential crew member would show signs of the type of abuse that occurs when catching fish by hand, e.g. cuts, calluses, scars from past infections.

Figure 5. Handline Ski-Boat Crew on their Way to the Fishing Grounds
source: author

Skippers who are new to the business tend to carefully distinguish themselves from what they view as the moral character of the typical fisherman. One white skipper, who only a year prior had retired from a white-collar job to start fishing full-time, made a sharp contrast between skippers and crew, assuming that "crew" and "fishermen" were synonymous:

> There is a significant difference between the fishermen and the skippers. They are two different kettle of fish. For the typical fisherman, fishing is an easier way of making money than working. They work when they want to. The majority drink too much and smoke drugs. Cape coloureds are the best fishermen. They are guys that grew up their whole lives fishing. They're experienced. White guys don't have the same experience; he's just a lazy guy who thinks it's an easier living. It's a happy-go-lucky crowd, not long-term focussed. They live hand to mouth. The top fishers eventually become the skippers. They have the experience, a gut feel for it. They handle the boat well, find their own path. You've got to be born with it. You're only as good as your last performance. I've had a shit day if I'm not in the top five. Some guys don't manage as well. You do your own thing and be judged by it.

This skipper describes the socialization process from crew to skipper as if it were a position earned by experience. But this socialization process seemingly only applies to other fishermen since, having only one year of full-time experience as a handline skipper, he considers himself to be one of the top five skippers.

On rare occasions skippers rank themselves lower than the crew in their construction of social hierarchy. One skipper who had been on a ski-boat full-time for the past four years gave the crew the credit for his success on the boat. When asked how he would describe his current crew, he replied:

> Alright. You don't get a good skipper. You only get a good crew. And they make a skipper. If you've got a good crew, then they say, "hey, that's a good skipper." It's only the crew that brings in the money. The more fish they can catch, they're not going to say that crew caught the fish, they say, "look at that skipper." You only get good up to a point. The crew makes your skipper. My crew is good.

Reliability is a virtue sought in an ideal crew by most of the skippers. One skipper in his late twenties had been fishing full-time on the handline boats for the past eleven years but only dependent on that fishing for the past three years. He believed strongly in his dependence on his crew:

> My crew are my partners. We are mutually dependent. Without your crew you are worth nothing. I can't treat them bad. The better guys always have sites. You don't want to be a guy who is constantly looking for a site. We call that guy a "paloepa." That guy is on a different boat every day. He doesn't care about the boat's catch. I try to make it nice for my crew, otherwise you lose good men. I'm basically a manager.

With the share system governing compensation, skippers are dependent on their crew for increasing profits on the boat. And in order for the skipper to retain a good crew, he had to regularly "put them on a piece of fish" (meaning to locate schools of fish). As one of the more experienced skippers bluntly put it when asked how he decides on a crewmember: "A good crew and a shitty skipper can go out, but you can't go out with a good skipper and a shitty crew."

The sister virtues to reliability are commitment and consistency. Many of the skippers placed these virtues above even the ability to catch fish. When asked how he would describe the ideal crew, a fisherman in his early forties replied:

> It's according to how good a fisherman he is, how regularly he… how committed he is. Are you a man that is too lazy to get up every day, and I have to come looking for you when I pick you up? You get men that are good fishermen, that don't catch the most fish, but they are there. That's very important. It's not always the man that catches the most fish. But that counts too. The man that catches the most counts too, because that's how you make your profit. You want that kind of guy.

While the ability to catch fish was a requirement for any crew wanting to retain their site, often skippers said they were willing to sacrifice profit for a good working environment on the boat.

A good working environment on the boat often meant a certain level of cooperation and teamwork. According to a skipper from north of Cape Town, an ideal crew member, "has to work regularly and be able to prove he's a fisherman. He has to be handy and helpful. He has to be willing to stand by the other guys. The guys have to have respect for each other." While the skippers did not take full responsibility for managing this mutual respect, most were willing to make concessions to ensure a certain level of harmony. Social harmony itself was thought to increase productivity. As one man who had been a professional skipper for more than half his life remarked, the ideal crew must be able to carry his load.

> If he can't catch, then we all suffer. He's going to hurt himself; he's going to hurt the boat. You have to remember one thing; the boat always has to get its share. My people

know that; when it's bad, when we just catch a few hottentot, then the boat will buy the fish from them. But then we won't go fishing there again. We scratch each other's back. You have to have good communication with your men.

He went on to describe the relations on the boat as quasi-familial. "We're like family. We work together well. Each one has his job. There's one guy that ties the boat off and loosens the boat. He's the man that says when. One guy has to make sure the daily maintenance is done, another has to make sure the fries are set aside and the fish are offloaded. They all do that."

Even though it was relatively common for skippers to have a complete turnover of crew in a matter of months, they constantly tried to retain a "permanent" crew. One of the more experienced skippers stated his preference in a more consistent crew: "I usually have a fixed crew. I'll pick one up at the harbor. You choose fishermen by their reputation. I won't take a new face. You have to see their tackle. I know who's who." Permanent crew were fishers who would fish on one boat more regularly than they did on any other over a longer period of time. But the "longer period of time" was always indefinite and open to change at any time and for any reason. Often crew would go in search of another "site" or position on another ski-boat in hopes of better returns. A crewmember is perfectly free to run "paloepa" (seeking a site) when his regular skipper has chosen not to go to sea. But the crew had to be careful not to switch sites too often for fear of getting a reputation for having "rubber boots," i.e., bouncing around from boat to boat (being unreliable).

Choosing a new crewmember was described as more of an art than a science. When the skipper did not have a full "permanent" crew, he had to rely on other, more casual crew. Skippers commonly claimed that the pool of crew was large, but that the pool of quality crew grew smaller with each new skipper on the water. More often than not new crew were hired based on their reputation. One skipper who had been a crewmember for at least as long as he had been a skipper was describing how he chose new crew:

I know the guys. I know who're good fishermen. It's always, through the years... you just know. The guys talk. "This guy, he's an old fisherman. He's caught a lot with me."

The guys' names float around through the fisher's community. You find out. You hear when a guy does good work, that the guy is prepared to do something extra.

A twenty-year veteran handline skipper put it this way:

> You move where the fish is, and he's got to come to where the fish is. You either see him when you go to sea or when you come from sea. You don't just go to sea, take your stuff and go home. You go sit around and there's a whole tactic of talking. You talk about where you were, about who went where, about how you baited your hooks, and all that stuff.

This tactical socializing served not only to circulate skipper and crew reputations but was also the time when critical information about a day's catch may be shared.

The true fisherman, according to the ski-boat skippers, is unequivocally dependent on the sea for his livelihood and is described almost invariably as poor. Even fishers who themselves only a few months or a few years prior had been "weekend" commercial fishers were quick to mention that a true fisher is wholly dependent on the sea for his livelihood. One of the skippers who has known work in no other industry was quick to point this out in his definition of a true fisherman:

> It's a fisherman that makes his living just out of fishing. You can't go part time and work part time and say you're a fisherman. You get a lot of guys that say they're fishermen, but he's catching fish on the weekends and they're all out at sea. But I regard a fisherman as a guy whose total income is dependent on the sea. So he doesn't have money from other places, except the sea. His whole life is fishing. A lot of guys work at the bank and he's getting an income there. But he still goes to sea on the weekends and says he's a fisherman. He is a fisherman for the day, but he's not a fisherman in the full sense. I wouldn't say he has to spend 100% of his time at sea, but his income is 100% dependent on the sea.

Many of the skippers said that a true fisher is one who goes to sea every day, but not even the most ardent handline skipper goes to sea every day. Such statements were intended as hyperbole—exaggerations to prove a point. A true fisherman was not only dependent on the sea for his income but his life did not permit him to take off more days than the fish or the weather would allow.

Skippers sought the respect of their crews. Most were quick to bemoan having any "lawyers" on the boat. A lawyer is a crewmember who would voice his own opinion a little too loud and a little too often. These lawyers reportedly always had a better idea than the skipper and often were the loudest to complain when the boat returned empty. "Lawyers" themselves gained reputations and were, according to the skippers, less likely to find a site on any boat in the future. Some of the more domineering personalities among the skippers demanded a little more than respect of their crew. They threw around terms like "obedience" and "respect" as if they were benefits that came with the role they played.

The most obvious criteria for selecting a good crewmember was not always at the top of the skippers' lists. As the oldest and most experienced of the skippers pointed out:

> Those that I have, that's a good crew. They can catch fish. If you take them to where there are fish, it's the way they catch fish. If you take them to where the snoek are, he can catch a lot of snoek. If you catch fifty, then he catches fifty too. But then you get men who say they're a fisherman, then the one catches fifty, and he catches two. Those aren't fishermen. Fishermen are guys that know how to catch fish, how to catch crayfish. You don't have to tell him how; he knows how to catch them.

Both skipper and crew were tested with each trip. Crew had to perform to retain their site; skippers had to perform to retain their quality crewmembers.

With few exceptions, skippers described the typical fisherman as morally suspect, a rough, rugged individual prone to licentious behavior. When asked how he would describe the true fisherman, a skipper of British descent, himself with a reputation of being a heavy drinker, gave this perspective:

> You can't bundle them all together. Some of them are pissed all the time, some on dagga; others work consistently and show up all the time. It's probably a good cross-section of the country, except there's a higher percentage of druggies. They are hard workers… not all of them, now. Everyone is basically working for themselves. But if they don't work well for me, it affects me and he's off. But I'm not a policeman, just no dagga on my boat. Others allow it, like [this other young skipper]. Many of them use mandrax mixed with dagga. They can do it as much as they want at night. Some guys can do their job "half-gesuip" [half drunk] and "half-gerook" [half doped up], just as long as they don't do it on the boat. I'm in charge and don't like the smell, that's all.

One of the skippers excused his crew's drug addictions as the price they pay for the difficult life they live: "I don't have a problem with them using drugs, unless they fall overboard. They work better when they're doped up. It's a cruel, painful, terrible world, a world of never having anything in life. One of my crew was killed in a car crash—he was a dealer." Of course, if

crewmembers "work better when they're doped up," there wouldn't be much incentive to prevent

the spread of drugs in the industry. Another young skipper connected his crew's lack of

trustworthiness to their tendency to drink and do drugs. While he was sure that there were only

two of his current crew who drank, there were also a few that smoked marijuana. He said he

refused to allow them to smoke on the boat, but that "a lot of the skippers give them dagga,

because they'll work hard for dagga."

The insidious use of drugs as an incentive to work sounds frighteningly familiar to the

"tot" system of the nineteenth century. Another skipper described the advantages of hiring those

who smoke marijuana over those who drink:

> The guys drink, smoke drugs like dagga, buttons [or mandrax] and crack. The guys that
> do drugs are more reliable than the drinkers. They tend to blow their money quickly and
> need to fish to get money for another hit. Those who are serious about it have kids to
> support, a house to look after, their own transport. But those guys are scarce.

Alcohol abuse itself tends to still be a cause for concern among the fishers. A man who had been

a professional skipper since he was nineteen said that he had more of a problem with drinkers and

hard drug users than with marijuana-addicts.

> No wine drinkers or mandrax; my crew had better not come to sea half drunk. Pot
> smokers, on the other hand, make for the best crew. They are more content but still retain
> all of their faculties. My guys don't take drugs onto the boat, but I know many of them
> smoke dagga. Dagga costs R2 for two little sticks. Mandrax costs R50 a "button" [pill].
> There were three of us that were able to kick the mandrax habit. It is too expensive a
> habit. Money comes in and out of the pocket equally fast. But it's even worse with
> druggies. Now I'm a God fearing man, and I'm trying to teach others.

The reality of the drug trade in the fishing industry is hard to deny. It is a social ill that members

of the fishing industry are working hard to combat. It is not necessarily a problem of their own

making. It becomes obvious that the analogy to the "tot" system is more than coincidental when

there is proof that the prevalence of drugs in the fishing communities can be traced in part back to

the scheming of the apartheid regime. In his trial before the Truth and Reconciliation

Commission the infamous apartheid "biological warfare expert" Wouter Basson, admitted to flooding coloured communities with mandrax pills and ecstasy, both synthetic and highly

addictive drugs, in an attempt to "control the enemy" (Suggot 1997).

Myth of the Colour-Blind Fisher

There is a strong belief among the handline ski-boat skippers that the ocean is the great racial

equalizer. The snoek are no respecter of color; I was told. They only discriminate between

various types of bait. A forty-three year-old coloured skipper who had been fishing full-time

since he was seventeen assured me that there has never been racism at sea:

> No, really, we've always been one. We've always worked together. Years ago, they
> used to charge us different. You work for your fish and you charge me [while I'm
> catching fish], you [call me] hotnot, and that kind of thing. But that passes. When we get
> to the shore we're pals again. There always has to be a little fight. But on the other side,
> in PE, Mosselbaai, etc., those people on that side, those people from the Transvaal,
> they're not like that with the blacks. But as white and black we stand together. We
> always stand together.

One of the younger coloured skippers was also convinced that work at sea did not allow for

discrimination. When asked to describe the true fisherman, he said:

> With us at sea, you can be white, black or whatever. Us fishermen look out for each
> other. We have a big respect for each other. Color doesn't make a difference. You can go
> to sea to work, but there are days that you don't make anything. Then you hang around
> each other. It isn't like we argue; that's not something you're allowed to do at sea. But
> you "skel" [call names; scold] your friends. Let's say I throw my line over yours, or I
> catch your line. If I cuss you out, then you'll get mad. Then there's an argument. That's
> now with the ski-boats. On the big boats there was racism. That's where the blacks...
> You see, from the eighteenth century people were catching snoek already.

An older white skipper who had been fishing on ski-boats for more than the past thirty years

agreed: "Now it's the new South Africa. It's just the way it is. I've got no better advantages than

a coloured person. In the fishing industry, we take everyone. But that was the case in the

apartheid years too. We never made a distinction between workers. The one gets treated like the

other one. So it's about the same. There was no distinguishing." While many were careful to

construct this myth as an exception to the exploitative race relations under apartheid, it wasn't

long before cracks in their idealist construction began to show.

A forty-five year old white skipper who had been fishing for thirty-two years but only as a full-time skipper for the past four years, said,

> It's nothing strange for me to work with blacks and coloureds. I have less problems with the bantu and the coloured than with the whites. There is no racism in the industry. The coloureds are your better fishermen. They grow up with it. They're uneducated and have lived from the sea, for example all the Kalk Bay men.

Having "worked with blacks and coloureds" in his previous profession, he was quite comfortable with the changes in the "new South Africa." Perhaps in the spirit of the new South Africa, white skippers tended to pride themselves on the fact that they had worked hand-in-hand with "anderkleuriges" (lit. persons of other color) long before political changes made it expedient to do so.

In describing his personal history, a fifty-three year-old coloured skipper from the Saldanha region shared his views of the racialized history of the industry:

> In those days there weren't so many whites in the fishing industry. The majority were coloureds, every now and then a bantu. I have uncles that were skippers. Then the Portuguese came over, and he had to teach them how to catch the crayfish. They came out of Madeira, and he was the one that taught them. The whites brought in the ski-boats. When they brought them out, they were only for pleasure. And afterwards they found out that you could put skippers on the ski-boats. I never worked for a white. I've worked for my own people this whole time. I've worked in Saldanha. There I learned on the chakkies. Only later the ski-boats came in.

This skipper correctly notes the role that white recreational fishers played in the introduction of the ski-boat and points to an historical reason for the dominance of white skippers in this sector of fishing. The consensus from both fishers and Marine and Coastal Management (MCM) seems to be that there are an increasing number of white skippers and crew entering the ski-boat handline industry. MCM knows that these new entrants place increased pressure on the resource; the skippers know that it places increased pressure on their ability to make a living.

Despite the common belief among the handline fishers that there has never been any racism at sea, the insidious tentacles of the apartheid racial schemes found their way into this most traditional of lifestyles. The racial categories of the apartheid system remain a dominant form of social distinction both structurally and culturally. Both white and coloured skippers use race as one of the primary building blocks in constructing their social reality, both in their cognitive construction of the "other" and in their social networks.

A forty-eight year-old white skipper who left his white-collar job five years ago to fish full-time described his perspective on the relationship between white and coloured fishers:

> We've always had respect for each other, but we think better than they do. We can handle different levels of responsibility. The lower their education, the less they worry about other's property. We maintain our stuff. What we've got we worked for. They're getting everything free. They'd rather dance in the street to parliament than work. I bought my boat from my father and had it built up from there. A coloured fisherman today even said if only he could get out of the country—here and there you get a good one.

Attitudes toward the racial other are mediated by the reputation that coloureds have for being good fishers. One ex-teacher who recently entered the industry at the time had six white and two coloured crew with him on the boat. When asked how he decides whom to hire, he said: "The best man gets the job. You just know. The crew brings crew. Mine would die if I brought a kaffer [sic] along. Sometimes I'll take 'papslange' [weaklings; guys who don't pull their weight]." The matter-of-fact reference to a black person as a "kaffer" is not uncommon among the white skippers in particular. This dehumanizing, derogatory type of slang reflects and reinforces what Harry Hoetink (Oostindie and Hoetink 1996) called the "social distance," reflecting what how some whites view themselves as a plane above those of other races. A forty year-old skipper from the suburbs of Cape Town who had been fishing full-time for the past four years described how he decided whom to hire:

> A guy that can catch fish well, not a drunk ass. A man that can catch his day's pay. I need to know him. I can't just take anyone. Like take the kaffers [sic]. The other man catches 100 fish, and he catches 30 fish. No, I take coloureds because they're good fishermen. And if I don't know him then I'll take him along, but I'll look at his gear. You can see from his lines if he's okay.

Just as attitudes toward coloured crew are mediated by their reputation for being good fishers, the general assumption is that individuals identified as black would not make for good crew. This assumption is often justified with references to the historic paucity of those classified as black working in the handline industry.

When asked what he looks for in a crew, one young college educated skipper, who had only been fishing full-time for a year, said:

> Honesty. Hard working. Sincere or upright. Good manners; punctual. I need to be able to count on my crew. No drunks; those stay at home. It's very hard to find good crew. The crew basically has nothing. They live from day to day. They don't have too many responsibilities. Everyone smokes dagga. But I'm lucky. I have a white crew.

He assumed that white crew, in general, were above the poverty and moral turpitude that reportedly plagued the coloured fisher. Moral vices are often directly associated with race. Rarely do the white skippers point the causal finger in the direction of poverty or institutionalized discrimination.

On occasion white skippers voice their preference for coloured crew to the exclusion of other whites. When this retired navy mechanic with nine years of full-time handline fishing experience was asked how he would describe the ideal crew member, he said: "Coloured. Whites have an attitude. They think the world owes them a living. There are a lot with drug cravings to feed. But the ideal crew is reliable. You don't have to phone them. They're punctual. He doesn't drink. He's respectable, not quarrelsome. He can take the conditions, even if he's old." But even the preference for a coloured crew can reveal how race influences the skewed nature of power relations on the boat. One young white skipper made the following point: "I'd rather work with coloureds. I can't work with a boat full of whites. Whites just don't want to do some things. You can't swear out older white men. A lot of these white guys are just like the "skollies" [roughnecks; beatnicks], but they don't want to be classified with coloureds." This skipper reveals his internalized estimation of social hierarchy by equating coloureds and "skollies" and contrasting them with older white men who he "can't swear out." But he also gives us insight into the social dynamics between coloured and white crew. He perceives white crew as attempting to distance themselves socially from their coloured counterparts.

Race is also a key component of coloured skippers' constructions of the other. Relations of power tend to dominate as a theme when coloured skippers refer to whites. One of the oldest and most experienced coloured skippers commented on the benefits he saw in the "new South Africa": "I've had my own ski-boat all the years. For me it's a benefit to be coloured. But for the other people that first had to work for the white man, for the factories, he still has to work the same as always. He has nothing for himself." A twenty-seven year old coloured skipper who had been fishing full-time since he was fourteen explained the changes in South Africa this way:

> I've always been a coloured. Nothing has changed. Even though I look like a white man. But that was in the apartheid years. With the new administration it's different. Let me put it like this, there's a big difference. In the beginning, before I started fishing, there were people that got quotas for crayfish and so on, but like today they're giving the quotas to new applicants. But, the people that already have, like people that are white, people that have boats, they that already have, that have enough, they want more. They're complaining to MCM. They already have boats and stuff. They bought trawlers and stuff. They got sardine quotas. Now like us, that are just beginning in the industry, we just work for someone else. And the people don't even work with you honestly. They take more away from you, that little piece of bread, they take an ever bigger piece from you. It's changing a lot. In the fishing industry, there was so much stuff hidden from us. Now we have the information about the quotas. See, there's a structure now, channels you can go through. See, we scratched kind of deep, and they got hurt. So the information got out. So we on the ground woke up. We began with a little group, and now we're coming by something.

This skipper was acutely aware of the effect that the discrimination of the past has on his life at the present. Even though he was optimistic about the potential benefits the structural changes in the country as a whole will bring for him in the future, he also recognized that his opportunities are limited not only by the disparities in access to resources that existed under apartheid but by the disparities that past limitations continue to cause.

Protesting Rights, Constructing Identity: Who is the True Fisher?

At 11h00 on February 17, 2000 a group of interested parties representing the "*bona fide*" fishers of the Western Cape marched through the streets of Cape Town protesting corruption in the government's fishing quota allocation system. Organized by leaders of the Artisanal Fishers Association and the Food and Allied Worker's Union (FAWU) and supported by the Wildlife and Environment Society of South Africa, Earthlife Africa, Cape Town, and the Congress of South African Trade Unions (COSATU), an estimated five hundred men and women gathered to protest the lack of fishing quotas for those previously denied access. In official memoranda they demanded the legal recognition of artisanal fishers, protested the granting of fishing rights to foreign companies and generally challenged the government's "reluctance to drive transformation and redistribution in the fishing industry" (FAWU 2000). The specific focus was on rights for small-scale fishers.

Figure 6. Protesters March on Parliament for Local Fishers' Rights
source: author

While the protest was designed to make a political statement regarding access to fishing rights, the social significance of this march goes far beyond its political aspirations. This march was as much about contesting identity as it was about political economy. Taken in the context of the promises made by the government concerning transformation and the redistribution of resources, this march was about whom should be recognized as truly historically disadvantaged.

With the assumption that the reallocation of fishing rights should go to those with a history in the industry, this march was about whom should be recognized as *bona fide* fishers.

The primary organizer of the march was Andy Johnstone, chair of the Artisanal Fisherman's Association, lobbyist and consultant to a rural, mostly coloured fishing constituency. Flanking Johnstone was the local chair of FAWU. He, along with three representatives from the COSATU, secured two bus loads of factory workers to increase the crowd to an estimated five hundred marchers. Flanking Johnstone on his other side was Andy Gubb, director of the South African Wildlife and Environment Society. Gubb provided the environmental justification for defending the rights of small scale fishers, promoting the long term sustainability of small scale versus industrialized fishing methods.

But most of those in the protesting crowd were far from the image of the "Cape Coloured Fisherman" so carefully constructed above. The crowd included a handful of people who would remotely relate to this image, the skippers and crew of handline boats, coloured, black and white. The protesters also included a number of people who could be described as subsistence fishers, a category the Living Marine Resources Act, 1998 describes as: "a natural person who regularly catches fish for personal consumption or for the consumption of his or her dependants, including one who engages from time to time in the local sale or barter of excess catch, but does not include a person who engages on a substantial scale in the sale of fish on a commercial basis" (1998:Section 1, (lv)). The bulk of the marchers came by bus and had taken half a day off work from a few of the local fish factories in Cape Town. There were more women in the crowd than there were men. And from the majority of protest songs that were sung during the procession through the streets, it was apparent that the majority of the marchers were Xhosa speakers.

It is ironic that the major trade unions in the area were responsible for the majority of participants in this march. The previous year FAWU, COSATU and the ANC fishing desk presented their case together as an aligned group to Marine and Coastal Management, the branch of government responsible for quota allocations. Their strategy was to maintain stability in the form of jobs, income and exports of the formal market sector. This move by the aligned group would appear to be in line with the government's RDP and GEAR strategy. However, by protecting their own interests, these unions compete directly with persons from the rural fishing communities for the rights to the reallocated resources. "The reluctance of formal unions to support the Informal Fishing Community might arise from the present position of organised labour in South Africa. The condition of work and remuneration of South African fish workers is fairly good in big companies. These workers might fear that their hard-earned benefits would get dissipated in any transition from the known to the unknown future" (Isaacs 1998:77).

Figure 7. A Diverse Crowd Marches in Solidarity with Local Fishers
source: author

At one point in the march an interesting concession happened for the Afrikaans speakers in the crowd. An elderly coloured member from one of the handline fishing crews took hold of the megaphone and started to sing his life's story, in Afrikaans, to the tune of the Xhosa freedom songs that were being sung as they marched along. The crowd toned down its song and, from that point on, at least for a time, started using Afrikaans words of protest. The crowd began to sing over and over again, "Ons wil ons kwota hê, Ons wil ons kwota hê" (lit. we want our quota, we want our quota). It was as if in this lyrical gesture the marchers were respecting the image of the Cape coloured fisherman

For many of the fishers interviewed over the course of this research, race relations in South Africa seemed to be so much simpler under apartheid. The competing sides and issues were more black and white then. An oppressive white regime limited blacks from access to legal and economic resources, constructed laws to protect white employment, property and privilege, and excluded black South Africans from all the major decision making processes in society. Class and race were correlated by design. In post-apartheid South Africa the relationship between race and class has become arguably more complex, more nuanced, but no less significant. While this increased nuance and complexity has significantly widened the crack in the door to social mobility for many previously disadvantaged South Africans, it has also made it more difficult to know who or what should be held accountable when change does not come as expected.

No longer de jure, a de facto correlation between race and class continues to heavily influence the structure of relationships in South Africa. It is now arguably even more difficult to disentangle the multiple social strands that are woven together to ensure access to important economic and political resources. There is perhaps no better context to highlight this increased nuance and complexity than in the fishing industry of the Western Cape. By examining the structural and cultural construction of race relations in this industry it becomes possible to tease out the more prominent strands and discuss the relationships between them. A careful analysis of specific events and specific interpersonal relationships in the fishing industry is the next step forward. When we look at events like this protest march, perhaps even more important are the voices that were absent from the protest march, those too busy earning a living to march through the streets of Cape Town, the rural fishers with few means and no transportation to the event...

The Construction of Gender in South Africa's Handline Fishing Industry

Gender Relations in Fishing

It is commonly assumed that the commercial fishing industry is a testosterone driven industry. The sea is thought of as men's domain. and land is women's domain (Davis and Nadel-Klein 1992). In South Africa, men dominate the most visible positions, from the captain's chair to the chair of the Marine Fisheries commissions. Commercial fishing is associated with intense independence, rugged individualism and physical prowess, all constructed as stereotypically male virtues. Men and women in commercial fishing families tend to view the male as the head of the household and often claim to be dependent on "his" income even when he admits to the kind of seasonal fluctuation in income that causes the family to rely on her employment to meet basic needs for a substantial part of the year. Despite the fact that fishing family women are most often involved at multiple levels in the world of fishing, more often than not both husbands and wives speak of the business as "his" business.

Women in South Africa, as in most of the rest of the world, have had to bear the "double burden" of labor in the marketplace and at home. As late as 1983, the home life of the average female worker in South Africa was described as: "Endless rounds of providing tea and food for her husband; making the bed; cleaning the house; carting the baby around; making the fire; ironing, etc. ... in contrast to her husband who feels free to read the newspaper and watch t.v. ('always with his 'little darling' bottle of whiskey beside him') on returning home from work" (Berger 1992:298). Berger makes note of how black women in particular were always at the bottom of the scale when it came to the jobs and compensation that were available. She notes how in the fish canning factories, historically women worked in only two jobs, gutting and packing.

Iris Berger (1992) teased out the complex relationship between race, class and gender in South African industry between 1900 and 1980, and no place did she collapse the categories or oversimplify the relationship between these variables. She notes how in the first quarter of the twentieth century there were many commonalities among women, regardless of race. "Treated as dependents of their fathers and husbands, although in radically different socioeconomic contexts, their contributions to domestic life were paramount. Apart from the pivotal place of African women in rural agricultural production, women's formal role in the economy was limited" (1992:17). Through the 1980s, this paternalism remained a powerful limitation to women's freedom and their participation in the market economy. Not only were women stereotyped into domestic roles by their male family, but the state supported this paternalistic control over women's labor power. It has not been until recently that marriage laws have been changing to allow women more control over family property and labor.

The significant absence of women's voices in this project will quickly be apparent to even the most casual observer. A deep exploration of the construction of gender, gender identity, gender roles, gendered notions of time and space and the impact of gender on race relations and social networks is beyond the scope of this current project. In the most general sense, this project follows in a long line of anthropological representations where men talk to men about men. I did not start out with the intention of avoiding in-depth conversations with women. What I discovered was an exclusively male occupational category that strongly limited the range and kind of information I was given. It is not that women are absent from the lives of these skippers, but the voices of women in the fishing industry have been muted by the marginal presence of women in the skippers' perceived social networks. The only women usually included in skippers' social networks were identified as wife, mother or girlfriend (included as family if she was in residence). Occasionally someone mentioned a close friend, but even then the relationship was linked to a male friendship, e.g. as part of a married couple friendship. This perception of women as marginal to fishing activity is reflected in the analysis I offer.

In most of the literature on fishing families we find descriptions of a very clear, though not always expected, division of labor between husbands and wives (Thompson 1985; Nadel-Klein and Davis 1988; Davis and Nadel-Klein 1992). With few exceptions, men captain the boat, hire the crew, supervise the crew, sell the product and do most of the manual labor directly connected with the physical activity of catching the fish. In general, women typically work on the less publicly visible aspects of the business. Women do most of the accounting, purchase supplies, run errands, pay the bills and, in general, keep the business organized and efficient. Few women gain access to the upper levels of fisheries management (although the same applies to commercial fishers in general). "The public/private dichotomy, which associates men with the public spheres of organization and women with the more private spheres of domestic life, has served as the predominant framework for studies of commercial fishing families. In maritime communities, the environment is specifically tied to gender" (Smith, Jepson and Lee 1993:2).

For most families, women are an integral part of the fishing business, even when they hold other jobs. To call it "his" business is a misnomer. This is true particularly considering that most fishing families integrate their family and business lives. Fishing requires more flexibility from all family members for business to survive. The unpredictable and seasonal nature of the business, combined with the need to keep costs as low as possible, makes it more attractive to have the entire family involved in the business.

Gender and the Patterning of Social Networks

The patterning of social networks is strongly influenced by the construction of gender. Male skippers network predominantly with other males in their personal and professional worlds. Unfortunately there were no women skippers in the handline industry who could act as a source for comparison with the male skippers. Consequently, this study focuses on how men structure and construct gender relations and relationships. The structure of skipper's social networks reveals some interesting constructions of gender and also shows some interesting gender patterning that varies by the race of the skipper.

Table 3. Skippers and their Alters: Percentage of Alters by Gender

	Coloured Skippers	White Skippers	All Skippers
Female	14.2%	10.3%	11.6%
Male	85.8%	89.7%	88.4%
Total:	*100%*	*100%*	*100%*

Table 4. Skippers and their Alters: Percentage of Kin Relations by Gender

	Female	Male
Family	76%	14%
Non-Family	24%	86%
Total:	*100%*	*100%*

Table 3 compares the gender composition of the networks of white versus coloured skippers. Despite the fact that 94% of the skippers interviewed were either married or lived with a female partner, on average only 11.6% of the skippers' entire networks were female, i.e., their social networks were heavily male. There was no statistically significant difference in the percentage of skippers' social networks identified as family when analyzed by race (see Table 4). Interestingly, however, there was a significant difference in the percentage of the networks that white and coloured skippers identified as female. Although their respective percentages were still relatively low, coloured skippers identified a significantly higher percentage of women in their network than did white skippers. An average of 14.2% of the ties in coloured skippers networks were female, while the percentage of females in white skippers networks is significantly lower at an average of 10.3.

Table 4 compares gender and kin relation in the average percentage of alters that skippers mentioned. The women that were in the social networks of skippers were predominantly family members. On average only 21.5% of the alters skippers mentioned were identified as family members. Of the 11.6 % of the skipper's networks that were female, skippers identified 76% as family members. This means that on average, only 24% of the females, or 3% of all the possible ties skippers mentioned, consisted of women who were not family members. In addition, the few women who were not included as family member were often identified as "couples friends," i.e., a friend in part due to their connection with another male friend. Only 14% of the men in skippers' networks were identified as family.

Perceptions of Gender in the Skipper Fraternity

In the specific context of the work that takes place at sea and on the harbor, the work directly connected with the act of fishing itself, men paint women out of the picture. "In maritime communities, space is not only defined by physical boundaries, but is socially constructed by individuals with particular psychological and emotional perspectives on the meaning of physical space" (Smith, Jepson and Lee 1993:12). Since the meaning of physical space is socially constructed, it is the contextualized variations in the construction of that meaning that are most interesting. With Collier, Bloch and Yanagisako (1987), I seek to document the ambiguous and fluid perceptions of gender within a specific spacial and temporal context. Skippers in the handline ski-boat fraternity structure their work on the boat as male work, the space on the boat as male space and the language on the boat as male language. Asking men about what happens when women are brought into this protected gendered space brings out the strongest differences in their perception of what they believe men and women are and respectively should be.

Skippers constructed the space on the boat as male space. When asked what he thought the other guys would say if a woman were to want to work at sea, one thirty-four year-old white skipper who had been fishing for seventeen year replied: "I'd accept it. I don't want to take a woman with me. But I wouldn't say that a woman's place is at home. But if she asks to come to sea with me, she won't fit in with five or six other men, where everyone sleeps together, bath, and so on. Then it's a man's world. But if she had her own boat and crew, then maybe" (Skipper 65). This skipper differentiates between being on the ocean and being on his boat. His major concern is how allowing a woman would change the gendered social dynamic not only on the boat, but in the other areas where fishermen live and work together as fishermen.

The practical issue of toilet facilities was brought up time and again as a reason for denying women access to the boat. A skipper with a similar background, when asked the same question, said: "It's a hard life. There are no toilet facilities for them on the boat. And the men wouldn't just be able to piss over the side. And then there's the swearing..." (Skipper 14). It is fine for men to deal with the dirty physicality of fishing on the open ocean, but women are above all that. One of the central arguments of Timothy Burke's Lifebouy Men, Lux Women is that hygiene served as the "underlying logic of certain colonial institutions concerned with ruling and disciplining Africans" (1996:34). The attitudes reflected by these fishers toward women and cleanliness is not unlike Burke's description of colonial Zimbabwe where hygiene became a significant marker of social difference. For the skippers, women are often associated with higher levels of civilization, or "culture," and should not demean themselves for work on the boat. "I don't think it's a job for a woman. Women are in general soft creatures. A fisherman is rough. A fisherman will be standing there fishing and just whip it out, and a woman won't like that" (Skipper 65).

Beyond the paternalistic chivalry, women were often constructed as the objects of physical desire. Skippers feared that this desire would interfere with a man's concentration at sea. When asked what others would do if a woman wanted to come along, one skipper noted: "They would call those women rough, physically robust. The guys have trashy mouths. The men are totally different here. Women are not seen as crew but as tit and ass" (Skipper 53). Women are in part dangerous to the men because they construct them as objects of sexual desire. Men fear allowing women onto the boats in part because they fear the power of their own sexuality. One of the older coloured skippers spoke about the possibility of women coming with him on the boat: "They have a lot of manners. I'm a man, a warm blooded man. Now if she had to pee, then I'd see everything and I'd have three legs. It's man's work. Women's work is in the factory" (Skipper 81). A young white skipper was worried about the effect a woman would have on his crew: "She would have to perform. But they'd all be thinking about sex. I guess she could if they'd make an oilskin for her..."(Skipper 51). It is ironic that men who pride themselves on physical strength and endurance view themselves (or, at least, others they work with) as helplessly driven by the force of physical desire. "Ooooooh, you know what happens on the ski-boats. You know what a fisherman is like, if he saw a woman on the sea water. He'll whistle and he goes crazy, he forgets to catch fish. It's not every day you see such creatures on the sea water" (Skipper 42).

In specifically male gendered space, men give themselves permission for conversations they would normally not have in a mixed gender environment. More specifically, skippers thought themselves free to use highly sexualized language and images about women when no women were present. One skipper acknowledged, "Fishermen are a breed of their own. They'll just use the toilet at will on the boat. The language on the boat is real rough. They talk about women, about screwing. The language is rough, crude. The guys would have to change" (Skipper 46). Highly sexualized language was used to categorize behavior on the boat. It was common, but only in the company of other fishers, to call the person who had caught the least amount of fish on the boat for the day the "piel" (lit. penis). Skippers and crew worked hard to avoid this phallic designation.

When asked about why they couldn't see a woman fishing for a living like they do, skippers were quick to point out the physical differences between men and women. Women were seen as physically unfit for the kind of dangerous and difficult work that fishermen do. When asked why he thought there were so few women who go to sea for a living, one of the most experienced skippers said,

> It'd have to be a crazy woman. A woman can't do the work that a man does. Even if she thinks she can stand on the shore and do it, or at home, she can't. She can't do the work a man can. That's laughable. Laughable. A woman doesn't have the power a man has. A fisherman works with power. That snoek is THIS BIG. Give it to a man to pull in…a woman can't do that. She has to think about that one. Those big, big fish, they have to be picked up and put over there. He has to be pulled over the side of the ship. Where do they fit in? Do they think there are toys at sea? Do they think it's like cleaning the house? (Skipper 12)

Physical prowess is often the first category of distinction raised in the gendered division of labor, particularly when physically demanding labor is at the heart of the task. Women are not supposed to be able to compete with men physically. When they do they are often placed in a separate category. One skipper described women that didn't mold to the generally accepted roles: "There are a lot of women in the hawking industry, but only a few on the handline boats. They are lowlifes. They could pass for a man. It is very physical work, not mechanical. It is very dangerous work. You have to be able to take the pounding on the sea (Skipper 46). With a similar point, another skipper confirmed the position he thought women should take: " The guys need a hell of a lot of support from their wives. He's gone 95% of the time. It's a physical job, beyond the strength of a woman. The one woman I know who fishes, she might as well be a man" (Skipper 100).

The roles these male skippers construct for women are not necessarily outside the fishing industry, just not on their boats. When asked why there are so few women that go to sea to make a living, one skipper noted:

> It's physical, hard work. With the whole emancipation, you can do what you want, but a woman can't do it. I wouldn't want it to be someone close to me, or far from me either. There are a lot of the factory ships that women work on, but they do factory work; they're not catching fish. They're not working with ropes and nets. A lot of women mend nets, much better than a man can do... you have to decide where your strong and weak points are, male or female, and you should stick to that. They can't make a man out of a woman, and they can't make a woman out of me. I'm not saying they won't make it at sea. Every one has their place, like on a factory ship, they have their place and they work, they work on a factory ship. They are very safe. But I can't conceive of a woman who has to put gloves on and catch fish with me. She'll enjoy it, but she won't do it every day. I won't allow a woman to crew with me (Skipper 16).

Women are often thought of more as supporting the work done by the man. When asked the same question, another skipper laughed and said, "Probably because they're scared. There are a couple that go to sea, but not by us. There was one that went to catch crayfish with the men down there. There are a lot of women that give the men advice and that stand by the fishermen, but not on the sea. A lot of women help the fishermen" (Skipper 87).

Race also played a factor in how some skippers constructed gender on the boats. When asked why there are so few women who go to sea to make a living, one young white skipper commented on his coloured crew: "The crew's language is bad. They've not been brought up well. The guys pee while on the boat. The one guy we know who takes a woman has a white crew, so it's not a problem" (Skipper 38). His assumption that a white woman would not be safe on the boat with a coloured crew was explicitly stated by another young white skipper when asked what he thought the other guys would think of a woman coming to sea: "Mixed feelings. Some will be very supportive. Some will just act as if they're being supportive. A white woman on a boat with coloureds would not be good" (Skipper 32).

Some of the skippers constructed myths about women that are consistent with ancient fears about women, the sea and bad luck. As one experienced skipper said when asked why he wouldn't take a woman to sea, "It's superstition. It's bad luck to have women on the boat. It's the truth. It comes from years ago. They say a woman calls the storms. It's an age-old story. Plus you don't want them to take away your men's attention" (Skipper 41). Another experienced fisherman elaborated:

Fishing has always been traditionally for men, especially among the coloured. I don't know how the whites feel about it. But among the coloureds it's always been traditional; the man goes to sea and the wife stays at home or whatever, and she prepares whatever must be done. In the past it was very... Fishing has a lot to do with luck. And they always feel that a woman is not good luck on the boat. Because if you really go back into Genesis, back many years, with the old type fishermen, they never wanted a woman to get on the boat. "A woman needs to be at home!" Sometimes you get, say I go to sea and this guy goes to sea and all of a sudden he catches a lot of fish. Now another guy will go there the same day, minutes later, and he won't catch. And he'll wonder, "how did you catch that fish?" He'll tell you, it's luck. If you're on the boat, you can't really see what's underneath. You've got equipment to tell you , but you can't really see. So basically, you say it's just luck. So with luck, and with all the bad luck, and what fishermen believe about, like don't put on the right jacket and it's bad luck for the day, things like that. It's more that women are bad luck. You'll find a lot of fishermen mentioning something like that. So when they believe it, it's probably better... "We don't want women at sea." You leave them at home (Skipper 1).

This skipper recognized the pragmatic consequences of a common myth. Whether he believes that women are bad luck or not, he is influenced not to take a woman to sea due to what he perceives to be the social pressure from those fishing with him.

On rare occasions I was able to get a glimpse into how some of the skipper's wives felt about gender and fishing. Consider the following interaction. During one of the interviews with a relatively young but experienced white skipper, his wife joined us for the interview and joined in on the conversation:

Skipper: About six years ago my wife crewed for a living. It's a very hard life. Ask my wife. You can ask her that question. It's the cold and stuff.

Skipper's wife: No, it's the competition. It's very great with them. They always look down at you.

Skipper: It's not the kind of job for a woman to do.

Skipper's wife: Ooh, don't go there.

Skipper: It's not their line of work. They can't put up with the strain that we do. Take her, she can't sit with a rod for four hours, or three hours, with one fish on the end of the rod...

Skipper's wife: But you're generalizing now.

Skipper: But there were a lot of days that we went to sea and you got hurt. They're not made for that kind of thing. The days we go to sea in thirty/thirty-five knots of wind and you get banged around, and my body is sore, if she's gotta be there, she won't get up this morning.

Skipper's wife: It's also a mental thing. I remember, every single day we came into the harbor, the guys always said to me, "how much fish did you catch?" And boy, oh boy, I'm talking the men were into the comparison. It wasn't a case of saying to [my husband], "how much fish did you catch?" They didn't want to know how much he caught. They wanted to know how much I caught. That kind of thing. Out of your five crew members, what did she catch; that's what we want to know. High competition. It was a case of, can she handle it or can't she.

Skipper: It doesn't boil down to that. The crew boils down to…they must be able to catch fish. Otherwise…otherwise, if I put somebody in that laaitjie and somebody in another one, and he catches fifty every day, and that one catches five, he's actually a burden, not an asset. He's actually wasting my bait, wasting my time having him there. I can rather leave him off for that few fish he's giving me at the end of the day. He's wasting more bait than what he's actually giving me money (Skipper 5).

Competition was prevalent between the skippers. In an industry where many of the skippers themselves had formerly been sport or recreational fishers, competition with other skippers was often an unspoken measure of success. While many of the skippers minimized the importance of competition in their interviews with me, this skipper wife's presence highlighted how important competition was. Other confirmed this importance informally. What she also brings out in this conversation is the gendered nature of the competition. Having the highest "tallies" (catch) for the day was cause for bragging rights among the crew, but it was particularly important to catch more than a woman did. The male fisher's success is measured against what they believe a woman should be and should be able to do, even when she is not with them.

CHAPTER 6

THE HISTORICAL AND SOCIO-ECONOMIC CONTEXT FOR HANDLINE FISHING

A Snapshot of South Africa's Fishing Industry[1]

Introduction

South Africa has a coastline of some three thousand kilometers, extending from the Orange River in the west, on the border with Namibia, to Ponta do Ouro in the east, adjacent to Moçambique. The western coastal shelf is highly productive in terms of the volume of sea life in common with other upwelling ecosystems around the world. The east coast is considerably less productive but has high species diversity. The living marine resources of South Africa have been exploited for many centuries with some evidence of abalone having been exploited 125,000 years ago (Marine and Coastal Management 1997). Approximately six thousand years ago, the "Strandlopers" (lit. beach-walkers) were already exploiting many marine species, as shown by studies of middens along the coastline (Hutton and Lamberth 1997). Industrial fisheries started just before the turn of the twentieth century and escalated rapidly thereafter. By the 1960s, catches in several South African fisheries had exceeded sustainable yields, and there were sharp declines in some key stocks. This led to initiatives to improve the scientific standard and base for management of the major fisheries.

Globally, fisheries management has utilized both input and output controls to limit the exploitation of marine life while managing productivity and employment in the fishing industry. "*Input* controls limit such things as the number of participants in fisheries, the type and amount of gear, and methods of fishing" (Committee to Review Individual Fishing Quotas 1999:1). Input controls may include closing off certain areas to commercial harvesting or limiting the length of fishing seasons for particular species. "*Output* controls use various means to limit catch to some level determined to be sustainable over the long term" (Committee to Review Individual Fishing Quotas 1999:1). Managers in industrialized fisheries often set limits, including the Total Allowable Catch (TAC), with recommendations of marine scientists. Since the early 1970s, South African fisheries management has been committed to use of TAC management through the use of quotas.

The South African commercial fishing industry has quota and non-quota sectors, the former being significantly larger in terms of value and quantity. Quotas (output/catch controls) to catch a stipulated quantity of a specific species are allocated to individuals or companies. In addition, permits are granted to individuals or companies to catch unlimited quantities of non-quota species using defined technologies and subject to other limitations (input/effort controls). The quota sector of the industry is made up of a few large companies and a number of smaller ones. Both types have, however, invested large sums in plant and machinery, with the consequence that some sectors of the fishing industry are overcapitalized (Kleinschmidt 2000).

Fishing in South Africa consists of four main components:

- the formal industrial component that is made up of a number of large and small companies, who harvest, process and market marine recourses on a commercial basis;
- the informal component, made up mainly of small operators and independent boat owners, engaged in subsistence fishing;
- the recreational fishermen; and
- the new entrants, mainly comprising of members of historically disadvantaged communities, who wish to take advantage of the new opportunities offered by the arrival of democracy. (FAWU 1997)

While the bulk of this project is aimed at understanding the social relations in the informal sector of South Africa's fishing industry, it is important to understand the industrial context that parallels this informal economy. Those in the informal sector will often move in and out of the formal sector in the course of a fishing career.

Table 5. Nominal Commercial Catches (Tons Nominal Mass) by Fishery and Species

Fishery and species	1985	1990	1993	1994	1995	1998
Trawling	186 040	240 506	211 885	186 328	177 778	203402
Hakes	139 889	134 821	141 202	144 071	137 616	149116
Kingklip	10 187	2 547	2 567	2 867	2 861	3409
Monk	4 230	5 405	4 281	5 047	5 941	7902
Panga, reds	634	572	798	1 161	647	885
Sole	882	868	846	978	813	890
Snoek	5 387	13 091	12 519	6 149	6 875	6913
Cape Horse Mackerel	13 439	43 875	12 348	11 987	9 321	19264
Other	11 392	39 327	37 324	14 068	13 704	15023
Purse seining	377 464	259 343	357 040	314 461	366 456	321683
Pilchard	32 986	56 740	50 717	92 806	113 748	128019
Cape Horse Mackerel	816	7 199	11 646	8 210	1 985	26661
Chub Mackerel	156	23	371	2 037	2 671	101
Anchovy	272 642	150 100	235 830	155 554	170 261	107548
Round Herring	39 871	44 710	56 331	54 145	76 486	52476
Other	30 993	571	2 145	1 709	1 305	6878
Rock Lobster	4 210	4 544	3 194	2 932	2 850	2596
West Coast	3 728	3 491	2 176	1 956	1 858	1726
East Coast	32	11	33	10	-	6
South Coast	450	1 042	985	966	992	864
Line, small net	18 336	24 717	21 857	24 629	26 083	147471
Snoek	3 493	7 753	2 757	7 302	9 174	7222
Tunas	4 375	4 929	4 903	4 069	3 816	8902
Yellowtail	414	612	818	825	777	521
Mullet	1 801	1 380	1 310	1 153	1 338	908
Squids	3 100	3 281	6 308	6 441	6 826	6354
Other	5 153	6 762	5 761	4 839	4 152	123564
Other activities	9 784	15 517	4 404	7 819	6 316	929
Prawn, Langoustine	1 085	952	521	609	512	405
Abalone	961	624	599	613	616	524
Other, Guano, S.weed	7 738	13 941	2 384	6 597	5 188	
GRAND TOTAL	*595 838*	*545 717*	*598 380*	*536 169*	*579 483*	*673485*

Source: Stuttaford (1996, 1998, 1999)

As shown in Table 6, South Africa's most valuable fishery commercially is the demersal fishery, a fishery dominated by deep-sea trawling for the Cape hakes. The fishery developed at the start of the twentieth century and grew rapidly after World War II to peak at more than

300,000 tons in the early 1970s. The mid-water trawl fishery is relatively small and targets exclusively adult horse mackerel, which are also caught by the inshore and deep-sea trawl fisheries.

The pelagic fishery is South Africa's largest in terms of volume landed. From 1975 until 1990, total catches fluctuated between 350,000 and 450,000 tons, except in 1987 and 1988 when catches averaged 675,500 tons, the largest since the inception of the fishery in the late 1940s. In 1990 and 1991, they dropped to 250,000 tons, the lowest level since 1958, recovered to 453,000 tons in 1992, and then declined again, to only 214,000 tons in 1996. Pelagic catches fluctuate because anchovy, a short-lived species prone to massive recruitment swings, dominated the catch from the 1960s until 1996. Used for the manufacture of fishmeal and oil, it has been the single most important species since 1966, when over-fishing caused the pilchard stock to collapse.

Table 6. Nominal Commercial Catches (Rounded Mass) and Wholesale Values

INDUSTRY SECTOR	1993		1995		1997	
	Catch (Tons)	Value (R,000)	Catch (Tons)	Value (R,000)	Catch (Tons)	Value (R,000)
Offshore Trawl	196,605	570,373	162,543	744,508	182321	989744
Inshore Trawl	15,280	43,455	15,235	60,722	15150	68736
TOTAL DEMERSAL	211,885	613,828	177,778	805,230	197381	1058480
Purse Seine (Pelagic)	357,040	232,134	366,456	403,835	272111	439224
Rock Lobster	3,161	138,270	2,850	185,901	2,570	167021
Crustacean Trawl	554	12,667	512	11,261	7715	225975
Line Fish	20,114	145,118	24,745	216,946	17221	128239
Demersal Longlining	0	0	1,696	26,520	4753	46373
Abalone	599	32,777	616	54,054		
Miscellaneous Nets	1,766	3,197	1,338	3,895		
Oysters	52	408	160	1,431		
Mussel and Oyster Farm	2,237	9,481	2,082	23,586		
TOTAL	597,408	1,187,880	578,233	1,732,659	304,370	1,006,832
Seaweed	995	2,819	1,250	4,215		
Guano	0	0	0	0		
GRAND TOTAL	598,403	1,190,699	579,483	1,736,874	502832	2070283

Source: Stuttaford (1998)

South Africa's commercial rock lobster fishery is based on two species, one on the south and one on the west coast. The latter is caught inshore by traps and hoop-nets deployed from small vessels, and it is also harvested by recreational divers. The south coast lobster is a deep-water species caught by means of longlines and traps set by larger freezer vessels. The South Coast rock lobster fishery has been in existence since 1974.

South Africa's commercial abalone fishery remained relatively stable for many years and had been controlled by a total tonnage quota since 1983. The lucrative market in the Far East has, in recent years, stimulated an escalation in illegal fishing activity. At the same time, the number of recreational divers has been steadily rising, so that the total recreational take is now almost as large as the commercial take. Scientific prognoses for the future, given the current lack of control over poaching, are bleak.

Table 7. South Africa's Imports and Exports of Fish in 1998

	Imports		Exports	
	1000 Kg	R,000	1000 Kg	R,000
TOTAL	52,831	421,683	130,299	1,353,921
MAIN PRODUCTS				
Live fish	112	6,202	107	1,176
Fresh fish, excluding fillets	139	3,126	11,376	156,358
Frozen fish, excluding fillets	19,781	68,866	66,968	388,238
Fish fillets, fresh and frozen	670	5,102	24,249	347,092
Fish dried, salted, smoked, etc.	378	9,400	3,361	41,295
Products of fish, crustacea & mollusks; corals; sponges; shells	102	1,193	1,464	2,545
Prepared, preserved fish	17,086	191,723	5,200	42,770
Crustacea and mollusks	6,540	114,653	29,547	352,457
Fishmeal and fish body oil	8,024	21,428	9,066	21,992

Source: Stuttaford (1998)

The South African linefishery is split into three main components: the squid-jigging fishery, the tuna fishery and the general recreational and commercial linefishery. The squid-jigging fishery targets chokka squid. After its initiation in 1983 the fishery grew rapidly until a permit system for vessels was introduced in 1987 to limit fishing effort. Today the jig-fishing fleet consists of about three hundred mostly small vessels, such as skiboats and catamarans, but effort is creeping up and catch rates are declining. The commercial fishery for tuna began in 1960 when longlining was introduced. Despite annual catches of two thousand tons, the fish fetched a poor price and operations ceased in 1964. The poling method (in which a baited hook or lure is attached by a short line to a pole) led to a renewed interest in commercial fishing for tuna in the late 1970s. In 1979 there was a massive run of yellowfin tuna, and more than six thousand tons were landed, prompting heavy investment in boats and tackle. But the large shoals failed to reappear the following year, and the new industry came close to collapse. Effort was subsequently redirected at albacore (longfin tuna), which, with smaller contributions from yellowfin, bigeye and skipjack, has since provided the bulk of the South African tuna catch of four thousand to six thousand tons per year.

Catches in the commercial linefishery peaked at 18,000 to 20,000 tons in the late 1960s and early 1970s but then declined steadily to an estimated 7,300 tons in 1985. This was despite an increase in fishing effort as smaller, faster and more transportable skiboats replaced the earlier lineboats. The newer vessels enabled fishers to concentrate effort where fish were available and to follow migratory species along the coast, so effectively increasing pressure on the declining resource. The dropping catches, together with a decrease in the mean sizes of fish caught, led to calls for the protection of linefish stocks, and in 1984, the South African Marine Linefish Management Association was formed. Today, management measures include minimum size limits, bag limits, closed seasons and closed areas (marine reserves), but catch rates continue to decrease as the numbers of fishers (commercial and recreational) rise annually.

Tables 5 (Nominal Commercial Catches (Tons Nominal Mass)by Fishery and Species), 6 (Nominal Commercial Catches (Rounded Mass) and Wholesale Values) and 7 (South Africa's Imports and Exports of Fish in 1998) provide a snapshot of the current activity in South Africa's commercial fishing industry. The most obvious observation to be made from this data is the dominance of capital-intensive fishing effort in the industry. Purse seining and trawling dominate the industry in both catch and value. For the purposes of this study, it is also important to point out the relative marginality of linefish in the general industry, both in terms of catch (Table 5) and value (Table 6). Fishers in the handline sector view this marginality as a Janus-faced dilemma having two somewhat contradictory outcomes. On the one hand, the relative economic marginality of the most commonly caught handline species, snoek and yellowtail, has meant that few of the major industrial companies have shown significant interest in controlling the markets for these species. This has allowed small-scale operators like the handline fishers to develop niche markets. On the other hand, the industrial marginality of these species has meant that the activity of the handline fishers remained largely outside of the government management and support structure for market development. Market prices for these species are erratic and remain relatively low.

The current quota system is unpopular at the industrial and the grass-roots levels of the fishing industry. Although the Quota Board makes its allocations according to agreed criteria, the quotas are generally perceived to have been allocated arbitrarily and often unfairly. Neither large nor small operators trust the system that had been in operation for almost thirty years. The Marine Living Resources Act of 1998 was an attempt to redress some of the socio-economic imbalances in the industry, improve the efficiency of fisheries management and stabilize what is increasingly perceived to be the unsustainable harvest of South Africa's marine life.

Prior to 1652

Little is known about fishing in South Africa prior to the arrival of the Europeans. "Fishing has long been carried out in South Africa, but its history as an industry spans only this century and its really intensive development into the large-scale enterprise of today has taken place [since just prior to World War II]" (Irvin and Johnson 1963:4). The origins of the South African linefishery can be traced back to the fishing activities of the indigenous Khoi and European seafarers from, at least, the 1500s. When Van Riebeeck came to the Cape and ordered fish brought in for the crew, he was not, by any stretch of the imagination, the first to fish these waters. Long before 1652, "Bushmen, Hottentots and Strandlopers fished both rivers and seas and superstitious mariners voyaging around the Cape considered it unlucky not to pause to throw a line into the rich waters of the Agulhas Bank" (Lees 1969:4).

According to Lees, the historian G.M. Theal showed how some coastal Khoi clans supplemented or replaced their cattle economy with harvest from the sea: "They had neither boats nor hooks, but they managed to catch fish by throwing light assegais with lines attached to them from rocks standing out in deep water" (1969:4). These early fishers were known to have harvested shellfish from the rocks and built stone fish-kraals (weirs) to capture fish as the tide went out. Some of the tidal pools built for bathers in the late nineteenth century, e.g. the tidal pools at Kalk Bay, were constructed on top of rough tidal pools built by Khoi "strandlopers" prior to European settlement (Walker 1999). Middens found in the area around the small coastal town of Struisbaai include shells and Khoi tools and ten thousand year old 'fish fyvers' (human-made tidal pools for catching fish) (Hutton and Lamberth 1997).

The Portuguese were the first Europeans to make significant contact with people living on the southern tip of Africa.[2] In his attempt to find new trade routes, in 1497 Vasco da Gama brought the first European foreigners to land and catch fish at a bay that he called St. Helena. While sailors and those stationed at the ports would most likely have made use of marine products to support their diet, evidence for the social or economic implications of fishing during this time is scarce. It is likely, however, that hooks and seine-nets were first introduced to this part of the continent by the Europeans, as most of the reports of fishing activity with the arrival of the Dutch excluded mention of such technology.

Dutch Settlement

There were no radical changes brought in the patterns or technology of fishing by the Dutch occupation of the Cape. Early Dutch settlers saw very few incentives for exploiting the marine resources beyond the level gained from trading with the Khoi.

> Development of fishing in the Cape was initially slow, both because it was discouraged by the Dutch East India Company in the newly established settlement and because the garrison could offer little protection to those burghers who attempted colonization of the inhospitable and hostile coastline. (Pulfrich and Griffith 1988:223)

Taking into consideration the lack of support from the ruling body, the perception of a dangerous coastline and the limited technology available at the time, the newly arrived Europeans restricted their fishing efforts to the inshore waters of Table Bay and False Bay. In the earliest days of settlement, those who were interested in fishing beyond the shore's edge used ship's boats and canoes for netting and linefishing. "As the Company began importing larger vessels and the demand for the larger, delicately flavoured line-caught species increased, handlining became the preferred method" (Pulfrich and Griffith 1988:228). With local demand easily met and fish the cheapest of foods, there was no true incentive for further effort (Lees 1969:10).

British Colonization

With the British colonization of the Cape came the expansion of the frontier and the possibility for further development of the coastline by the Europeans. When the British captured the Cape Colony in 1795, all fishing restrictions were lifted, and by the mid 1800s the linefishery had become a thriving industry. The statistical register for 1830 showed that 40 boats and 200 men were exclusively engaged in fishing (Lees 1969:11). Salted snoek was becoming important as South Africa's first Marine export commodity, but only as cheap food for slaves on the islands of Mauritius. This trade to Mauritius was important enough to have Cape Town nicknamed "Snoekopolis (Van Sittert 1992:35). Snoek, the first species exported from South African waters in significant quantity, is also the most commonly caught species for today's handline fishers (see

Figure 8). "Snoek was first mentioned by Van Riebeeck as having been caught in Saldanha Bay and, owing to its similarity to the fresh-water pike or snoek of Holland, he named it 'Zeesnoek'" (Lees 1969:11).

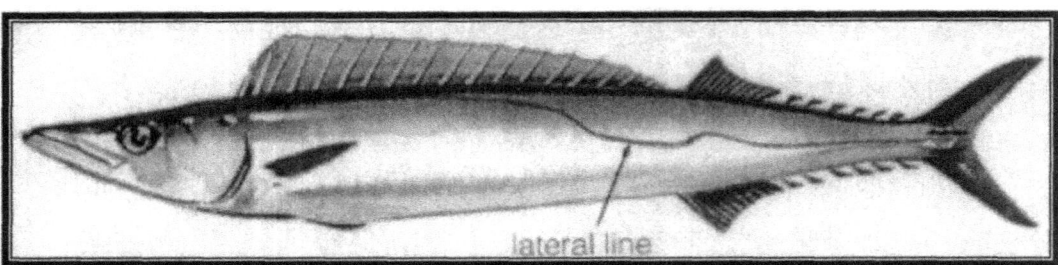

Figure 8. The Southern African Snoek *Thyrsites atun*
source: van der Elst (1981)

An 1830 painting in the Cape Town Museum, *Fishmongers* by HC de Meillon, shows vendors carrying fish on wooden poles across their shoulders, an image often repeated by artists depicting coastal Cape life. This suggests a local food fishery in South Africa in the early nineteenth century, perhaps with the participation of the original slaves from Indonesia. The current Fishing Industries Handbook (Stuttaford 1999) logo, which has been adopted by the South African Fisheries Museum, is derived from a painting titled *The Snoek Seller* (see Figure 9). The original appeared in "Sketches of various types of the Cape of Good Hope" and is now in the Pretoria National Library (Stuttaford 1999:157). The barefooted, dark-skinned hawker is dressed in what would have been easily recognized as Cape Malay garb. The June 1884 edition of the *South African Illustrated News* contains a picture of a dark-skinned, tattered-clothed man in a small fishing boat in Hout Bay. He is depicted in the process of clubbing a snoek, a practice commonly employed to avoid the potential dangers of the razor sharp teeth of a wriggling game fish. Common to all three of these representations is the identification of the impoverished fisherman as a coloured man. Race and class are conflated with such presumption as to make the identification seem natural.

Figure 9. The Snoek Seller
source: Stuttaford (1999)

From the earliest days of harvest, snoek was thought of as food for the poor. Its export to

Mauritius was for the purpose of feeding the East Indian sugar plantation slaves the British had

placed there after taking the island from the French in 1810. Trading for sugar, this export-import

relationship developed slowly until snoek became economically the most important Cape fish.

But the stigma of snoek as a slave fish meant that it would serve well as a staple for the poor of Cape Town and for cheap farm labor food, but not as a delicacy for the European palate (Lees 1969:11–12). Today many of the fishermen refer to snoek as the Cape Coloured fish.

Until the 1880s Cape Malays dominated the catch and sale of fish in the western Cape Colony. But from about 1880 onward, European immigrants played an increasingly important role in the fishing industry.

> [This immigration] started with an influx of Greeks, followed in later years by Italians (mostly Sicilians) and Portuguese. England, Denmark, Sweden, Norway, Spain, France, Holland—in brief, every European country with a seaboard—all contributed a quota of citizens to try their luck at this new and faraway venture. (Franck and Robb 1975:64–65)

Others increasingly involved in the fishing industry from this time included Chinese and Indian laborers, the crews of merchant and fishing vessels from America, Norway, Japan and Korea. On the larger fishing vessels, particularly the deep sea factory ships, Southern African fishing companies would eventually employ black Southern African laborers like the Hereros from Namibia, Zulus, Sothos, Swazis and Malawians.

In 1892 a formal report was presented to the government by a Commission appointed to inquire about the status of fishing in the Cape Colony. The chairman of that committee, C.A. Wolfe, reported some twenty years earlier that fishermen were "a mild, patient and a very poor section of our community, they work very hard, know little intermission; their gains are very small; they die in numbers from diseases engendered by cold and exposure ... they seem to accept their fate as a predestined thing, and know little better" (Lees 1969:26–27). And at this point in history, Wolfe was not referring to the numerous European immigrants flooding into the fishing industry, nor was he speaking about the Hereros, Sothos, Swazis or Malawians who would eventually be employed by the fishing industry giants of the mid to late twentieth century. The radical demographic shifts in the industry lie in the next century. Wolfe did not have to mention the race or the ethnic background of the fishermen, for it was commonly assumed that the fishermen, in general, were coloured (Lees 1969; Van Sittert 1992).

In 1893 investigations into the fishing industry lead to the Fisheries Protection Act. The act provided for the protection of seals, sea birds and the economically important guano islands. The act also provided for the registration of all commercial boats and nets. But the act protected the rights of the new industrial trawlers over against the small-scale line fishers. Local line fishers were protesting the operation of trawlers in False Bay from the time of their introduction. The debate was carried on to some degree in the *Cape Times*. "It was claimed by some people that the problem was that the line fishermen were inefficient, lazy and drank too much, 'using their primitive methods of hooks and lines and stopping work for the rest of the week if they make a good catch!'" (Stibbe and Moss 1998:34). The local fishermen were accused of standing against any development of the industry by private enterprise or the government. Ultimately very few restrictions were placed on the trawlers, aside from a three mile from the shore limit. "The future for the industry was seen to be in trawling" (Stibbe and Moss 1998:34).

Rarely has fishing been considered an upper status occupation. Men and women in fishing families often supplemented their incomes through other means. Fishing itself was seasonal and provided insufficient financial and social capital for individuals or families to move up the social ladder. From the mid-nineteenth century on, the entire family was increasingly required to become involved in the formal economy to make ends meet. But the kind of work available for these families tended to be entry-level service occupations. "The uncertainties of fishing (weather and resource) made a range of other economic pursuits a basic necessity—the most common of which was seasonal farm labour during harvest time" (Van Sittert 1992:xxiii).

An old postcard, on view at the Sea Fisheries Museum in Hout Bay, depicts Kalk Bay[3] washhouses in the foreground and the Rex, a 244 ton trawler that had run aground on October 3, 1903 in the background. These washhouses were "the laundries in which fishermen's wives did the washing for the local community on a commercial basis" (Walker 1999:142). The Muizenberg municipality, established in 1895, bought the washhouses in 1901 and upgraded them in 1903. Although they had no ownership in the property or control over the construction of the new facilities, the laundry work of the fisher wives not only provided a stable income for a family dependent on the seasonal income, but proved central to combating outbreaks of the Bubonic Plague and Typhoid (Walker 1999). For the typical fishing family, the wives and daughters worked as domestic servants or as laborers in businesses such as the washhouses. While boys were quickly socialized into fishing, in their pre-fishing days they were responsible for tasks such as blooding the lines,[4] drying fish on racks, fetching water and wood, and collecting sea products from the beaches for their family's use.

Fishing vessel and code	Length (m)	Propulsion	Range of operation (nautical miles)	Maximum number of craft operating between 1880 & 1900
WHALING BOATS (a) Barque-decked 	> 20	Square-rigged on fore and main mast. Mizzen mast fore-and-aft rigged	?	6
(b) Brig-decked 	> 20	Fore and main masts square-rigged	?	±5
FISHING BOATS (a) Schooner-decked 	15–20	Fore-and-aft rigged on all masts	±40	±45
(b) Cutter half-decked with centreboard 	7,5 8,5	Fore-and-aft rigged mast with mainsail and two jibs, oars, 5–6,5 m	±30	±45
(c) Dinghy 	4,5–6,5	Fore-and-aft rigged single mast. Mainsail and jib, oars, 4,5–6 m	15	±500

Figure 10. Fishing Vessels in Operation in the Cape between 1880 and 1990
source: Pulfrich and Griffiths (1988)

On the rural west coast to the north of Cape Town, fishing and fishing communities fed and were fed by the development of agriculture. Farms needed fish, and fishing needed seasonal labor. One of the primary needs for the colony's developing agrarian economy was the supply of cheap food for farm labor. Fish filled this need as it was plentiful and easily accessible. When dried, fish tended to preserve well in hot climates and, therefore, was easily stored and transported over long distances. As farming and fishing are both seasonal, the one became an important source of labor for the other. The fishing communities themselves were populated by a diverse group of persons alienated from these west coast farms, alienated from the land and from the capital to improve their circumstances. "The effects of subdivision and land shortages on small farmers, ongoing dispossession of the indigenous population and the abolition of slavery and ex-slave's apprenticeships all contributed to the creation of a rural underclass in the western coastal districts of the colony" (Van Sittert 1992:13). The numbers of this multi-racial underclass were "swollen by deserters, maroons and other castoffs from the coastal shipping trade, whaling and guano industries, a miscellaneous flotsam of seaborne humanity which collected in the eddies and backwaters of the coast" (Van Sittert 1992:14).

The need and ability to seek other forms of employment during the non-fishing months was even more pronounced for fishers who lived outside the coastal fishing villages. In late nineteenth century Cape Town, fishing was a significant source of employment for both artisans and unskilled labor. Yet in the 1875 census only 280 Capetonians described themselves as fishermen. The likelihood of the underreported nature of this statistic is evident from a government report of 1892:

> In regard to fishermen themselves, those at Kalk Bay and at places distant from towns usually adopt that calling when young and follow it all their lives; but in Cape Town many of the men are ... half carpenters, masons, or coolies who only go out fishing when they cannot get other work, and even when fishing pays best they frequently prefer to remain on shore lest they be unable to obtain employment when the fish are scarce. (a fisherman quoted in Bickford-Smith 1995:18)

There were also one thousand Cape Town residents who reported in the 1875 census that their sole income was from fishing. "Although fishing may have provided residual employment for many artisans, there seems to have been a hard core of fishermen and their families who did nothing else but catch, cure and sell fish" (Bickford-Smith 1995:21).

Bickford-Smith views the fishing industry as evidence of the imprecise division of labor in the employment patterns of late nineteenth century Cape Town. Employers benefited from the seasonality of fishing work through the manipulation and use of casual employment. Fishers knew there were higher wages available from more consistent jobs on land and were reluctant to take full-time fishing employment for fear of not having work in the off seasons. However, even though class positions in general at this time did not translate in any simple or automatic way into class consciousness, fishermen were an exception.

> Among [fishers] the sense of occupational solidarity was informed by community.... Fishermen fought for the preservation of their way of life, and thereby for the preservation of their community, when fish-curing at Rogge Bay was threatened by municipal and central government interference in the late 1870s. (Bickford-Smith 1995:22–23)

Snoek fishing was a highly skilled and labor-intensive activity. Because snoek is such a fast, agile fish, it proved impossible to be caught by nets. They were enticed by nothing less than a hook and a line. They were most often caught by men in small dinghies with a single center mast (see figure 10). When hauling fish into the boat, the fishers kept themselves from harm's way by killing the snoek with a sharp blow to the head or by breaking its neck. It took particular skill not to be torn up by the razor sharp teeth of this rapacious predator. As the snoek trade boomed in the second half of the nineteenth century, skilled handliners were in high demand. Calling themselves "snoekers," it was believed that these men were so committed to their craft that they would throw even more valuable fish overboard if it interfered with catching snoek (Van Sittert 1992:41).

The sense of community that fishermen claimed was reinforced by more than occupational interdependence. Bickford-Smith argues that the solidarity of fishers as a group was in part enhanced by a shared sense of history: the sense of common origins as emancipated slaves (1995). In the late 1870s a literate and relatively wealthy coloured fish-curer, Jongie Siers, used this sense of shared history in protesting against municipal and central government interference in Rogge Bay fish curing. Siers wrote to the town council in 1878: "We were always under the impression that we were emancipated in the reign of our most Gracious Majesty Queen Victoria, and freed from tyranny, but it seems that we are mistaken" (Bickford-Smith 1995:23). The "we" that Siers spoke of was a racial referent, not an occupational one. If coloured people were not free to be fishermen because of their race, because they were not white, then they were no more free than they had been under slavery. Historically, those most closely associated with fishing were coloured. While ownership remained in the hands of those with puted lineages of a lighter hue, those who did most of the manual labor in the fishing industry were coloured (Lees 1969; Van Sittert 1992).

The analysis of race relations in the fishing industry of the late nineteenth century is complicated by a tenuous correlation between race and class. Popular conceptions of fishing assumed it to be a coloured occupation. Coloured fishers in the western Cape were, by reputation, the most skilled. While divisions of labor or status within occupations, even in the 1870s, may have promoted ethnic identification when such a correlation was possible, such identification was not nearly at the level that the rulers of apartheid imposed on society. Still, in the fishing industry at this time, fishing was strongly considered a coloured occupation. As Bickford-Smith reports on the 1875 government census, "only 62 out of 284 fishermen and less than 100 out of over 1,000 washerwomen were White, which may help to explain the group consciousness displayed by the vast majority in those occupations who were not" (1995:33).

The fact that boat ownership was largely in the hands of whites should not lead one to the conclusion that whites avoided crew or labor positions in the fishing industry. Many of the artisan-turned-fishermen were white.

> Cape Town's artisans were Black as well as White, a legacy of the skills acquired in the era of slavery. This, together with the permeability of the colour line and the imprecise nature of the division of labour within many occupational categories, meant that even an ethnic division of labour was far from rigid. (Bickford-Smith 1995:29)

There is little evidence that the Cape Town of the 1870s included a powerful employer class pushing for state intervention to bring about segregated labor institutions, like what happened in the diamond and gold mines of Kimberley and Johannesburg.

At the end of the nineteenth century in the small fishing towns immediately surrounding Cape Town, tensions increased between fishing families and those not connected to the life of the sea. Originating most likely with the arrival of the railway in 1883, fishers on the Cape Peninsula became more of a nuisance as recreational beach activities became more popular. As the recreational use of seaside towns increased, property values soared, forcing the working class away from the beachfront properties that some had occupied for generations.

"Die land" was the area of the earliest fishing settlement in Kalk Bay. It was most likely chosen because of its close proximity to the beach and the easy access to the boats that this provided. However, "rising property prices and rates ensured diminished areas of residency for the fishermen and *die land* became increasingly overcrowded and slum conditions developed" (Walker 1999:153). Substantial improvements in housing and sanitation in this area only came about when Kalk Bay was incorporated into the greater Cape Town municipality. This lack of municipal response to the slum conditions in *die land* resulted in the segregation of the fisherfolk from the other inhabitants of Kalk Bay, a feature that remained throughout the village's social and church life. The white dominant class of the late nineteenth century Cape Town had little sympathy for the plight of thousands of casual laborers whose numbers were steadily growing in the slums. Even though some doctors would admit that overcrowding and squalor might be partly the result of bad sanitation and a shortage of housing, most blamed the slum dwellers for their own "ignorance" and "dirty habits." Slum dweller's "lack of economic resources was considered as a crucial part of explaining slum conditions, but this poverty was not deserving [of assistance] because it supposedly resulted from laziness, improvidence and overindulgence in alcohol" (Bickford-Smith 1995:97).

The lack of municipal response to the concerns of the fishing families was further evident from the lack of support for improving facilities used most exclusively by the commercial fishers. Concrete and iron gantries were finally built in 1906 for Kalk Bay fishermen to lift and protect their boats during high seas. "By 1910 these gantries had deteriorated so badly and with the erosion of the concrete footings, especially along the northern section, it had rendered them dangerous. Damage to the fishing boats in the frequent high seas was common and had a severe effect on the fishermen's limited earnings" (Walker 1999:155). The municipality threw the responsibility for repairs back at the fishers who responded by withholding their customary usage fees. The final compromise, after some political pressure from the minister of Railways and Harbours, was for the Municipality to build a full harbor and breakwater. "At the time of the laying of the first block 47 boats were utilized in the fishing industry in Kalk Bay, giving employment to 236 men and with an annual catch valued at 50,000" (Walker 1999:192). Even though the Municipality's motivation for this development was more tourist and revenue driven, these improvements eventually led to improved conditions for the fishers as well. Even so, the interests of fishing families, particularly those limited to the smaller, lower technology fishing vessels, continued to be increasingly marginalized in municipal affairs. It would be almost another century before fishing families could rely on the carefully marketed romantic allure of fishing boats on a working waterfront to win support from the municipalities.

Figure 11. Gantries for the Fishers of Kalk Bay, 1905
source: Stibbe and Moss (1998)

The wooden fishing boats of the early twentieth century handliners were between five meters and seven and a half meters and weighed approximately nine hundred kilograms. "There was little to distinguish the boats of Kalk Bay from those of Roggebaai, Hout Bay and the Strand, and they appear to have been built to a similar design as the beach boats in England of the same period" (Walker 1999:162). Usually a combination of oar and sail power, these boats would carry up to eight crew members but would need up to twenty muscular bodies to be carried up the beach slope at the end of a day's fishing. The need to carry these boats onto the beach meant that they had no keels or centerboards. The open style of the boat made for easier storage of the fish but increased the risk of sinking in high seas. The boats were divided into two compartments, called "laaitjies" (lit. little drawers), for each fisher, one in which to stand, the other in which to place the catch. Each fisher was compensated for the amount caught, a practice still universal on today's handline boats. Although later motorized, there are a couple dozen boats of the same style still in operation in the western Cape. Called "chakkies," these modern wooden boats were built in the 1950s and can be found moored in Arniston, Struisbaai, Hout Bay and in a few of the other coastal towns further up the west coast.

The division of labor on handline fishing boats was clearly defined. Each crew member had specific tasks to perform at specific times.

> Duties varied from 'turning to' the crew at 2:00am, checking the boat prior to leaving, organising the ballast and anchor, collecting fresh water, loosing and furling the sails, distributing the fresh water once at sea, tying the fish, bailing the water and balancing ballast with fish or sand. (Walker 1999:165)

When the sea was too rough for the small, open boats, most of the skippers and crew would spend their time in repairs or fishing from the rocks or shore.

The skipper, who was often the owner of the boat, was responsible for selecting a reliable and profitable crew, checking the boat and arranging for maintenance prior to departure, steering the boat and for making the most important decisions such as when to fish, where to fish, how long to fish, where and when to drop and raise anchor, and when to return to the harbor (Carse 1959). The skills of a good skipper were passed down from experienced veterans to their eager apprentices, normally a family member. The secrets of the sea were a prized bundle of knowledge and not shared lightly. The skill of the better skippers was thought to be beyond reason, a certain "feel" for fishing that was as much a gift as it was a learned set of skills. Once on shore the skipper was responsible for the sale of the catch and distribution of the earnings. It would also not be uncommon for a skipper to serve as the welfare agent for the crew and their families; crew would look to their skipper if any of them fell on hard times.

Wages for fishers at the beginning of the twentieth century were poor. The lack of transport and cold storage necessitated the immediate sale of the catch. This left the fishers at the mercy of traveling hawkers for their fish prices. The hawkers

> beat the price down to a bare minimum knowing that the fishermen could not withhold their catch and were in dire need of money. The hawkers, on the other hand, could withhold their bid knowing the fishermen's predicament and organised syndicates to exploit the fishermen. (Walker 1999:166)

Fishermen would occasionally pre-arrange for the sale of their catch in order to ensure better prices.

While the owners and skippers of the boats organized and managed the operations on the boat, remuneration operated on the share system. The share system recognized the independence of the individual worker, compensated fisher and skipper "according to contribution (skill and labour power versus boat/net/gear) and allowed both control over the product of labour" (Van Sittert 1992:xxiii). This egalitarian system encouraged individual effort, but it also provided for structural flexibility in light of the changing dynamics of a seasonal occupation.

> Thus, by the last quarter of the nineteenth century fishing labour had emerged as independent if transitory members of the rural underclass, occupying a tenuous niche on the underbelly of the dominant agrarian economy and dependent on the latter for both markets and seasonal wage labour. (Van Sittert 1992:xxiv)

With the rapid expansion of South Africa's industrial fisheries at the beginning of the Twentieth Century, fishers faced unprecedented competition and numerous new threats to this "independent if transitory" position.

The Early Decades of the Twentieth Century

The end of the nineteenth century also heralded the end of the dominance of small-scale handlining as the primary method for commercial fishing in South Africa. In 1889 an American schooner called The Alice arrived in Table Bay. "To the horror of local fishermen, this vessel began to scoop up quantities of mackerel, maasbanker and harders with a purse-net 60 fathoms long and 15 fathoms deep" (Lees 1969:21). "In the 1890s bigger fishing boats, manned by Italian immigrants, and trawlers undermined the position of Malay fishermen, as trams and (in the 1900s) cars undermined the position of horse-drawn cab-drivers" (Bickford-Smith 1995:189). In the first decades of the twentieth century motors were starting to replace sail and oar power on the vessels used for handlining themselves. By 1919 there were sixteen motor fishing boats registered for fishing in Kalk Bay as against none before 1913; six other open fishing boats were converted into motor craft that same year (Walker 1999). Trawling dominated the development of the South African fishing industry from the Union in 1910 until the Second World War.

The main development of South Africa's industrial fisheries began in the first decades of the twentieth century, pioneered by the union of a Swedish born entrepreneur and the son of an English family firmly established in the trawling industries of the North Sea. Charles Ocean Johnson and George Driver Irvin set wheels in motion that would eventually lead to the marginalization of the linefishing industry in the context of an industry dominated in volume and value by pelagic trawling. In their early years, Irvin and Johnson faced stiff competition from the handline fishers (Lees 1969). Where once handliners were on the economic center stage of fishing, they now struggled even to get a back stage pass. Almost immediately the larger inland and export markets were closed to handline fishers; handline fishers were to remain dependent on shrinking local markets.

With the rapidly increasing dominance of trawling in the fishing industry, handline fishers struggled with an unprecedented level of competition. Line fishers had been in continued opposition to trawling since the latter was introduced in False Bay in 1897. As an increasing number of steam trawlers began operating in False Bay, line fishers complained that trawling activity was destroying the seabed and depleting their stocks at a rapid rate. "The trawling industry responded and accused the line fishermen of being against 'progress.' They stated that the line fishermen were jealous of prices received by the trawlers for their catches. They claimed that hand line fishing was an 'out of date method of fishing'" (Stibbe and Moss 1998:62). By the mid-1920s evidence for the depletion of the stocks in False Bay was so overwhelming that, in 1928, the government Administrator announced in the *Government Gazette* that False Bay would be closed to all bottom trawling. This seeming victory for the line fishers came about twenty years too late. "The Bay by this time was no longer used to any significant extent by the trawlers. They had moved to other new fishing grounds that had been discovered since the resources in False Bay had diminished" (Stibbe and Moss 1998:63).

The industrial development in Hout Bay started in 1903 with the Hout Bay Canning Company. A canning factory was opened aboard an old wrecked sailing ship. It supplied a growing overseas hunger for canned lobster. Up until this point, fishing in this area was mostly informal. Handline fishing consistently put food on tables, albeit a subsistence income. But this abundant crustacean that was for so many years used as food for slaves and farmworkers suddenly became an international commodity. And as the industry in South Africa developed this market, many a handline fisher supplemented their income on the crayfish boats. Some even converted their operations into full-time crayfish operations. To this day, crayfish remain an important supplement to the income of those who consider themselves full-time handline fishers.

In the years just prior to World War II the fishing industry continued to be influenced by European immigrants. "The pioneers in the 1930s and 1940s were fishermen who settled in Woodstock because it was conveniently close to the harbour" (Bickford-Smith, van Heyningen and Worden 1999:72). These were Portuguese immigrants from the island of Madeira who settled in Cape Town. Although many of these immigrants eventually moved out of the fishing industry, preferring the independence of small businesses, fishing remained a part of their local economy. The role of Portuguese fishermen in Cape Town was strengthened when Luisitania Sea Products, currently one of the largest companies in South Africa's fishing industry, was established in the 1960s. The Portuguese owner made a point of hiring people from his own ethnic/linguistic group:

> I looked specifically for Portuguese fishermen and skippers because I wanted my company to get a name as a Portuguese company.... As a "Portuguese," I felt the company could be run better with Portuguese labour because we could communicate in our language and relate to each other better. (Bickford-Smith, van Heyningen and Worden 1999:72)

Those still interested in fishing but not tied into the factory networks often opted for work in the handline industry.

Significant national government involvement in the inshore fishing industry started in 1944 with the formation of the Fisheries Development Corporation (FISCOR), based on the Fisheries Development Act of 1944 and provided for in the Fisheries Industries Bill. FISCOR was designed to glean excess profits from the highly lucrative deep-sea trawling sector to finance aide programs to upgrade the inshore sector.

> FISCOR were to take complete control over the marketing and distribution of fish. All boats were to be required to sell their catches to FISCOR. This financing would then enable boat owners to take out affordable loans for new vessels, equipment or engines. Factories were to be financially assisted in upgrading facilities. Schemes for fishermen's housing, lights and water were to be undertaken. (Stibbe and Moss 1998:73)

But with considerable opposition from the trawling industry, the "excess profits" were never gleaned from the industry. Instead, FISCOR was to be dependent on financing from the government itself for its various programs.

Post World War II and the Beginnings of the Apartheid Era

World War II brought about prosperity for the fishing industry that it had yet to encounter. A boom in technology combined with expanded international export relations for the large industrial companies ensured that production and profits soared. Boats were getting bigger, were more likely iron than wood, and were more technology driven. The need for inexpensive, preserved food for the troops caused an explosion in the canning industry, and thousands of workers flooded into the fishing factories. Both fishing effort and linefish catches increased substantially. This resulted from the simultaneous introduction of motorized vessels, the construction of small-boat harbors along the coast and the availability of echo-sounding technology. The total annual catch peaked in the late 1960s and has declined steadily since then, despite a continual increase in the number of fishers (Sea Fisheries Research Institute 1997–1998:12).

Fishing in South Africa saw its most significant industrial boom continue in the years immediately after World War II. The World Wars gave South African marine products an unprecedented exposure to international markets, particularly for its canned products. Large purse seine trawlers had been scooping up sardines and pilchards for over a decade. As stocks were depleted further north on the west coast, these trawlers moved back into the government restricted False Bay. In 1956 large shoals of pilchards and maasbankers were found in False Bay, prompting a rush of purse seiners. Local conservationists, residents and particularly the line fishermen were quick to respond to this "invasion." Urgent appeals to local government representatives produced a quick response. The government amended its 1928 prohibition on dragnet trawling in False Bay to include "any net for the catching of pilchards, maasbanker or mackerel for canning, or the production of fishmeal, fish oil or fish fertiliser or for sale to any person for these purposes" (Stibbe and Moss 1998:76).

Figure 12. Purse Seining
source: Stibbe and Moss (1998)

While the development of the fresh fish markets that were to impact the linefish industry were still more than twenty years in the future, commercial handline fishing remained socially and economically significant to local communities. But the prosperity of the post-war years brought with it new technologies and new sources of competition for the traditional handline fishers. Not only was there an increase in the competition from the industrial fishing industry, but the white middle-class discovered the pleasures of owning personal access to the ocean's riches in the development of the recreational boat-based linefishing industry.

The explosion of small boat operators was made possible by the introduction of the ski-boat. "In 1944, the development of the ski-boat, powered by an outboard motor, signaled a widespread change to offshore fishing in Natal as it was instrumental in allowing beach launches to be made from various sites around the coast" (Guastella 1997:16). While older commercial fishing boats were being converted from oar and sail power as early as the 1920s, the boom in small, motorized boats began in the decade of the Second World War. On the Natal coast a handful of relatively wealthy recreational fishing enthusiasts installed small (less than 5hp), two-stroke engines on the sterns of the precursors ski-boats. These smaller boats were easily transported to remote sites and proved to be more maneuverable at sea.

In 1947, ski-boats were struggling to make their way into the industry. Port officials were reluctant to allow these small (four to five meter) boats onto the water. One port official in Durban refused to endorse the use of ski-boats. When one of the pioneers of ski-boat fishing went to register his boat, he was denied an inspection.

> As a matter of fact, as from the end of December (1947) no ski-boats at all will be allowed to operate from any beach which falls under my jurisdiction…. These boats are a menace to shipping and the signal station commander on the Bluff has his work cut out having to keep an eye on them and, finally, they're not seaworthy. (Mara 1973:70)

What he was not told at the time was that a well-known local commercial fishing company had complained to the Port captain that fish were being sold openly on the beaches by ski-boats and that this was affecting their business. The line between recreational and commercial fisher was blurred from the introduction of the ski-boat.

By the mid-1950s handline and rod fishing from ski-boats was becoming a popular middle class leisure time preoccupation. According to most accounts, ski-boats and their associated technologies diffused from Natal to the Cape. Dr. V. Taylor, current chair and long-time member of the South African Marine Linefish Management Association (SAMLMA), saw the first ski-boat in the eastern Cape come to Jeffrey's Bay in 1955 (personal communication). It was a motorized flat five meter aluminum boat with two twenty-five horsepower outboard engines. This boat, and the ones common in Natal by this time, were the forerunners of the Cape Craft ski-boat, the style most common today. But what started out as a recreational activity became, for some, an opportunity to generate more than just a casual, supplemental income.

Right about the time that ski-boats were rising in popularity, a well-known trawl skipper from the small fishing village of Velddrift introduced the fishing industry to their first echo sounder. In 1955 J. Eigelaar installed this electronic device that would allow fishers to take a peek at what was under the water and would revolutionize catch effort (Eigelaar 1999, Lees 1969). Based on the sonar technology used to detect submarines in the First and Second World Wars, echo sounders were known as the "magic eye." Known by his friends and family as "oom Johnnie," Eigelaar recalled years later,

> It was truly a miracle to be able to see the bottom under the boat, and to know how many fish there were. In the evenings many boats followed the *Bokkeveld*, and when they saw I turned on a school of fish, they'd all want to know just how big the school was...We caught a lot of fish—and it proved difficult to get the Echo Sounders into South Africa fast enough, because then everyone wanted one. (Eigelaar 1999:32–33; author's translation)

The first commercially available echo sounders in South Africa were large and cumbersome and served primarily the larger commercial vessels. It was not until the 1980s that technological advances made it practical and affordable for echo sounders to find their way onto ski-boats.

But the social and political changes of the 1950s were to have a far greater impact on fishing families than any radical change in the technology for fishing. When the National Party came to power in 1948 and the era of apartheid began, sweeping social programs designed to protect white privilege were forced on all South Africans. The fishing hamlets of the western Cape coast were far from immune to apartheid social engineering.

A typical example of how apartheid affected social and residential relations in the traditional fishing communities can be found in the rural coastal village of Struisbaai.[5] Commercial fishing has been a part of this community for at least the last century and a recreational fishing industry since the early part of the twentieth century. Prior to the 1960s, Struisbaai was a fishing village of approximately forty coloured families. These families lived in the immediate harbor area on land rented from a local white family. Abundant game fish were attracting anglers to the region since the first half of the twentieth century. Even though the neighboring town of Agulhas, famous for being on the southern most tip of Africa, provided some services to these visiting fishers, the tourist industry provided little to no income for the coloured residents of the area.

The South African National Party's Group Areas Act of 1950 seemed to have had delayed effects in Struisbaai. In 1960 that act was used to declare the harbor area for use by 'whites only.' The existing coloured families, about forty in total, were relocated to an area some four kilometers from the harbor. This new community was dubbed 'Molshoop,' or 'Mole Heap,' by local residents. Shortly after the Struisbaai relocation, a small coloured population from a nearby town called SkipSkop was also relocated to Molshoop. Since that time, the population of Molshoop has grown to over an approximate three thousand coloured residents (Lindsay 1998).

The harbor area was cleared of most of the previous residents' homes as they were demolished. The only remaining architectural legacy of pre-apartheid arrangements include a cluster of houses on the road between Struisbaai and Molshoop (known locally as Hotagterklip), as well as the small Anglican church and one house near the harbor. These have since been restored and have been declared heritage sites. The harbor and other coastal areas were developed for white residential and business use.

The legacy of apartheid's notions of space still lingers in Struisbaai/Molshoop as the white and coloured communities remain socially and residentially segregated. In this way, Struisbaai is typical of the rural coastal communities in the Western Cape and thus warrants a more detailed analysis. Molshoop is a low-income area of small, single-story houses and an increasing number of informal shelters. The residents are almost exclusively coloured. Amenities include a community center, a sports field, elementary school, nursery school, general grocery store, and an Anglican church. A new library designed to serve the whole of Struisbaai was constructed in Molshoop in 1997 and, in 2000, was still the most pristine building in the area. In the Struisbaai community of the nineteenth and early twentieth century, Anglicanism seems to have been the sole religion. Over half of the residents of Struisbaai as a whole identified themselves as Anglicans in 1993 (Schutte 1993:10). Today, other Protestant denominations, many of which are in the evangelical tradition, are also gaining adherents. Islam has had little impact on this community.

The area of Struisbaai around the harbor and along the shore towards Cape Agulhas consists largely of holiday homes owned by families living in all parts of the country. These homes are usually empty for the better part of the year. "There is, though, a growing permanent white population which is made up of retirees and those involved in a range of local businesses, many of which cater to the needs of seasonal tourists" (Lindsay 1999:14). Naturally, the Municipal Council is interested in actively promoting the area as a site for continued retirement and tourist development. They are also increasing their efforts to exploit the popularity of this area as a recreational fishing site for future development.

Although largely thought of as a fishing town, and with little other industry of note, the past decade has brought an increase in tourist-related development to Struisbaai, including job opportunities for the residents of Molshoop, mostly in building, masonry, roof thatching, plumbing and housework. In some cases, people have found full-time, permanent employment in these fields. More often, they provide a supplementary income during the fishing off-season, along with farm labor jobs and cutting the surrounding bush into firewood (for personal use and local sale). Thus, most households in Molshoop continue to be dependent on the fishery as a primary means of income.

Three local, white-owned fishing companies have secured a virtual monopoly on the Struisbaai fishing industry. While a few local fishermen are independent boat owners, the overwhelming majority of commercial fishers are, in fact, hired labor employed by one of these three companies. The share system allows a skipper to fish for one of the companies for a percentage of the catch. The skipper and crew are responsible for supplying fuel and bait (sold to them by the company) and for the daily maintenance of the vessel. Usually the catch is then sold back to the boat owners who themselves have wholesale or retail networks as far away as Cape Town (a good three hour drive away). The few independent commercial fishers in Struisbaai who own and operate their own ski-boats, on the other hand, are theoretically at liberty to sell to whomever can give them the best price. In practice, however, most independent fishers have unwritten agreements with one of the companies, which can offer to supply less expensive bait in return for remaining regular clients.

The Struisbaai fishery is almost exclusively a handline fishery. The fishery is highly seasonal due to its dependence on migratory shoaling species such as yellowtail, cob, Cape salmon and silverfish. Struisbaai is particularly well known for its seasonal abundance of yellowtail. This species is popular among recreational and small-scale commercial fishers alike for its relatively high commercial value and its strength as a 'fighter.' During the yellowtail season the local fishermen face stiff competition from a flood of recreational fishers and transient or 'roving' commercial fishers who haul their ski-boats from harbor to harbor over the course of a season, following the migratory fish stocks. But this same influx of fishers also provides local fishers the opportunity to network for sites on other boats in other communities. Most of the boats that operate consistently out of the Struisbaai harbor are the old style wooden chakkies, much like those in Kalk Bay.

Figure 13. The Traditional "Chakkie" Used for Handline Fishing
source: Stibbe and Moss 1998

Improved housing for the coloured fishing families of Kalk Bay had been an important municipal issue since 1919 when the Fisherman's Union petitioned the town council for assistance in building new houses (Stibbe and Moss 1998:57). In 1925 the housing problem received a great deal of publicity when hundreds of members of the Coloured fishing community presented a signed petition to the Housing Committee of the City Council. "The plight of the fishermen was desperate, because many of them had been evicted when inspectors had condemned several houses" (Stibbe and Moss 1998:57). In 1936 the Health Department condemned and bulldozed many of the fishing families' cottages, and there was serious talk of moving the fishing families from Kalk Bay. Instead, interested members of the community lobbied the council to replace the housing rather than remove the occupants. So, beginning in 1940 the council built the fifty-five flats that are still in use today by many of Kalk Bay's coloured residents.

But the housing question for fishing families of Kalk Bay was to take on much larger socio-political significance with the implementation of apartheid policies. When, in the 1950s and early 1960s, the apartheid government forced thousands of families from their homes to make way for racially exclusive residential areas, many of the coloured fishing families in Kalk Bay escaped the removals. This exception was in large part due to the growing commercial fishing interests in Kalk Bay and the integral part that coloured fishing families played in the local economy. Since the actual work involved in fishing was considered dirty, hard labor, there was little competition for this work from the increasing number of middle- to upper-class families moving into the area. Most of the families involved in the fishing industry here on the peninsula had been involved in fishing for generations.

Then in 1967 there was a fifteen-year extension given on the date for removal of the coloured families of Kalk Bay. Exceptions such as what happened in Kalk Bay are often used as proof of what historians call Cape "exceptionalism" or the triumph of the Cape liberal tradition.[6]

According to one account, members of the Kalk Bay community united against the removals: "Over 60 per cent of the families sentenced to lose their homes put faith in the future, lives in the present and stayed" (Iggulden 1982:13). Coloured and white residents united in opposition to the removals. And on February 9, 1982 the government announced that there would be no more forced removals in Kalk Bay (Iggulden 1982).

The narrow escape from the bulldozer of forced removals in Kalk Bay was due in part to the strength of the inter-racial social networks developed over time in this small community, particularly among those involved in fishing. The earliest local resident's association was formed in 1964 and was comprised mostly of fishermen. The chair of the Resident's Association, Councillor J. Heeger, enlisted the help of M. Ritchken, a member of the Black Sash and later founding member of the Kalk Bay Rate Payer's Association. The Black Sash and the Rate Payer's Association, which incorporated the earlier organization, along with local fishers, led a letter campaign to raise objections to the implementation of the Group Areas Act in Kalk Bay. In public hearings held, the romantic image of the traditional fisher was put to good political use. "On the second and last day of the inquiry a 15 minute film *The Fisherfolk of Kalk Bay* was shown, at the request of Monica Ritchken who described the film as 'depicting the fisherfolk so beautifully and movingly that it was guaranteed to move a heart of stone'" (Iggulden 1982:15).

Of course, the fact that the residents of Kalk Bay had a powerful National Party stalwart in their corner did help. J. Wiley, Member of Parliament for the Simonstown constituency from 1966 through the mid-1980s and Kalk Bay resident, believed that the fishing community of Kalk Bay should be recognized as such, and as such deserved to be exempt from the removals in order to preserve its identity as a fishing community. His argument that won over the Minister of Community and Development was ironically far less specific and had potentially far more universal implications, but somehow was never applied beyond this very specific situation. He told one interviewer:

> When the period of grace came up for review again, I was asked my views. ... And I gave them. [They] listened most sympathetically to my representations as there has been an appreciation, in the course of time, that it would be inequitable to move out Coloured fishing families who have lived in Kalk Bay longer than most Whites. (Iggulden 1982:18)

The universality of the argument was seemingly apparent to neither the staunch Nationalist Wiley nor the Minister of forced removals.

Recent Developments in the Management of South African Fisheries

Prior to the Marine Living Resources Act of 1998, the first comprehensive legislation framed to protect marine resources was the Sea Fisheries Act of 1940, subsequently superseded by new Acts in 1973 and in 1988.[7] Approaches to the utilization of the living marine resources, including the issue of access rights to marine fisheries, have varied little in the past thirty years. In earlier years, quotas were granted by the responsible Minister acting on the advice of officials stationed mainly in Pretoria, officials who were not dedicated solely to fisheries' matters and dealing with problems on an *ad hoc* basis. This state of affairs led to severe criticism by successive commissions of inquiry, notably the Du Plessis Commission in 1971 and the Treurnicht Commission in 1980 (Marx 1998). In 1982 the control post in Cape Town was upgraded to Chief Director and that local establishment was henceforth regarded as a component of the head office in Pretoria (Verheye 1998).

With the passing of the 1971 Sea Fisheries Act the government also established the Sea Fisheries Research Fund. This fund was used to coordinate and fund a consortium of marine biologists and economists who would be responsible for gathering scientific data related to marine life and its exploitation. The Sea Fisheries Research Institute (SFRI) was founded that same year. Initiation of the lucrative South Coast Rock Lobster fishery in 1974 was one of the first important industry decisions supported by the research of the SFRI. In November of 1977 South Africa joined most other countries with industrial fisheries in the declaration of a two hundred nautical mile national fishing zone, broadening the scope and political impact of the

SFRI's responsibilities. South Africa's declaration of a two hundred mile fishing zone was consistent with what other nations, like the United States, were doing at the time and with negotiations tendered at the United Nation's Convention on the Law of the Sea. This UN convention argued for the same extension of jurisdiction for all coastal nations (Committee to Review Individual Fishing Quotas 1999).

The 1986 Diemont Commission gave considerable thought to access rights and proposed that the allocation of quotas be entrusted to a statutory board. This recommendation was accepted by the Government as recommended in the 1986 White Paper. The Sea Fishery Act of 1988 made provision for the establishment of a Quota Board. The first Board then became operative in 1990. At the time, the Quota Board (like the Sea Fisheries Advisory Committee) was appointed by the responsible Minister. This Minister determined the number of members and the quorum. No person with interests in the fishery was supposed to serve on the board. The Act also stipulates that "a person in the employment of the State" may not serve on the Board (Sea Fisheries 1997).

But not everyone was satisfied that these rules were being followed. The Quota Board had tremendous power over access rights in the industry and was constantly beset with accusations of corruption and nepotism (Johnstone 2000). On September 26, 1996 Andy Johnstone and members of the Artisanal Fisherman's Association staged the first of a number of sit-ins at the Sea Fisheries headquarters. They held the quota board hostage, demanded the reallocation of quotas and complained of nepotism and racism. While the demands of the artisanal fishers were not met immediately, leaders from their association were allowed to participate in the drafting of the White Paper proposal for a new marine fisheries policy for South Africa.

Under the Marine Act of 1998 Sea Fisheries has been renamed the Department of Marine and Coastal Management. While research is still funded by monies voted by the legislative assembly, the current Act also provides for the continuation of the Sea Fishery Fund established in 1973. Apart from other sources specified in the Act, the Fund is supplemented by levies on the industry. In 1997 the Sea Fisheries global operational costs were some R60 million, of which 20% is consumed by administration, 17% by the operation of marine vessels, 29% by marine control and 34% by the activities of the research institute. A total of some R9.5 million of these global costs, or 16%, was obtained from fisheries-related fees and levies channeled through the Sea Fishery Fund. The balance came from Central Revenue. In light of the mounting accusations, provisions were made in the new Act to increase the transparency of the process for allocating these funds (Stuttaford 1999; Kleinschmidt 2000).

While major protests were still to plague the 1998 fisheries legislation and its eventual implementation, this latest Act received input from an unprecedented diversity of stakeholders in the industry. For the first time in the history of management, the socio-economic conditions of the participants in the industry were given consideration. In keeping consistent with the government's priorities as reflected in the Reconstruction and Development Programme (RDP), this Act commits to:

> Provide for the conservation of the marine ecosystem, the long-term sustainable utilisation of marine living resources and the orderly access to exploitation, utilisation and protection of certain marine living resources; and for these purposes to provide for the exercise of control of marine living resources in a *fair and equitable manner to the benefit of the citizens of South Africa*; and to provide for matters connected therewith. (Department of Environmental Affairs and Tourism 1998:1, italics mine)

The legislative priority on equity is undoubtedly unique, but it remains to be seen just how "equity" will be interpreted and implemented programmatically.

On February 17, 2000 the Artisanal Fishermen's Association, the Western Cape branches of the Food and Allied Workers Union and the Congress Of South African Trade Unions, the South African Wildlife Society, members of the Green Party and several other fishermen's organizations (SACFC included) organized a march on parliament to protest the slow pace of transformation in the fishing industry.[8] In part, this protest march came in response to an internal audit report released on November 12, 1999 finding major mismanagement of MCM funds, "to the tune of R24m" (Department of Environmental Affairs and Tourism 1999:2).

The challenges for the restructuring of the fishing industry in South Africa continue. On March 5, 2000 the Fisheries Transformation Council resigned. The Transformation Council replaced the old Quota Board and was responsible for redefining the priorities in the industry. All the members of the board resigned the week of a court-ordered deadline forcing them to reallocate the all-important longline (hake) quoatas. Massive restructuring of Marine and Coastal Management is still underway, and commercial fishers anxiously await the outcome to determine their fishing rights.

A Historiographical Footnote

Most of the secondary literature on the history of South African fishing belongs to one of two genres: hagiographic company histories or nostalgic area monographs. As the historian Lance van Sittert has commented, company histories typically glorify founders and laud successors and dazzling posterity (and potential investors) with output volume, sales figures and profit margins (e.g. Lees 1969, Sacks and Silverman 1993, Irvin and Johnson 1964). "Richly anecdotal, boringly parochial and meticulously uncritical, this work constitutes a corpus at once tantalizing and frustrating to the academic historian" (Van Sittert 1992:xvi). So much of the evidence in these works remains without citation, leaving the reader dependent on the authority of the ones who penned the stories for the veracity of stated evidence. The area monographs are infected with a similar uncritical perspective (e.g. Carse 1959; Tredgold 1965, 1985; Walker 1999). Often written by self-proclaimed local historians, the area monographs are more often written as if to attract tourists to the area, describing the vistas in picturesque language and the people in romantic harmony with each other and nature itself. The serious academic has to sift through the narrative in search of appropriate historical detail.

A critical weakness of these works is the glaring lack of any detailed analysis of social relationships in the coastal towns or in the various sectors of the fishing industry. Of particular concern is the racial bias inherent in what is written and, perhaps more importantly, in what is omitted. These company histories and area monographs describe their respective subjects from the perspective of white South Africans. As with reading any other historical document, the reader has to keep in mind the limitations of the author's orientation.

These works serve as windows into the values of the authors, sponsors and intended readership at the time of their publication. They "reflect their producer's and reader's own conceptions of the past, for free enterprise is an article of faith and history an act of obeisance" (Van Sittert 1992:xvi). Since the progress of technology and civilization is assumed to be the irresistible force driving the expansion of the fishing industry and the individual heroes valorized in these works are portrayed as the primary movers of this progress, hard work, determination and ingenuity are seen to triumph over all obstacles, including the environment, the state and a resistant labor pool.

Van Sittert's analysis of the industry histories provides some insight into the hidden social dynamics often omitted from the available histories:

> In seeking to legitimate the post-war status quo in the fisheries, the fishing company histories also amplified the twin themes of pioneering white industrialists and the decayed "coloured" fishermen. Whites were pioneers and industrialists because they were innately gifted, dynamic and hard working. "Coloureds," on the other hand, were labourers because they were lazy, drowned their genetic inheritance in a wine bottle and were simply unable to adapt or keep pace with the rapidly developing industry. As a result the companies had to exercise a benign paternalism over their fishermen, employing and housing them and their families and ensuring that access to liquor was strictly controlled. (1992:xvii)

The weaknesses in these works do not negate the important information they do contain. The industry histories are histories from above; they reflect the power hierarchies of a country deeply divided along racial lines. Taken in perspective, these works provide important background information about those described in the respective works. Often the best information is gained by reading between the lines. Until historians take the chance to analyze the mountains of

archival data available in the storehouses of Marine and Coastal Management and the personal

collections of those vested in the industry, these references are the best available.

Notes

---

[1] The following general statistics are taken from an industry summary given by the Department of Sea Fisheries in the 1997 White Paper on the development of a marine fisheries policy for South Africa.

[2] A number of sources refer to a report from Herodotus in the seventh century that raises the possibility that people from the northern hemisphere had fished in South African waters as early as 610 B.C. Herodotus reports that Pharaoh Necho sent

> Phoenicians with ships, bidding them sail and come back through the Pillars of Hercules to the Northern Sea and so to Egypt. The Phoenicians therefore set forth from the Erythrean Sea and sailed through the Southern Sea. ... In the third year they turned through the Pillars of Hercules and arrived again in Egypt. And they reported a thing which I cannot believe, but another man may, namely, that in sailing round Libya they had the sun on their right hand. (Lees 1969:5)

But the myth of the Phoenician voyage has long served as justification for white domination in Africa and cannot be taken at face value.

[3] Kalk Bay is one of the oldest and most romanticized fishing communities in the Western Cape, and it is also historically one of the most significant. It "has the distinction of having been South Africa's first seaside resort" (Iggulden 1982:15). Located on the southwestern side of the Cape Peninsula, Kalk Bay is a small village trapped between the mountains and the sea. Just north of Fish Hoek, this little town is historically significant as one of the few areas in South Africa that escaped the strict segregation-based land-use policies laid out in the Group Areas Act of 1950.

[4] "Blooding the lines" was a common practice for preserving and strengthening cotton and other natural fiber fishing lines and nets. The lines were soaked in animal (usually ox) blood, drained and put out to dry.

[5] Most of the information about Struisbaai was gained through personal visits and informal interviews with members of the community. I am also indebted to Lois Lindsay's detailed fieldwork.

[6] See Worden and Crais (1994) and Keegan (1996) for detailed discussions on the Cape Liberal Tradition.

[7] Information for this brief history of the management of South African fisheries is taken from the 1997 White Paper presented for discussion by the Division of Sea Fisheries housed under the Department of Environmental Affairs.

[8] This march and its social significance is described in detail in Chapter 4.

CHAPTER 7
CHASING A LIVING: COMMERCIAL HANDLINE SKI-BOAT FISHING ON SOUTH AFRICA'S WESTERN CAPE COAST

Introduction

There are about eight large firms that currently control the South African fishing industry. These also have business interests in other food products like potato chips, canned tomatoes and olives. Some of them are also involved in diamond and gold mining. These companies are essentially subsidiaries of large South African multinationals and are controlled by a handful of families. Almost the entire catch comes from industrial trawling and purse-seining. Mainly controlled by white companies, control over the industry is highly skewed by race. With hake, the most valuable of the South African fisheries, three white companies controlled 72% of the TAC in 1996. Irvin & Johnson Ltd., set up by the pioneers of industrial fishing in South Africa, is one of those three companies (Mathew 1997).

Table 8. Quota Distribution in Some Key Fisheries in South Africa in 1996

FISHERY	TAC (TONS)	NUMBER OF QUOTA HOLDERS	% OF TAC HELD BY LARGEST QUOTA HOLDERS		
			3 TOP	10 TOP	20 TOP
Hake	148 300	49	72	82	87
W Coast Rock Lobster	1 500	104	23	51	73
S Coast Rock Lobster	427	6	82	100 (6 all)	-
Abalone	615	16	75	95	100 (16 all)
Pilchard	105 000	59	30	55	63
Anchovy	70 000	18	36	79	100 (18 all)
Sole	872	11	71	100 (11 all)	-

Source: Stuttaford (1997)

Non-whites and relatively poor whites have participated in the coastal fisheries local market in a rudimentary capacity for centuries, in addition to working on board white-owned fishing vessels and in white-owned processing plants. Throughout the twentieth century a small scale fishery, very limited in scope and mainly for the local market, continued to co-exist with an industrial fishery that dominated the export market. When the quota system was introduced to South Africa in the late 1960s and early 1970s, those in the small-scale inshore fisheries found their way of life increasingly threatened. The access enjoyed by non-whites to the lobster fisheries, for example, was taken away at the time by the quota system of the apartheid regime and given to the white companies. "This forced many people from the coastal communities to fish illegally for rock lobster and supply clandestinely to the black market at cheaper prices. The right to fish non-quota species like snoek, however, is still open to all, both non-whites and whites" (Mathew 1997:4).

Although Marine and Coastal Management (MCM) is currently in discussions over how to formalize this sector of the industry, it remains largely outside the scope of government monitoring and intervention, as has been the case for centuries. In the context of the South African fishing industry as a whole, the small-scale commercial handline ski-boat operations fit somewhere between the fully commercialized small businesses and subsistence fishing. Due in part to the fact that handline fishing has thus far remained below the radar of government intervention, the handline fishing industry serves as an important context for the study of the informal development of socioeconomic relations.

Estimates on the number of commercial handline fishers on the Western Cape coast vary greatly. Official government statistics do not allow for the distinction between those who fish full-time commercially and those who use fishing to supplement a more stable income. According to researchers funded by South Africa's Marine and Coastal Management, the South African linefishery is currently a multi-user fishery that exploits more than 200 species (Verheye 1998:12). Ninety-five of these two hundred species contribute to the bulk of catches. The fishery includes significant recreational and commercial sectors. The commercial sector, i.e., those boats licensed by MCM for at least part-time commercial activity, is made up of some three thousand boats that operate on the continental shelf in depths of five to one hundred meters. The recreational sector includes estuarine anglers who fish from boats or riverbanks, rock-and-surf anglers and a recreational lineboat sector that operates in an environment and manner similar to the commercial sector. It is estimated that the linefishery, excluding the estuarine component, is estimated to provide employment for more than 13,000 persons and generates a calculable revenue of around some R2.2 billion per annum for the coastal provinces (Verheye 1998:12).

As there had been no new commercial or semi-commercial fishing licenses issued by the government since the Living Marine Resources Act of 1998, these government statistics proved an unreliable source for determining who the active members of the handline ski-boat network were. So, by visiting each of the harbors, interviewing local fisheries officials, fish factory management and fishers themselves, I was able to identify the active network of handline ski-boat fishers who traveled the coastline in search of their prey.

Race, Class and the Handline Fishermen

Personal Histories

Of the 102 skippers interviewed, 31 identified themselves as coloured and 71 identified themselves as white. The youngest of these skippers was 21; the oldest was 74. White skippers tended to be a little younger than coloured skippers on average (average age: white=39.1; coloured=42.5). The average years of formal education for the entire group was 10.5, with 4 being the fewest number of years and 19 the most. Forty-three percent of these skippers graduated from high school, but only 13% did any further schooling. All of those with more than a high school education were white. Although most were fully bilingual, and some even trilingual, the dominant language spoken in the home and at work is Afrikaans. The difference in the average age of white and coloured skippers in the handline ski-boat industry is statistically insignificant. The average age in general is 40.2 years old with the average age for coloured skippers slightly higher at 42.5 years, ranging between 27 and 74 years of age, as compared to the average white skipper average age of 39.1, ranging between 21 and 68 years of age. As would be expected, there was a slightly negative correlation (-.33) between age and years of education. Younger skippers in general were more likely to have more education.

The average years of education differed significantly between coloured and white skippers. Coloured skippers reported an average 8.1 years of formal schooling while white skippers reported an average of 11.5 years. Only 10% of the coloured skippers matriculated (graduated from high school, i.e., finished standard 10) as compared to 61% of the white skippers. While only 12% of the skippers had any schooling beyond high school, all of these were white.

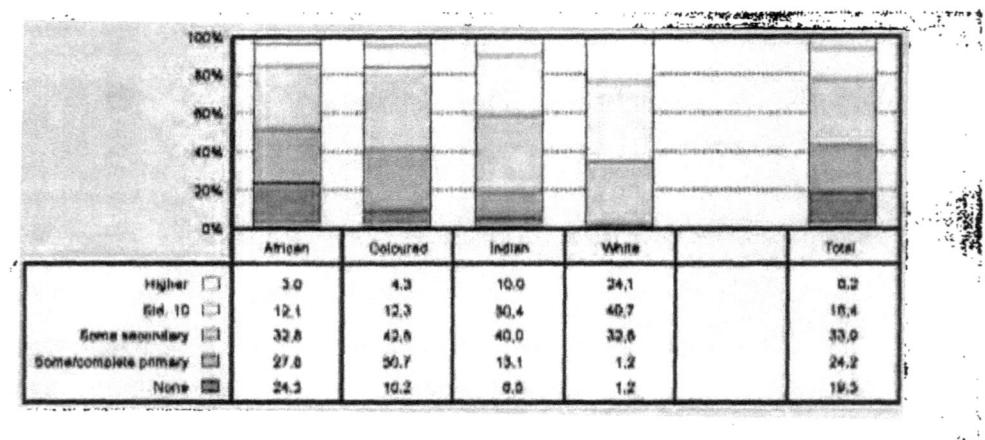

	African	Coloured	Indian	White		Total
Higher	3.0	4.3	10.0	34.1		8.2
Std. 10	12.1	12.3	30.4	40.7		16.4
Some secondary	32.8	42.6	40.0	32.6		33.9
Some/complete primary	27.8	30.7	13.1	1.2		24.2
None	24.3	10.2	6.6	1.2		19.3

* Excluding other/unspecified

Figure 14. Education Levels by Population Group (percentage)
source: Statistics Council, Minister of Finance (1996)

Although all of the skippers in the handline ski-boat fraternity reported some level of bilingualism, the majority by far are primarily Afrikaans speakers. Eighty percent of the group as a whole reported Afrikaans as their primary language. Only 13% of the coloured skippers and

22% of the white skippers reported English as their primary language. The only other variation was the one white skipper whose primary language was Portuguese.

Almost all of the skippers are either married or live with a partner. Only 6% of coloured skippers and 17% of white skippers reported being single. But the difference in household size by race is quite significant. Defined as all those who are living at the same home, household size (reflective of economic conditions and family size) is highly skewed by race. Coloured skippers reported an average household size of 4.5 members while white skippers reported an average of 2.9 members. This difference in household size can in part be explained by the significant difference found in the number of children living at home with coloured skippers, an average of 2.3, compared to those living at home with white skippers, and average of 1. For the 65% of the skippers who had children at home, the overall average age of those children was 12 years, with no significant difference by race. What accounts for the remainder of the difference in household size is that coloured skippers tended to have a number of extended family members living with them in their household, while white skippers tended to reside solely with their nuclear family.

All of the skippers interviewed considered their fishing job as their current full-time occupation. On average, skippers across the board reported themselves responsible for approximately three-quarters of their household income. Two-thirds of the skippers reported that their wives or significant others also supported the household through a cash income. Skippers also reported on average that 87% of their own income came from their work as skipper on the handline ski-boat.

Religious affiliation tended to be more important for coloured skippers than it did for white skippers. All but one of the coloured skippers claimed to be a member of a community of faith, with one attending a mosque and the rest some Christian denomination. Eighty-three percent of white skippers reported being members of a Christian congregation, with a full 42% of those claiming membership in the Dutch Reformed church (Nederduitse Gereformeerde). For skippers themselves, membership in a religious organization was more common than participation in the activities connected to that organization. On average, coloured skippers reported that they gather with other members of their faith community a couple times a month as compared to white skippers who on average said they gather a couple times a year. Church attendance was affected by the amount of traveling the handline ski-boat skippers did. Church became a significant context for socialization only when they were home with their families over the weekends, and this rarely happened during the fishing season.

Skippers were reluctant to talk about their political affiliation. The majority of skippers claimed not to belong to any one party. During the course of the year the New National Party (NNP) and the newly established Democratic Party (DP) merged to form the Democratic Alliance (DA), the strongest opposition party to the African National Congress (ANC). There was a lot of uncertainty about the political future in the country, but over half of the skippers said they were not interested in politics, that they probably would not vote in the upcoming elections.

There is a significant difference between coloured and white skippers in the amount of recreational time they estimate they spend with other commercial fishers and their families. When asked to rate the amount of time they spend with other fishers and their families on a four point scale, white skippers reported on average that they "occasionally" spend time with other fishers outside work (an average of 2 on the 4-point scale), while coloured skippers reported on average that they spend "a lot of time" with other fishers outside work (an average of 3 on the 4-point scale). One factor that may contribute to this variation in how skippers spend their free time is the fact that a higher proportion of white skippers live in suburban Cape Town and commute to the various harbors, while a slightly higher proportion of the coloured skippers live in the coastal fishing towns. One would assume that persons living in fishing towns would more likely interact with other fishers. But the variance can also be explained in part by the differences in the social networks of coloured and white skippers. As will be shown in a later section, the race of the skipper is by far the strongest predictor for the racial composition of their personal networks. White skippers tend to have white friends and coloured skippers tend to have coloured friends.

Since the majority of crewmembers are identified by these skippers as coloured, one could expect there to be fewer fishers in the friendship networks of the white skippers.

One other explanation for the variation in levels of socializing with other fishers and their families can be found in a qualitative analysis of the interview data. As will be shown shortly, virtually all of the coloured skippers have had no significant employment other than fishing, while almost half of the white skippers came to fishing from some other form of employment. The friendship networks developed by these white skippers over years of employment outside the fishing industry continue to influence current socialization patterns, making it less likely that white fishers become a part of the social network. Many of the skippers who were formerly blue-collar and white-collar workers were used to divorcing work and recreation, punching a time clock and rushing home to relax on the weekends. It was not uncommon to hear suburban white skippers talk about fishing as a job nor to hear their priority on making it home in time for dinner.

Work Histories

When categorizing distinctions among themselves, one of the most salient categories of difference was the previous employment of another skipper. The most important major division was between those who had been fishers for all or most of their lives and those who had other significant jobs prior to entering the fishing industry. Over half, 54% (55/102), of the skippers as a group had no significant work outside the fishing industry (see Table 9). But this statistic was highly skewed by race. A full 90% (28/31) of the coloured skippers had never had significant work outside of the fishing industry as compared to 38% (27/71) of the white skippers who had never had significant work outside of the fishing industry. A forty-one year-old coloured skipper with no significant employment outside of the fishing industry had been dependent on the fishing industry for twenty-five years and skippered six of those years. When asked to describe the true fisherman, he said:

> You get all different kinds of fishermen. You get men, like us that began as fishermen. Then you get a fisherman that only started a few years ago, and they had a craft to begin

with. What I would describe, us fishermen that left school in standard 5, standard 6 that have been fishing from the time we were little, I'd describe them as good fishermen. A guy that's been fishing a long time is the true fisherman. He didn't go into a trade.

Often the skill of the skipper was related to the length of time he had spent in charge of a ski-boat.

Table 9. Chi Square Distribution for Previous Jobs by Race

Frequencies
PREVJOB (rows) by RACE (columns)

	0	1	Total
0	28	27	55
1	3	34	37
2	0	10	10
Total	31	71	102

Row percents
PREVJOB (rows) by RACE (columns)

	0	1	Total	N
0	50.909	49.091	100.00	55
1	8.108	91.892	100.00	37
2	0.000	100.00	100.00	10
Total	30.392	69.608	100.00	
N	31	71	102	

Percents of Total Count
PREVJOB (rows) by RACE (columns)

	0	1	Total	N
0	27.451	26.471	53.922	55
1	2.941	33.333	36.275	37
2	0.000	9.804	9.804	10
Total	30.392	69.608	100.00	
N	31	71	102	

Column Percents
PREVJOB (rows) by RACE (columns)

	0	1	Total	N
0	90.323	38.028	53.922	55
1	9.677	47.887	36.275	37
2	0.000	14.085	9.804	10
Total	100.00	100.00	100.00	
N	31	71	102	

Test statistic	Value	df	Prob
Pearson Chi-square	23.995	2.000	0.000

Source: Systat (1998) output

Some of the young white skippers attributed their decision to go into fishing as the result of the changing racial politics in the country. A twenty-five year-old, university educated white skipper who had been fishing for less than a year described his decision to go into fishing full-time:

> I went to a university in Tygerberg for five years after high school. Then I worked in marketing management for Golf for a year. I bought a boat with my father and got out of the marketing business. I got out of business because of Affirmative Action; there are no advancement opportunities for me because my skin is the wrong color. I've been fishing full-time now for the past eight months.

When another young skipper was asked what it meant to be white in the new South Africa, he also referred to the pressures of racial politics:

> Nah, it doesn't mean anything to be a white. It just means you don't have any special privileges. That's the only thing it means. Like with the fishing boats, with all the affirmative action they don't want the whites to work. They're trying to get more and more blacks working. So you, as a white... I've got one guy that works for me, my crew. He's just finishing school, and he's trying to make a living. And the other people work, too. They don't want him on the boat. So if you can't learn this industry and get a qualification behind your name and become skipper so that you can get experience, then I don't know what you'll do.

The younger white skippers relied on assistance from their families to get their feet off the ground. When asked how he got into fishing for a living, one of the younger hired skippers said, "I graduated matric not too long ago and have been having a problem finding work. Even with matric, white guys won't find a regular job—too much affirmative action. I still live with my parents."

Non-fishing jobs held previously by these skippers could be broadly categorized into blue-collar and white-collar jobs. Thirty-six percent (37/102) of the skippers surveyed had previous employment in blue collar jobs. The jobs categorized as blue collar include: plumber, rail road trade (2), sheet metal, electrician, operator, welder (2), engineer (2), teacher (3), police (5), mining, woodwork, mechanic (4), municipality, assistant accountant, bricklayer, military (4), farmer (3), cane factory manager, diamond diving. While 10% (3/31) of the coloured skippers had previous employment in blue-collar jobs, **48%** (34/71) of the white skippers had previous employment in blue-collar jobs.

Jobs categorized as white collar include: Harbor Master, Telkom management, SonChem management, Atlantis management, frozen foods management, Railways head of training, filling station owner, aquarium fish shop owner, chief draftsman for the Cape Town city council and a high ranking naval officer. A total of 10% (10/102) of the skippers had previous employment in white-collar jobs. All ten of those who came out of white-collar jobs were white.

Table 10. Skipper's Race and the Jobs they Held Before Entering the Fishing Industry

	Only Fishing	Blue Collar	White Collar	Total
Coloured	90% (28)	10% (3)	0	100% (31)
White	38% (27)	48% (34)	10% (10)	100% (71)

Skippers who considered themselves veterans in the industry felt threatened by the many new entrants, men they called "package guys."

> You get two types of fishermen, one that has his heart and soul into fishing. He's the real fisherman. Then you get the fisherman who just likes to fish. The real fisherman has to make a living for his house, sends money home. He stores money by me. Some of the guys who live from day to day are also good fishermen; they're drinkers, drinkers and smokers of dagga and buttons. Then there are the package guys, the guys that used to be weekenders. They're the ones that took the golden handshakes. But there are fewer weekenders left now. A ton of these guys are running to the sea. The guys fear losing their right to fish, and they're streaming in left and right. Some pensioners sneak into the coops through the back door.

"Package guys" were described as men who had "taken the golden handshake" from an employer, often a severance or retirement package, and invested it in a boat and tow vehicle. This category included men who left their jobs voluntarily and those who were forced out of their jobs. In either case, the capital they gained from a previous employer gave them a sizable advantage over those who bought their own boats out of their fishing money.

One of the three coloured skippers who had previously developed a trade as a mason but has been fishing full-time for the past twelve years, explicitly excluded these "package" guys when describing the true skipper:

> He makes his living out of the sea. That's what a fisherman is, whether it's crayfish or handlining, 100% of a fisherman's livelihood comes from the sea. It's not a guy that took a package. There are a lot of guys that took package and bought themselves ski-boats and now think they're fishermen.

Even those who themselves had other employment, at one time, but who had been dependent on fishing for a considerable time now considered the "package guys" a threat to their livelihood.

A forty-seven year-old white skipper who had retired from a lucrative white collar job and had been fishing full-time for the past three years admitted that his severance package gave him a significant leg up. When describing the true fisherman, he said:

> You get many kinds. For example, me and my crew, we're non-drinkers. Only two of them smoke. We all took package together; now we're just working for our houses. The real fishermen work for their homes, they have responsibilities, like us. The others smoke dagga, booze. Whenever their money is up they go to sea again. They live from hand to mouth. The bad ones are always drunk, but they won't get a site from me.

Ironically there is no connection in such descriptions between the relative poverty of the "bad ones" and their addictions, even though this skipper acknowledges many a crew's hand-to-mouth existence.

Not all of the "package guys" retired with lucrative severance packages. A fifty-one year-old white skipper cautioned against painting all of the package guys the same:

> I'm a South African citizen. It does mean something to be white. These other people are getting resources, and you're getting nothing. That's not right. A fisherman is a poor white. I was a plumber in those days, with the railways. In those days you did a five year trade apprenticeship. After three years you can apply, or you can take your trades test before the five years is up. If you pass then you're automatically a tradesman.

While training as a tradesman kept many white men in South Africa from starving, for those who went into fishing it rarely provided for significant upward socioeconomic mobility.

One older coloured skipper commented on his frustration with those who "bought" their way into the industry: "I won't train the bosses how to catch fish. Owners hire [one of the better coloured skippers], learn from them, then let them go. We have no real money to buy boats, but they'll exploit our skills. ...The guys that give me the hardest time are the AWB guys [right wing Afrikaners]." A number of the white skippers acknowledged their dependence on formerly hired skippers for teaching them how to fish. In describing his personal work history, one of the wealthier "package guys" who had been fishing full-time for the past five years acknowledged this dependence:

> In 1981 I bought my first boat, a small four-man boat. In 1983 I bought a six-man boat from my cousin. We fished weekends. In 1989 I hired a skipper to work my boat commercially. I fished weekends and during factory shutdowns. It was during those times that I got to know the guys. In 1994 I bought a nine-man boat and hired a skipper. In 1995 I had to ask myself what I really wanted out of life. I decided I didn't want to sit in an office. When I took package from my first job in 1995, [another company] offered me a fantastic salary to come and work with them. I decided to take the job so I could finance my second boat. In 1998 I resigned from [that job] to start fishing full-time. The skipper I hired on [my other boat] taught me how to fish. He used to have his own boat, but it was well out of warranty when the engines blew.

Some coloured skippers described this type of relationship as exploitative, others saw it as symbiotic.

A Dispersed Sense of Place

The Mobility of the Roaming Handline Ski-Boat Fishermen

Socioeconomic relations in the handline ski-boat industry are in part determined by the geographic range of the ski-boat activity. The communities of residence for the handline skippers are spread along a large portion of the Cape peninsula. These skippers reside in thirty-four different towns and suburbs stretching from Arniston/Waenhuiskrans, approximately 200 km along the coast southwest of Cape Town, to the town of Paternoster, approximately 150 km to the north-northwest (See Skippers' Residence Map, Figure 15). This geographical range makes sense in light of the need for proximity to the lucrative Cape Town markets and the moving concentrations of snoek (van der Elst 1981, Wilke 2000). Each skipper's more regular crew

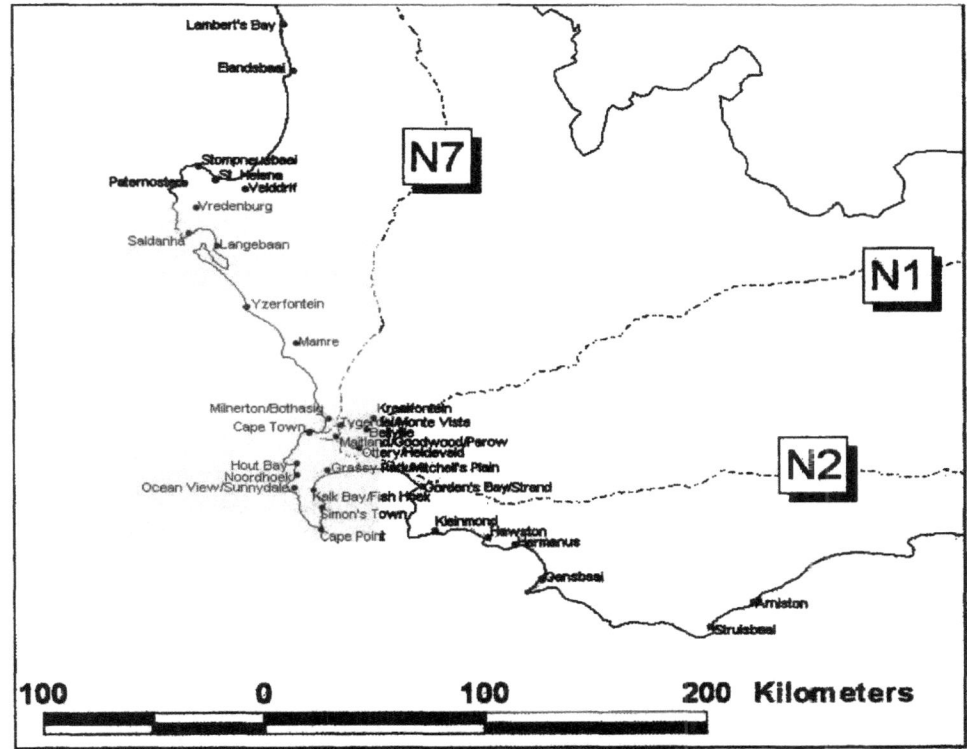

Figure 15. Towns of Residence for Skippers in the Handline Ski-Boat Fraternity

members most often reside either somewhere near the skipper's residence or closer to that skipper's most common fishing grounds. Crew for the fishers that live in the rural fishing towns tend to live closer to the skipper. Skippers who live in suburban Cape Town more often live in areas quite separate from their crew and will require their crews to meet them at the harbor that he decides to fish from for the day.

Figure 15 and Table 11 display just how spread out the residences of these skippers in the network are.

Table 11. Residence of Ski-Boat Skippers Interviewed

Town of Residence	# of Skippers	Town of Residence	# of Skippers
Yzerfontein	20	Langebaan	2
Strand	9	Ocean View	2
Goodwood	7	Vredenberg	2
Kraaifontein	6	Maitland	1
Hout Bay	6	Milnerton	1
Arniston	4	Monte Vista	1
Saldanha	4	Ottery	1
St Helena	4	Tyger Valley	1
Bellville	3	Tygerdal	1
Bothasig	3	Gordon's Bay	1
Heideveld	3	Hawston	1
Mitchell's Plain	3	Kalk Bay	1
Stompneusbaai	3	Kleinmond	1
Struisbaai (Molshoop)	3	Mamre	1
Grassy Park	2	Noordhoek	1
Parow	2	Paternoster	1
Southfield	2	Sunnydale	1

Rural vs. Suburban Fishers

When asked to describe the differences between the different skippers, one of the older skippers, relatively new to the industry, said: "No two are alike. There are groups of them divided by geography, like Struisbaai, Gansbaai, Hout Bay, Stompneus, Yzerfontein. You can see the difference but it's hard to describe. They're geographical differences." One of the categorical geographical distinctions made is between those who come from Cape Town and its suburbs and those from the small fishing communities all along the coast. One of the skippers from Cape Town's northern suburbs noted the difference this way: "We know the guys in Goodwood. Every guy tends to do his own thing. The Yzerfonteiners and the St. Helena fishermen, they've all got rich parents. They have the bigger boats, the bigger engines. We're struggling."

When asked about how he felt the current quota system worked, a twenty-seven year-old white skipper who had been fishing for a living since he was nineteen replied:

> Unfair. The guys from other places get quotas and they've ruined their areas. But the guys out of the Cape can't even get a quota for our own island [Robben Island] where the stuff lies thick all over the place. That's unfair. Why do they have to ruin us where we, the fishermen on the ground, can't even get a quota. But people can come from Gansbaai and Hermanus to come fetch our quotas. That's not fair. But then you go there to catch fish, just to catch fish there, then they chase us guys from the Cape, then we can't buy bait from them, we are chased away, they flatten our tires because us guys from the Cape are taking their fish. Their fish that they say are theirs. But they come fetch our quota. It's kaffer psychology that they're using. That's what I have to say. I don't know if it's right or wrong.

When asked who he considers his major competition, one long time resident of Cape Town said:

> ...the harbor masters can also be a problem. That's a bunch of nonsense. If it's his chommie [friend], he lets him through the gate first. Some places you're a foreigner; you're not allowed to come there. That's how they work. They're against each other. It's the same at Yzerfontein. The council said they don't want anything to do with the harbor master any more. So there's not any control there anymore. Now they say that only the fishermen that live there can catch fish there. You that live in the Cape, you're not allowed to fish there. That's what they're trying to do.

While as of the conclusion of this current research no such restrictions have been placed on non-residents of Yzerfontein, there have been major complaints about favoritism at this most desired of fishing harbors. Even residents of the town note how tight the social networks are in such a small, close-knit town. One relatively new resident noted: "There's a lot of gossip about us in this town. We're English. I don't mix much with the Afrikaans people. We mix more with the Cape Town people. There are lots of cliques in this town."

While the Cape Town skippers were quick to point out the disadvantages they faced when visiting the harbors in the rural fishing towns, skippers from the rural fishing towns were equally ready to point out some of their own reservations about the guys from town. One of the older coloured skippers who made most of his living by fishing in False Bay commented on the skill that it took to be able to fish for a diverse group of species:

> You get the fisherman that only catches big fish. You get the Cape fishermen. They'll only catch snoek and hotnots. In the Cape that's about all they have. Here by us you get everything. There's redfish, stompneus, kabblejou, geelbek, maasbankers, makriel, you get all of that here, but not in the Cape. A lot of those Cape fishermen, they'll only work on the snoek. But if they're not catching snoek, then they'll come out this direction and try for stompneus, red roman. But all in all, he's not a professional fisherman. A professional is a man that can catch every kind of fish, like what's in our bay. Kalk Bay guys, they're professional fishers. He can catch every kind of fish. He catches snoek, geelbek, kabblejou, geelstert. He can catch everything there is. But you get the man that can't catch, like the Cape men. He only concentrates on snoek. When it comes to the fish that we catch here, he can't catch them like we can. He can be a professional when it comes to catching snoek, but when it comes to our bay, then he's not. The true fishermen are the guys from this area. He can catch how he wants to, but if he can't catch like we do, then he's not a true fisherman.

Most of the handline ski-boat skippers focus their attention on the snoek for the greater part of the year. But there are certain times of the year, particularly when the lucrative yellowtail are biting, that a significant portion of the fraternity will move to the southern coast chasing the reef fish.

When the ski-boat fishers travel to different harbors, particularly when they plan to return to the same harbor for days or weeks on end, they will often rent space for themselves in the nearest town. More often than not skippers require their crew to find their own housing, or if they all decide to room together, they'll share the expenses of the rental. Some of the wealthier skippers, all of whom retired from lucrative non-fishing jobs, have combined their retirement plans with their fishing plans. They purchased holiday homes in the town they fish most often and regularly commute between their fishing house and their family home. Occasionally the family will join them at the holiday home if the fish are biting well for an extended period of time. But these holiday/fish homes are the exception to the rule. Most of the skippers in the handline industry rent the most affordable accommodation available for them and their crew, seeking to minimize expenses.

Members of the Informal Economy

The distinction between the formal and the informal components here parallels recent distinctions between the formal and informal economy in economic anthropology (Plattner 1989; Wilke 1996). In understanding the construction of economic systems, these distinctions refer specifically to Western divisions. In the informal economy, the primary participants "are producers of goods and services who provide some marketable commodity that for various reasons escapes enumeration, regulation, or other type of public monitoring or auditing. The category includes any economic activity... that eludes, is discounted, or is ignored by the state's national accounting system" (Smith 1989:294). In the formal economy, on the other hand, "formal training is often required to enter, enterprises are large and capital intensive, corporate kinds of organizations are typical, formal management techniques prevail, and connections with national and international institutions are profound" (Dannhaeuser 1989:28).

Handline fishers have been dependent on informal economic and social organization for their survival since handline fishing was introduced to the Cape. This informal organization has had both advantages and disadvantages for these fishers. The lack of formalization has allowed for certain benefits to the fishers such as open access to the fisheries (e.g. no distinction between recreational and commercial fishers), development of niche markets (e.g. the roadside sale of snoek), a lack of restrictions on when and where to fish (independence) and limited exposure to taxation and the responsibilities of labor laws (e.g. each fisher is self-employed). But this lack of formalization has also allowed for little or no job security, a factor that increases uncertainty and stress in an environment where a host of factors are already beyond any individual's control. In addition, those with capital have a significant advantage over those without, those who are willing to organize have an advantage over those who are not organized, for those with quality formal education have an advantage over those with limited formal education. This situations has led to exploitation of both the workers in this industry and, arguably, the resource from which they make a living.

The Technology of Handline Fishing

Most modern linefishing vessels are owned either by individuals or small to medium sized fishing companies. There are individual owners/operators who fish commercially, take the boat to sea themselves and gain the majority of their income from that activity. Some boat owners employ a skipper to take the boat to sea. The owner may or may not gain most of their livelihood from fishing and, more often than not, has primary employment not related to the fishing industry. Finally there are the owners/operators who the commercial handline skippers call "weekenders." These are skippers who take their vessels to sea for pleasure or to supplement a more stable income. As mentioned earlier, there is significant animosity between the "commercials" and the "weekenders" in the competition for the resource.

The Department of Marine and Coastal Management adopted the classification of entities as outlined by the Department of Trade and Industry and it is as follows:

Table 12. Classification of Fishing Companies by the South African Government

Size or class	Current full time Paid employees	Total annual turnover	Total gross asset value (property excluded)
Large	Over 100	Over R4m	over R4 m
Medium	50–100	R2-R4m	R2-R4m
Small	10–49	R0.4-R2m	R0.4-R2m
Very small	Less than10	Less than R0.4m	Less than R0.4m

Source: Kleinschmidt (2000)

According to many critics, this classification is not suitable for the fishing industry. MCM is consequently debating on how to change this.

Fishing vessel and code		Length (m)	Propulsion	Range of operation (nautical miles)
ROCK LOBSTER BOATS (a) Large commercial with 10-12 dinghies CFBa		15-20	Single screw diesel	< 100
(b) Small commercial CFBb	(i)	10-15	Single screw diesel	< 75
	(ii)	5-10	Single screw diesel	±15
LINEFISH BOATS (a) Decked, commercial lineboats LFBa		8-15	Single screw diesel	< 40
(b) Small decked lineboats LFBb		5-10	Single screw diesel	±15
(c) Small undecked or partially decked motorboats LFBc		4-8	Short-shaf. diesel	±12
(d) Skiboats LFBd		4.5-8	Twin outboard or Z-drive	< 15
(e) Dinghies LFBe		3-5	Single outboard (18-25 hp)	< 6
(f) Rowboats LFBf		3-5	Oars	3-4

Figure 16. Fishing Vessels Operating in the Western Cape
source: Pulfrich and Griffiths (1988)

Some of the line fishing fleet have been formally incorporated as small. This is becoming the norm as the government continues to avoid issuing fishing rights to non-incorporated individuals. There are owner/operator vessels where the skipper/owner has formed a Closed Corporation (formally recognized business) and is running the vessel through its accounting records. Some fishing businesses that have broader interests than handline species will employ a company skipper on their boats. Small to medium sized fishing companies will often employ a skipper to work the vessel for them.

The vessels used for handlining primarily include "chakkies" or crayfish boats and ski-boats, but may also include deck boats and pelagic boats that are used intermittently for handline fishing. The chakkies, so named reportedly as an onomatopoetic reference to the sound of their slogging inboard diesel engine, are one of the oldest types of vessels still in use for small-scale commercial fishing on the Cape coast. Chakkies are usually geographically limited to the range they can travel by sea from their home port in a day. Since the rise in the popularity of ski-boats as an option for handline fishers, few new chakkies have been manufactured. Most of the chakkies currently in existence have been around for more than twenty years and are often bequeathed to family members.

Ski-boats reached up to twenty-eight feet with as many as twelve crew (including skipper). Powered by up to two 200hp outboard petrol motors, or more expensive yet more efficient diesel inboard motors, these vessels are capable of carrying a maximum of approximately four tons of fish (e.g. over 1,000 individual snoek). The most popular pair of outboard motors among the commercial ski-boat operators tended to be the 85hp Yamahas. With their twin outboard motors, ski-boats allow for a greater range of mobility and ease of maneuverability at sea than the chakkies and thus have the reputation for being more efficient when fishing for fast-moving shoaling species like snoek. Ski-boats are easily loaded onto a boat trailer and transported to where the fish are biting best. When the lucrative yellowtail run hits the southern shores and competes for the fisher's attention with the concurrent snoek runs on the western shores, it is not uncommon for ski-boat skippers to be in Yzerfontein for snoek one day and to be a three hour drive away in Struisbaai catching yellowtail the next.

In the ski-boat sector, skipper-ownership status is highly skewed by race. Only 13% of those who own their own boats are coloured; 63% of the hired skippers are coloured. While only

41% of the coloured skippers own their own boat, 82% of the white skippers own their own boat. Analyzing the distribution via Chi-square shows that this ownership distribution is not likely to happen by chance. One of the explanations for this distribution is the historical economic discrimination against non-whites. In 1999 the initial investment for a new commercially rigged ski-boat, engines and tow-vehicle was somewhere between R150,000 and R300,000 ($25,000–$50,000), far beyond the reach of most South Africans. Very few of the skippers operated with new equipment, but still the investment was substantial.

Table 13. Chi Square of Skipper's Boat Ownership by Race

	Coloured	White	Total
Hired	22	13	35
Own	9	58	67
Total	31	71	102

Test statistic	Value	Df	Prob
Pearson Chi-square	26.546	1.000	0.000

Most of the skippers who owned their own boat either bought the boat with money from a severance/retirement package or had major assistance from family members. For those who had no severance package to aid in the initial investment in a boat there were few alternatives for capital financing. In 1987 the government disbanded FISCOR, the primary and government-sponsored financing agency for the fishing industry, and allowed the existing loans to be bought out[1]. The Small Business Development Corporation (SBDC) was formed to take over the money for smaller businesses, including businesses in the fishing industry. Loans were made available for upwards of R5,000, and some small scale commercial fishers took advantage. In 1996 the government did away with the Fisheries Development fund, thus cutting new loans to small scale operators in the fishing industry. The SBDC kept the debtors but restructured their lending practices in favor of larger businesses. That same year 80% of the SBDC was privatized and renamed Business Partners, keeping R40 million invested in the fishing industry. In 1999, R26 million was approved to fund the Marine Investments branch of Business Partners, with 55% of the funds slated for owners of "disadvantaged" businesses.

In the late 1980s and early 1990s small loans were made available to white and coloured skippers for the purchase of capital equipment such as new boats, new motors and electronic equipment. According to Anton Roelofse, director of the Marine Investments branch of Business Partners, 90% of the ski-boat operations that borrowed money from them lost money. The investors decided that the ski-boat industry was too risky an investment. The cost of capital was too high for most of these small businesses. "The problem is that you have the informal sector seeking formal capital. Most of these guys can't manage that kind of money. Our solution at Business Partners is to help them change from fishermen to businessmen. They can't do that if they're solely dependent on handline fishing." (Roelofse and Gates 2000). Currently Business Partners will only fund loans over R150,000 and refuses to invest in the ski-boat industry.

Skippers know the limitations of their options. A number of the skippers commented on the foreclosures that happened on fishing loans in the mid-1990s. One of the oldest coloured skippers in the business gave his perspective on this process:

> There is no one that helps the fisherman. Look, the fisherman is poor; he has nothing. Nothing he can give. If you go to the banks, they won't give you money. There were some that helped the fishermen, some helped a few in Hout Bay. It's a company, I can't remember the name. They lent a few of us money. The Small Business. That's it. But when the fish became scarce, and the man didn't have the money to pay, they came and got his boat. They took it away. The boat, the engines, the trailer...

Many others spoke of the impossibility of obtaining loans from a bank. A fifty-two year-old skipper who had been fishing full-time for the past eleven years tried to explain: "Fishermen have a bad name. 'There goes another drunk.' But we're not all like that. It's very difficult for us to get a loan. We have no fixed income, nothing to prove that we can pay. One day the fishing is good, the next day not so good." Anton Roelofse said that, as far as he knew, they were the only source of financing to which those in the fishing industry could turn, and if they didn't finance the ski-boat industry, no one would. The only assistance reported as coming from a bank by any of the skippers interviewed was through pre-existing personal credit lines.

Spurred on by the technology available for larger vessels, most of the technology on ski-boats was first introduced to the industry through the heavily resourced recreational industry. The technological sophistication of the electronics used on the commercial ski-boats has exploded in the past fifteen years. As one skipper with over a decade of experience in the handline ski-boat industry said:

> A few years ago without some of the new equipment and technology it was different than what it is now. Regarding how hardened a fisherman is, the technology has made it easier. Years ago they didn't have echoes on ski-boats. Now there's an echo. Earlier there was no such thing as a GPS or plotter. You only had a compass. Now you've got those things. People got lost because they couldn't read their compass. The technology has made everything so much easier. But the line fisherman works physically with his hands. He doesn't have any equipment. Everything is done with his hands.

While the skill of the skipper who can make his catch without modern instrumentation remains a common thread in the fabric of fireside fishing stories, competition has forced even the older skippers to adopt much of the latest technology.

Most commercial ski-boat skippers in the Western Cape use the following electronics: compass (97%), a long range VHF radio (60%), a shorter range High Frequency radio (90%), cellphone (81%), echo sounder (95%), Global Positioning System (85%), plotter (33%). Skippers have appropriated these technologies with very little formal training. They tend to learn in the process of using the technology and will most often either read product manuals or be shown by others how to use it. What is particularly striking about this phenomena is that all of this technological sophistication is in use despite the cost of the initial investment and the maintenance of the equipment. The edge they add in the competitive world of handline fishing reportedly outweighs the cost of the technology itself.

Table 14. Electronic Technology On-Board Commercial Ski-Boats

N=102	Communication			Direction/Fish Finding			
	HF	Cell	VHF	Compass	Echo	GPS	Plotter
Use (%)	90%	81%	60%	97%	95%	85%	33%
Use (n)	92	83	61	99	97	87	34
Formal Training(n)	20	6	26	37	7	7	3

The primary purpose for the investment in these technologies was reportedly to increase a skipper's competitive edge at sea. But electronic technology on-board these ski-boats also has significant social implications. The owners of the boats are responsible for the purchase and maintenance of this technology. Owners who hire skippers to run their boats often commented on the need to hire trustworthy skippers who would watch over their expensive equipment. White boat owners who stereotyped coloureds as untrustworthy often used the protection of their investment as justification for hiring only white skippers. One of the outliers in the network of skippers had a reputation for having a crew that often helped themselves to the electronic technology from other boats. Whether or not this reputation was true, skippers knew that when certain boats were around, it was time to keep the electronics locked up in the bakkie.

The use of the cellphone has become ubiquitous in handline fishing over the past two to three years. Because the ski-boats normally do not range more than 25 kilometers from the shore, the 16 nautical mile offshore range of the more popular 5- and 8-Watt phones operate quite effectively in clear weather. Since the introduction of the ski-boats in the 1940s the widespread use of radio technology served as the primary means for communication at sea. Skippers would keep in contact via VHF and HF radios. Some of the skippers still prefer to use the radio due to the public nature of the medium. Cellphones have become particularly important in the communication networks for handline skippers. Cellphones enable skippers to contact family members on shore, pre-arrange markets for the fish and contact those trusted colleagues for important information on where to find fish. One of the wealthier skippers who recently retired from a lucrative white-collar job explained how the cellphone helps his business: "David, one of my crew, does our bidding. He takes no shit. The cellphone has radically changed the ways we sell. Buyers phone at sea and pre-arrange buys. The langaaners get cross at me. Their buying power is split when guys fish out of more than one port."

Of the 18 skippers (19%) who did not use cellphones, 12 were coloured and 6 were white. This means that 39% of the coloured skippers did not have this technology available to them for their work as compared to 8% of the white skippers.

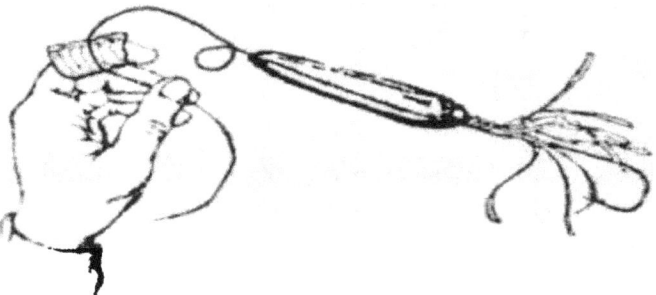

Figure 17. A Fisherman's Hand, Protected by a "Vingerlappie," Casting a "Lood"
source: Stibbe and Moss (1998)

Ironically, with all of the sophistication of the navigational and fish finding technology on board these ski-boats, they catch the fish with technology not much different from what was used in the eighteenth century. Even the largest of fish they catch by hand. Although they have substituted wooden spools, blood let lines and iron hooks with plastic spools, synthetic gut and steel hooks, the basic techniques for catching by hand have been passed on through generations of fishers. Each fisher will commonly have three lines in the water at any one time. The hooks are commonly baited with sardines, although a more effective and more expensive bait, pike, is used when the snoek really need to be enticed. In addition the fishers will often use a "lood" (a stainless steel spinner) to skim the surface when the snoek are shoaling. Crew sometimes estimate the depth of the snoek via consensus on how deep they are biting, but most often skippers inform the crew of the depth via their electronic fish finder (echo sounders). Lines are reeled in hand over hand. As indicated above, handline fishers protect their fingers with neoprene tubes called "vingerlappies" (lit. finger rags) (see Figure 17).

The Resource

Most handliners are dependent on seasonal catches of species such as snoek, yellowtail, Cape salmon and hottentot. These species have been neither formally exploited by corporate fishing industry interests nor, as of 2000, carefully regulated by the national marine resource management plans. But this is soon to change.

> Analysis of historical *cpue* [catch per unit of effort] for the commercial linefishery revealed that, in spite of massive technological advances, such as vessel motorization, nylon lines, echo-sounders, electronic navigational aids and on-board freezer facilities, the current catch rates of demersal linefish are dramatically lower than historical values, with most falling way below the 25% level. ... The recorded declines in *cpue* and those stock assessments which have been completed indicate that the majority of bottom-dewelling linefish have been heavily overexploited. (Naidoo 1999:15–16)

The economic and cultural bedrock of the handline fishing industry has always been, and continues to be, the southern African snoek. Fortunately for the handline fishers, the catch rate of pelagic nomads such as yellowtail and snoek have not demonstrated the same dramatic declines as the demersal species. "The key to the resilience of the latter is presumably their unpredictable movement patterns that effectively reduce fishing effort" (Naidoo 1999:16).

Snoek is a medium-sized, pelagic predator inhabiting the coastal waters of the temperate Southern Hemisphere. It is found from the surface to the seabed, to depths of 550m and occurs off southern Africa, Australia, New Zealand, the east and west coasts of southern South America, Tristan da Cunha, and the islands of Amsterdam and St Paul. Snoek is an important food fish throughout much of its distribution, supporting moderate fisheries (<1,000 t/yr) off southern

Australia, Chile and Tristan de Chuna, and substantial fisheries (>10 000 t/yr) off New Zealand and Southern Africa (Griffiths 2000).

Southern African snoek have been recorded from northern Angola to Algoa Bay on the South African east coast but are mostly found between the Cunene River and Cape Agulhas, i.e., in the Benguela ecosystem. Snoek has been an important commercial species in this system since the early 1800s, caught initially with handlines but also trawled after 1960. Total catch peaked at about 81,000 tons in 1978 but dropped substantially with the exclusion of foreign trawlers from the Namibian fishing grounds in 1991. Current annual-catch ranges between 14,437 and 22,920 tons (1991–1995), with 93% of it made in South African waters (Griffiths 2000).

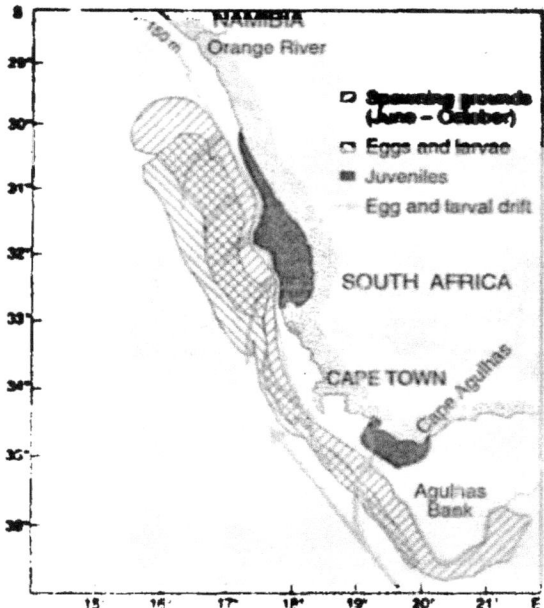

Figure 18. Primary Habitat for Snoek *Thyrsites atun*
source: Griffiths (2000)

Snoek is by far the most important species caught by the South African commercial-linefishery, comprising 39% of the 1986–1997 catch, according to MCM. It is also targeted by recreational anglers, for which catch statistics are not available. Around 40% of the South African catch (1990–1996) is made by commercial handline-fishers and 60% by trawlers (Griffiths 2000). However, the commercial line-catch may be under-reported by as much as 75% (Sauer et al., 1997).

The seasonal nature for the handline ski-boat fraternity is, for the most part, controlled by the movement of its primary target species: snoek. Their movement is, in one sense, determined by the prevalence of the primary species they follow. But in another sense, their movement is highly dependent on information about this species from each other. The fraternity follows its prey up and down the west coast, relying on information from each other in determining when and where to fish.

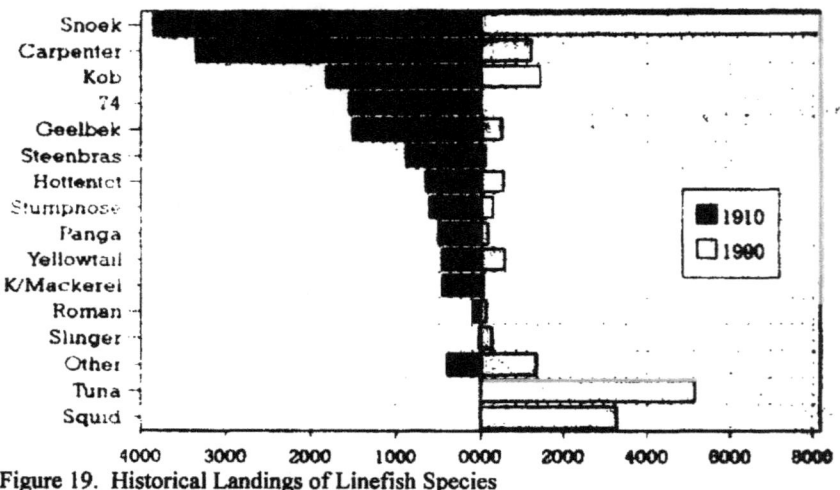

Figure 19. Historical Landings of Linefish Species
source: Penny (1993)

Fishers and historians alike praise not only the ecomic but the cultural value of snoek as well. As one industry historian put it, "The same delicious madness infects the fishermen toward the end of April every year. Sick fishermen leave their beds and drunk fishermen become sober to plead for a place on a boat…It's holiday fishing with all the excitement of the chase—and good money to be earned at the end" (Lees 1969:209). The end of April tends to be a boom season for the snoek fishers and langaaners alike. Snoek is relatively scarce but the demand is high. Cultural observances surrounding the Christian celebration of Easter reportedly cause a bullish market for the sale of snoek. The taboo against eating red meat for Good Friday is satisfied by the substitution of fish. In Cape Town, the fish of choice is snoek.

When asked about the upcoming regulations on the linefish industry, one of the white skippers with more than ten years of experience as a skipper said, "Snoek is a culture in the Cape. They mustn't commercialize it. It's part of the coloured culture. Your major consumers are the coloureds. It's a source of cheap food." More than one skipper mentioned the value of snoek to the coloured communities. Another skipper was attempting to explain the importance of the work he chose when he said, "We supply the people with food. Snoek goes directly to the table, 60,000 tons of snoek from my fleet alone. All the poor people eat together on one snoek for R10."

The Informal Marketplace

Handline fishing is purely a cash enterprise. Skippers are paid in cash by the hawkers for their fish, and they in turn pay the crew on the day of the catch. The crew is paid on the half share. They are paid 50% of the price garnered at the market for the fish that they caught for the day. The remaining 50% of the gross value goes to the skipper and the owner of the boat. In addition to their 50% share, most skippers allow crew to take one or more "fries" for the day. A fry is a fish whose total value belongs to the fisher who caught it. There are slight variations to the fry system, but it is most common for a skipper to offer one fry after the tenth fish caught, then another after the 25th fish caught, a third after the 50th fish caught, and perhaps a fourth or fifth if more than a hundred fish are caught per crewmember in one day. The only other financial benefits mentioned by the skipper are holiday bonuses. A number of the skippers said that around Christmas time they would allow their crew to choose their holiday bonus day. On the day chosen, the entire value of a crew's catch was his to keep.

The owners of the ski-boats were invariably responsible for the upkeep and repairs on the boat and tow vehicle. More often than not the owners would provide the petrol money for the boat. It was not uncommon to charge the crew R20 each per day for petrol money if they had to travel long distances. On many of the boats, the owners passed half of the cost of the bait on to the crew as well. Owners were more often willing to pay for the cheaper bait, sardines, but when the crew chose to use the more expensive bait, pike, they were usually required to pay for half the box they used. When snoek were plentiful and moving fast, there was no need to entice them to the surface with the better bait. Often a simple "lead" (shiny stainless-steel spinner) would do.

When the skipper was not the owner of the boat, his compensation would be much like that of the crew. Most often the owner would agree to give the skipper 50% of what he caught for the day plus a percentage (most often 10%) of the total gross on the boat for the day. Alternative arrangements were made for compensation when the skipper had to "hou riem[2]" for the day. Depending on the weather and how the snoek were biting, skippers either threw anchor over a school of fish or they held the boat steady over a school of fish by keeping the nose into the wind and the throttle in hand. This latter tactic they called holding "riem." Holding "riem" required the skipper to be away from catching snoek and would make compensation purely on the share system unfair.

The prices garnered for snoek varied erratically over time. Between October 1999 and August 2000, fishers were paid as much as R42 per snoek (during late April) and as little as R2 per snoek (during the winter months). In the winter months, when fishing days are few and far between, it is often not worth the price of the petrol it takes to go in search of the fish. Even though the prices for the fish are higher during times of scarcity, the supply is so limited that many refuse to risk the transportation costs. Skippers, particularly those with very limited resources, take a larger risk to search for fish during the slow times.

Crew

Despite the dominance of white skippers in the handline ski-boat industry, the true fisher is most often characterized as coloured. This may be due in part to the high percentage of coloured crew. Skippers identified a full 70% of the crew in this fishing fraternity as coloured. Only 7% were identified as black, while 23% were identified as white. The strong correlation between the negative stereotypes common to both "fisher" and "coloured" makes it difficult to tease out which are prior in the skippers' descriptions. It is uncommon to find a coloured skipper in charge of a white crew.

Weekenders

The marketplace is the site where the strongest battles are fought between those who consider themselves full-time fishers and the recreational fishers, or the ones the commercials call "weekenders." The market is greatly affected by the presence of "weekender" fish on the harbor. With the increased number of recreational fishers selling their catch on the harbor, prices are forced unreasonably low. Prices drop in part due to the supply and demand nature of the open market. The more fish thrown onto the market floor, the less the langaaners are willing to pay. When fishers find out that the snoek are biting at a particular harbor, the highly mobile ski-boat operators rush the fishing grounds. One skipper with more than a quarter of a century of experience as a fisherman complained about what he called the "trippers" (or the day-trippers):

> We're the fishermen. We make our living out of the sea. And there were trippers at sea, a bunch, and they came in before we did, with their 60s and 50s. So they threw it on the harbor, and one of the langaaners told them R7 for the fish. And they believed him. And there the price was in its glory. But a smart man that sells fish, he'll bring his own truck, or he knows what the fish are worth. But when we got in what they were offering was R7. So I had to take my fish in the bakkie to sell them myself. And you know, that's an effort. You have to go stand at night...

The abundance of fish attracts an abundance of fishers, which in turn attracts the hawkers to the harbors. With cellphone in hand, the hawkers arrange to buy just the right amount of fish for their market at the lowest price.

Hawkers can be seen coordinating their purchasing strategy among themselves prior to the rush of boats at the market area. When the fish are abundant, hawkers are more likely to offer lower prices. This forces the commercial line fishermen to leave the fishing grounds early in order to sell their product before the market is flooded and prices drop too far. Alternatively, commercial handliners are forced to fish longer hours to make up in volume what they will not get in price per fish. It is not uncommon for fishermen to get to the harbor and refuse to sell their catch before the prices they are offered rise. If prices do not rise they may attempt to sell their own fish to the public on the side of the road. In times when hawkers are offering ridiculously low prices, those with available freezing facilities will often store their catch in order to sell later when snoek are scarce.

Commercial ski-boat skippers also complained about the impact that increasing numbers of recreational or part-time commercial ski-boat operations were having on their livelihood. Some complain that the newer boats, bought mostly by new "package guys," are siphoning off the quality crew by offering bigger incentives. When asked to describe his current crew, a thirty-three year-old, college educated skipper who had been fishing professionally for a decade emphasized the importance of loyalty in a crew. He claimed that, "Chaps poach crew all the time. The bigger newcomers are luring the better crews. Their boats are more comfortable. They provide free bait. Sometimes a van is given. They're buying the crew away." This reportedly makes it more difficult to compete for those who have built their fishing business out of money made mostly from handline fishing.

Langaaners

The marketing of the fish caught by handliners at the turn of the twenty-first century is remarkably similar to the way handliners marketed their fish in the nineteenth century. Most of the skippers and crew operate with no formal letters of employment or protection that goes with this. The vessels mostly sell their catch for cash at the harbor, with few or no official records kept. The catches are largely sold to informal hawkers/traders called "langaaners." These langaaners pay cash for the fish and resell them for cash to the public. Often these sales will be from the back of a bakkie (pick-up truck) on the side of the road, from informal fish stalls, or to prearranged private buyers (e.g. fish shops and restaurants). When skippers are offered what they consider to be ridiculously low prices by the langaaners, they will often attempt to sell their catch themselves. In this situation, those with access to commercial freezer space are at an advantage over those with no such access. But most of the handline ski-boat skippers are forced by logistics to sell to the langaaners. As one of the Cape Town skippers noted, "The langaaners, we're ruled by them. They determine the price, and you have to unload. We've no time to stand on the road and sell our fish."

One of the langaaners shared his categorization of him and his colleagues. He said there were three types of langaaners, the big langaaners, the medium sized langaaners, and the rogues. There were only a handful of big langaaners (and many of them were of hefty girth) that sought the ski-boat snoek business. They tended to be big buyers, often organized with four or five different buyer and bakkies. The leader of this group of buyers would walk around with R10,000–15,000 in his pocket to ensure a good buy. The majority of langaaners fit into the medium category. They were the ones who buy 200–300 fish at a time and sell to specialized markets or from the back of their bakkies. Included in these are the "Portjies" or the Portuguese who buy fish for their own fish shops. Fishermen often talk more favorably about these Portuguese merchants because they have a reputation for paying higher prices. The langaaner interviewed for this categorization was willing to classify the "rogues" euphemistically as the independents. The independents were less likely to work with other langaaners. They typically transported fish to other factories and sometimes had contracts with the large snoek buyers like Snoek Wholesalers. When their contracts were not filled, they often also sold snoek from the back of their bakkies. The langaaner interviewed emphasized the interdependence of the fishermen and the langaaners. Describing it as a love-hate relationship, he admitted that the buyers often exploit the fishermen, knowing that most of them have few alternative markets.

Figure 20. Hawkers Bidding on Snoek at Hout Bay
source: author

Handline fishers complain that they are exploited by the langaaners on the informal market. Like the handline skippers and crew, the langaaners are themselves not subject to government controls and taxation. This situation provides for an environment where those with capital survive and do well; those without are at a disadvantage. Historically disadvantaged persons are particularly at risk of exploitation in such an unstructured market, primarily due to the lack of capital and the lack of quality professional networks. As one experienced skipper put it, "I'm dependent on the langaaners. I don't have my own markets, so I'm dependent on them. If I want to be independent, I have to get my own markets." The chief complaint against the langaaners is that they reportedly band together to control prices, give the fishermen poor prices for their catch, then turn around and make large profits at the retail end. Another skipper complained about the control the langaaners exercise over their prices: "They have meetings and dictate the price for the day. That affects our whole life. They have a monopoly. I even saw one stab another for paying a higher price."

Skippers will often distinguish between reliable langaaners and "skelm" (or crooked) langaaners. One of the well-connected Yzerfonetein skippers noted:

> There are some hawkers that know you, and you know them. And there's an understanding between you. You know that you can't bullshit each other. A Portuguese gives you a better price and doesn't want to stand in and among all the others; he doesn't worry about size. They stand off to the one side and don't form cliques with other langaaners. They make deals ahead of time while we're at sea. They buy from me even when I'm the only one going out. We establish the price while I'm at sea, and you have to keep your word!

Few of the skippers admitted to arranging prices for their fish ahead of time. It was also obvious from the activity at the boat ramps/fish markets that most skippers were taking the highest prices bid by the available hawkers.

Some of the white skippers believed that their race had an impact on how much the langaaners took advantage of them. One of the younger white skippers from Yzerfontein complained: "I have no pals among the langaaners; they're all coloureds, 'koelies,' non-whites." The implications behind his complaint was that he was at a disadvantage because he was not of the same race as the hawkers. When asked what it means to be white in the new South Africa, one fisherman said:

> We are going to struggle bitterly; we won't get rights. If I had a black skin or a brown skin today, then I would've gotten fishing rights. There are those brown skippers that get a better price from the langaaners. I believe, in any case, we all believe, the majority of

the boat owners and the skippers that are white, now with this license story, we'll be disadvantaged. How, I don't know, but that time is upon us. I may be wrong. ... Like they'd say now, regstellende aksies [corrective/affirmative action].

This forty-four year-old white ex-policeman applied his fear of the government's redistribution priorities to the activities of the langaaners.

Managing the Linefishers

With the dismantling of apartheid legislation beginning in the early 1990s, hopes ran high for greater participation in South Africa's fisheries, particularly for those who had previously been excluded from its benefits. The specific focus for these hopes was on the redistribution of the quotas allocated by the Department of Marine and Coastal Management. The mosaic of new claimants to fishery resources from within the non-white fishing communities include fishers who already hold quotas but who have no fishing capacity, fishers who have both quotas and fishing capacity, fishers from the informal sector, not legally recognized as fishermen, retired fishers from fishing companies, fishers laid off from fishing companies, widows of fishermen and women processing workers (Mathew 1997). In addition, there is a host of interest groups outside the fisheries sector that would like to benefit from the quota system.

The first attempt at managing the species most often caught by linefishers was the introduction of minimum size limits for selected species in 1940. But in the absence of biological data on the health of the stocks such as growth rates, fertility rates, etc. these limits were somewhat arbitrary. A few biological studies were initiated in the late 1960s, but it was not until the mid-1980s that the linefish species were to receive significant attention from government regulators. "With the exception of a closed season for elf (shad) in KwaZulu-Natal, and snoek in the Cape, no other restrictions were promulgated until a comprehensive management framework was introduced for the linefishery early in 1985" (Sea Fisheries Research Institute 1997–1998:12).

At the beginning of the 1980s the government was still in the early stages of taking control of the linefish industry. But 1985 marked a turning point in the government's involvement. It was in this year that Sea Fisheries crafted the first linefish management system into policy. Called the National Marine Linefish System (NMLS), this "system" is primarily a database designed to "enable the capture and analysis of the diverse and fragmented catch and effort data available for South African commercial and recreational linefisheries" (Penny 1993:68). The system developed from a need to coordinate and combine information to assess the impact that both recreational and commercial linefishers were having on the marine species. This linefish management system included the following measures: the introduction of a two-tiered license system for commercial fishers: full-time (named the A Category) and part-time (named the B Category); freezing of the commercial effort at the 1985 level; the introduction of minimum size limits based on the species size at maturity; the categorization of linefish species based on their perceived vulnerability to exploitation, with associated bag limits for commercial and recreational fishers; and the introduction of national closed seasons for specific species (Sea Fisheries Research Institute 1997–1998:12). One of the main objectives behind this initiative was to steer fishing effort away from "vulnerable" reef fish species to the more "resilient" shoaling species.

In 1984 the South African Marine Linefish Management Association (SAMLMA) was formed by a number of academic researchers (mostly marine biologists) and individuals with strong interests in the recreational angling clubs (Brunt 1993). The intention behind the creation of SAMLMA was to coordinate a network of researchers with interests in linefish species and to establish priorities for future research. The first step in the development of this research group was taken at a 1978 meeting of a steering committee appointed by the South African National Committee for Oceanographic Research the previous year. The Sea Fisheries Act of 1973 required the development of a Fisheries Advisory Council, chaired by the Chief Director of the Marine Development Branch of the Department of Environmental Affairs. But it was not until

1981 that this council gained its first representatives from the commercial and recreational linefishery (Brunt 1992:179). In that same year the government-sponsored Sea Fisheries Research Institute (SFRI) funded a post directed at linefish research, specifically the processing of catch information. The National Marine Linefish Committee was birthed from a 1983 meeting of the Marine Development Branch and members of the recreational fishing industry. The Sea Fisheries Act of 1988 replaced the Fisheries Advisory Council with a Fisheries Advisory Committee "which excluded direct representation of identified facets of the marine line fishery and also made the National Marine Linefish Committee redundant" (Brunt 1992:180). SAMLMA was officially launched in April of 1990 as a continuation of the interests of the original Linefish Committee, only now the group was a body independent of the government management system and responsible for its own infrastructure. While SAMLMA boasts representation from a broad range of stakeholders, including scientific institutions, regional conservation and management agencies, the sport/recreational linefishery and the commercial linefishery, commercial linefishers themselves have yet to be well represented in this association.

An interesting side-effect of the implementation of the A and B license system by the Department of Sea Fisheries was the informal market that developed for these commercial licenses. Within two years of the implementation of these new licenses, transfers of these licenses, obtained for a nominal fee from the government, boomed into a cash business. Since only a limited number of A and B licenses were available and the legal sale even of recreational catches was dependent on possession of these licenses, they quickly became a valuable commodity. Although the prices for these licenses fluctuated violently, brokers could expect to receive as much as R2,000 for a part-time commercial license (B-license) and R5,000 for a full-time commercial license (A-license). According to officials at the Sea Fisheries Research Institute, the transfer of these licenses in the late 1980s ran around 35% (personal communication). In an attempt to halt the free trade of licenses, motivated in part by the need to keep license holders accountable to management regulations, the government placed a moratorium on the transfer of all licenses in 1987.

The brief life of this informal market for commercial fishing boat licenses had important implications for the future of the handline fishing industry. Handline fishers who wanted to fish legally were bound to fishing from one of the licensed boats. Even though the license trade that developed allowed anyone with the right amount of money to purchase a license, the rising prices of the licenses on the black market made it increasingly difficult for fishers of few means to obtain such a license. This made it particularly difficult for most coloured fishers to obtain a license. What further complicated access to these licenses by coloured fishers is the fact that most of the boats were owned by whites. Since the licenses are attached to a boat, the best most coloured skippers could do under this system was to work for someone with a licensed boat.

In 1998, with the passage of the Marine Living Resource Act, the A and B license system was suspended. This act called for a revision of the linefish management system in general and the boat licensing system in particular. The government sent out a call for applications for this new system in 1998 and received thousands of responses. Due in part to political turmoil in the top management structure of the government and inertia in the bureaucratic wheels of government, no decisions were made regarding these applications. A second call for applications was made in 1999. As of the conclusion of this research no new official licensing system had been put in place. Since the passage of the Marine Living Resources Act of 1998, owners and skippers of handline vessels have been anxiously awaiting word on their possible continued existence in commercial fishing. They have, in the mean time, been fishing under the assumption that the rules of the old A and B license system remain in effect.

Fishing Associations

The handline fishers of the Western Cape have historically been unable to form lasting, representative associations that would enable them to unite for their own benefit. As early as

1908 the fishers of the Cape peninsula united to form an association for mutual support and to amplify their voice in public proceedings. The Fishermen's Union was designed to unite the fishers from Simon's Town to Muizenberg with the view to forming a co-op. "A committee was elected to consider various proposals regarding the transportation of fish, the use of tugboats to get to distant fishing grounds, the cold storage facilities and the possibility of taking over the premises of Kalk Bay Fish and Land Company" (Stibbe and Moss 1998:41). Instead of focusing on ways to decrease their common expenses and improve the markets for their product, the members of this union got involved in a protracted dispute over a steam tug, the Gnu, that often towed the small, non-motorized fishing vessels to the fishing grounds. Their inability to unite for a common cause became clear when a number of schemes to cut out the middleman and market directly to the public failed to materialize. Though the Fisherman's Union continued to be active in Kalk Bay, the idea of a co-op eventually failed.

The impact of fisher associations like the Fisherman's Union of Kalk Bay remained without any real teeth, confined to local, small-scale issues. The first significant attempt to unite fishers from across the western Cape was initiated by the government's Directorate of Sea Fisheries in 1992. The Directorate's Quota Board initiated an inquiry into the socio-economic conditions of West Coast fishing communities. The Human Science Research Council conducted the study (Schutte 1993). Impressed by the social needs of the poverty-stricken fishing communities on the West Coast, but in typical paternalistic fashion, the Minister of Environmental Affairs decided to pour development money into these communities. In order to do so, the Department of Sea Fisheries modified its commitment to a management system based on Individual Transferable Quotas (ITQs)[3] to include the allocation of quotas to specific geographical areas, not just to individuals. The Quota Board decided to establish what they termed Fishermen's Community Trusts. Money would be funneled from the industry through the government to these trusts explicitly for the purpose of social development. At the end of 1994 there were twenty-five officially registered Fishermen's Community Trusts while eight were in the process of being registered.

Fishermen's Community Trusts were established in 1992 to uplift and develop the fishing communities along the west coast. Most, if not all, of those involved in small-scale commercial handlining registered under one of these trusts. A certain proportion of the deep-sea hake Total Allowable Catch (TAC) was set aside for allocation to these trusts. In 1995, about 5% of the hake TAC and 4% of the anchovies TAC were set aside (Fishing Industries Handbook 1996). Since the harvesting of hake requires highly technical and expensive equipment, which the trusts did not have and could not afford, they were unable to participate in the harvesting, processing and marketing of quotas. Their quotas were therefore sold to established fishing companies.

There were a number of factors working against the success of the Fishermen's Community Trusts, including the top-down implementation by management, the lack of guidelines for the appropriation of funds and, most importantly, a lack of knowledge about the dynamics of power in the communities of interest. The top-down implementation of the Fishermen's Community Trusts doomed them to failure from the beginning. With a program reminiscent of the social engineering of the early apartheid years, the government failed to take into account the local political dynamics of the communities it intended to help. Protests and even violent action surrounded the implementation of the community trusts. "The offices of the Chief Directorate of Sea Fisheries were occupied on more than one occasion, and [at least] two incidents of physical assault which occurred during mass action were reported by the media" (Committee of Inquiry into Fishermen's Community Trusts 1994:7). The trusts were intended to fund projects such as study bursaries, educational monies for schools, home shops, community fishing needs (e.g. freezing facilities, a tractor for moving boats, community boats), small business loans, housing material for fishing families and emergency food assistance. However, fishers accused each other of manipulating the system for personal gain. The selection of trustees became a source of conflict in many of the communities, particularly the larger communities. A committee of inquiry into these problems reported at the end of 1994 that, "It is clear to the Committee that whereas the idea had been that Fishermen's Community Trusts should be an uplifting and reconciliatory factor in the communities, improving the quality of life, in certain communities they had become a source of division resulting in a lack of trust, sowing of suspicion and even violent action" (Committee of Inquiry into Fishermen's Community Trusts 1994:32).

The designers of the Fishermen's Community Trusts soon discovered their naiveté; they had not done their sociological homework on the communities they were interested in developing. Little consideration was given to the internal power dynamics in each of these communities and how these dynamics vary from one community to the next. The Fishermen's Community Trusts were designed to use money raised from the fishing industry for improving the lives of the poorest workers in the industry. Yet, at the most fundamental level, they had not carefully defined from the outset just who the real fishers are and who should benefit. They also neglected to carefully define what they meant by "fishing community." Some of the definitional vagaries were evident from the Committee's report:

> Line fishermen undoubtedly considered themselves "real" fishermen, and it is they who suffer the most from vagaries of the weather and fluctuations in fish supply. They too are the ones who put their hands and lines into the water and wet them. In spite of this nearly all discussions indicated that all fishermen and fish factory workers should be regarded as beneficiaries of the Fishermen's Community Trusts. Boat owners and factory managers, by consensus, should be excluded. In some cases it was felt that skippers, too, should be excluded, although this negative argument was usually only put forward when there had been rumours of the possibility of some form of cash payments. (Committee of Inquiry into Fishermen's Community Trusts 1994:33)

In this report, full-time handline fishers were assumed to be the most obvious group that should fall under the category of "true fisher." But the debate raged not over who is at the core of this fishing community but over what should be the boundaries for a fishing community. Which of the more than three thousand residents of Molshoop/Struisbaai, for example, most of whom claim some connection to the much smaller local fishing industry, deserved access to the trust funds?

The fact that the most obvious beneficiaries of the trust funds sought a broad definition for the "true fisher" is evidence of their identification with a broader community of disadvantaged people in the fishing communities. Yet for the purposes of the distribution of aide from the Fishermen's Community Trusts, the consensus definition of the "true fisher" contained a strong class component. Factory labor and fish hands in other sectors of the industry were readily included on the list of those who should benefit. Persons of greater means, including those from the communities mentioned, were not considered deserving: boat owners, factory managers and even some skippers were excluded. The bond of class, in this instance, proved stronger than other macro social bonds such as race or gender.

After numerous acts of violence and a major court challenge to the distribution mechanisms of the Fishermen's Community Trusts, the South African Supreme Court ruled in 1995 that it was illegal to allocate quotas to a trust rather than to an individual. With the swipe of a constitutional pen the Trust's quotas were revoked as hastily as they were allocated.

The government strengthened its commitment to allocating marine resources to individuals and companies through the quota system in the Marine Living Resources Act of 1998. This in mind, the tendency has been for handline fishers to formally incorporate as Closed Corporations (up to 10 members) or Pty. Ltd. (up to 50 members) with the primary focus being the application for quotas from MCM. Many of these small- to medium-sized companies are direct descendents of the Fishermen's Community Trusts and have inherited more than the membership rosters. Fraught with internal conflict like their predecessors, these organizations have a frequent tendency to splinter. The South African Commercial Fishermen's Corporation (SACFC), the largest of the commercial fishing associations in the late 1990s, was established in 1995 and has since split into at least three major groups that compete against each other for members. The Helderberg Kommersiele Vissermans Vereeniging (HKVV; lit. Helderberg Commercial Fishers' Association) broke away from the main group by 1997 in an attempt to gain quotas for a more select group of fishers. The Valsbaai Vissers Ko-op, Ltd. was established in

1997 after a conflict between members over the distribution of quota allocation rights to members. According to Valsbaai Vissers Ko-op members, the split also had to do with conflicting personalities of the respective directors.

By 2000 most of the small-scale commercial ski-boat skippers on the Western Cape coast had nominally joined the SACFC and were in the process of signing up crew members. But controversy within the organized CCs and Pty. Ltds was also not uncommon. Some of the members have complained that their names are being used on company membership roles when they have never signed anything nor received any part of the profit. In 1999 there was a court case pending in Vredenburg in which members had taken legal action against the misuse of their names. The majority of the skippers interviewed for this project complained that, although they had been members of the SACFC for the past three years, they had yet to see any benefits for their membership fees. Much of the SACFC's internal controversy surrounded decisions by the leadership of the SACFC to commit themselves to the development of the infrastructure of the business at the expense of short-term returns for the shareholders. Many of the over 2,500 shareholders felt slighted as they saw the company paying large salaries to the directors, investing in company vehicles and upscale offices and hand picking the few fishers who were to benefit directly from the catch of the company quota.

Tensions in the SACFC came to a head at what was supposed to be a company-wide chairperson's meeting on August 2, 2000.[4] The tensions erupted along a complex set of fault lines, with the major cracks appearing along the lines of race and class. A couple of weeks prior to this meeting a large group of the company's shareholders, most of them fishers, marched on the company's offices in Wynberg. The company had been warned of the march, and the riot police were waiting outside the offices to prevent access to the marchers. The march prompted a company-wide chairperson's meeting. Many of the shareholders understood the chairperson's meeting to be a general meeting and were determined to have their grievances heard. The largest faction, led by a handful of white ski-boat skippers based in the Strand, brought their own lawyer to the meeting to challenge the company's distribution of quota allocations. Many of these men had met the week before in a secret meeting in Hout Bay to discuss a protest strategy. When the company would not allow this faction's lawyer into the meeting, the Strand chairmen walked out of the meeting.

As the Strand faction was walking out of the meeting, an agitated busload of over eighty fishermen from the Cape Town docks arrived, most of them black and coloured laborers from the larger fishing vessels. According to one of the chairmen, shareholders from the Cape Town dock workers' faction were upset over being denied a Christmas respite from the company back in December. They were told by the managing director that the money was needed for the company's investments in the new fishing season. Multiple attempts at receiving some financial gain from the company were met with failure. As disenchantment with the company leadership grew, protest was inevitable. When the door was slammed in the faces of those who came to protest, it sparked violence against the company and its leaders. Two directors of the SACFC, including the one black member of the board, were physically assaulted. Company property was stolen and vehicles damaged. The crowd finally dispersed with an ultimatum: the company directors were to meet with representatives from the different factions in forty-eight hours. The meeting, mediated by leaders of the Western Cape Food and Allied Worker's Union, turned out to be a continuation of the same complaints brought in the first two protests, with a similar lack of response.

The collapse of the Fisher's Community Trusts and the constant friction in the SACFC are evidence that "fisher" and "fishing community" are both heavily contested, socially constructed domains. Tensions over who is and who is not a "bona fide" fisher are magnified by competition for the limited funds available from government quotas. This debate over who classifies as a bona fide fisher is ironic, given the fact that the Marine Living Resources Act of 1998 never mentions "bona fide fishers" as a category for special consideration in the reallocation of resources. The Act set specific guidelines to increase the allocation of funds to previously disadvantaged persons in South Africa. The Introductory Provisions of the Act specifically

prioritize equity and the redistribution of resources to the historically disadvantaged:

> 2. The Minister and any organ of state shall in exercising the power under this Act, have
> regard to the following objectives and principles: …
> (d) the need to utilise marine living resources to achieve economic growth, human
> resource development, capacity building within fisheries and mariculture branches,
> employment creation and a sound ecological balance consistent with the development
> objectives of the national government; …
> (j) the need to restructure the fishing industry to address historical imbalances and to
> achieve equity within all branches of the fishing industry. (Chapter 1; Department of
> Environmental Affairs and Tourism 1998)

But nowhere does the Act explicitly state that fishers as a category deserve special consideration.

The leadership of the Artisanal Fisherman's Association and the SACFC came to recognize that

"previously disadvantaged" was more often used as a racial euphemism and was not necessarily

designed to protect historically disadvantaged fishers as such.

Even though the Living Marine Resources Act does not specifically name fishers as

priority beneficiaries of the new allocations, there is a general assumption in the coastal

communities that the most deserving historically disadvantaged persons should be those coloured

and black fishers with a history in the fishing industry. The leadership of the SACFC

intentionally filled its shareholder roles with what it thought were "bona fide" fishers, many of

them of the "previously disadvantaged" category. The Artisanal Fisher's Association has been

actively lobbying MCM for the rights of those with a history in the fishing industry. Many

fishers interviewed over the course of this research complained that government quotas were

going to individuals with no connection to the fishing industry. Furthermore, they complained

that these rights were being treated like property, bought and sold to the highest bidder for cash.

These "paper quotas," as they are now known, are a major source fueling the fires of

discontentment over the allocation of fishing rights under the new Act.

Notes

---

[1] Information on the transition from FISCOR to the Small Business Development Corporation and now to Business Partners was gained on a detailed personal interview with Anton Roelofse, the financier in charge of the fishing sector for the SBDC and Business Partners since 1988.

[2] "Riem" was also a leather strap used to control oxen when working the fields. Keeping the "riem" taught gave the handler more control over the oxen. The connection between the metaphors of fishing and the metaphors of farming can be related to the historically intimate relationship between rural farmers and fishers as discussed in detail in Van Sittert (1992).

[3] For an in-depth analysis and discussion of the various forms of ITQ systems see Sharing the Fish: Toward a National Policy on Individual Fishing Quotas (1999).

[4] The summary of these events has been reconstructed from a handful of eyewitness accounts from participants interviewed by the author.

CHAPTER 8
THE IMPACT OF RACE ON THE SOCIAL NETWORKS
OF HANDLINE FISHING SKIPPERS

Introduction

In 1651 the philosopher Hobbes noted in <u>Leviathan</u> that to have friends is power. Max Weber (1968) built on this concept more formally in his analysis of social inequalities. Weber believed that persons varied in their access to three types of resources: economic, symbolic and political. *Economic* resources consisted of the wealth and assets that allowed for further accumulation. Prestige is the central form of *symbolic* resources that Weber discussed. The social importance ascribed to different jobs can act as a measure of prestige, regardless of the income that job generates. According to Weber, *political* resources govern one's access to power. Power is the ability to control both people and goods. So it is the availability of these three types of resources and the effective use of these resources that determine one's position on the social scale. It can be argued that social capital is defined by access to a combination of these three types of resources.

Rationalistic individualist assumptions about the nature of human social relations dominate the study of economic behavior in technologically complex societies. From this perspective, society consists of an aggregate of individuals seeking to maximize their personal gain while minimizing risks to themselves. Individuals are seen as rational decision makers in a world where the pursuit of one's own interest benefits *ipso facto* the society as a whole. When taken to an extreme, individuals are reduced to cold, calculating, utilitarian monads in a highly competitive dog-eat-dog world, the so-called *Homo Economicus* (Schneider 1974). One of the most well-known proponents of these assumptions in the latter half of the twentieth century is

Milton Friedman. While Friedman and other neoclassical economists are willing to admit that these claims about humanity may be unrealistic (Friedman 1962), they believe that the absence of realism does not diminish the value of their theory primarily because it "works;" it works in the sense that it generates valid predictions.

The structural analysis inherent in social network analysis assumes that at one level, norms in thought and behavior arise from the positions that individuals or groups occupy in the context of the whole. "Norms arise from the structural position of individuals or groups, because this position is sufficient to determine the opportunities and constraints which influence the allocation of resources and to explain the behavioural regularities observed" (Degenne and Forse 1999:2). Most researchers interested in the systematic study of social structure rely on the macro-analysis of attributional data aggregated across individuals or groups. Network analysis relies on relational data. Relational data "are the contacts, ties and connections, the group attachments and meetings, which relate one agent to another and so cannot be reduced to the properties of the individual agent themselves" (Scott 1991:4). In the 1950s John Barnes followed Radcliffe-Browne's lead from the 1930s and since then an increasing number of researchers have developed ever more sophisticated models to analyze network relations.

For the most part, anthropologists have shied away from structural analysis in part due to the assumption that its development remains stunted, stuck in the static theories of 1940s and 1950s social anthropology. Social network analysis does not rely on the nomothetic structures imposed on societies by distant researchers. Instead, structure is allowed to emerge from the measurement of actual or perceived relations in specific situations. By measuring concrete relations, or the way people perceive themselves to be related, we can explain why some people have easier access to information and resources than others. Current research in social networks has moved far beyond the limited study of dyads, the links between two people, and has expanded the analysis to include the complex interaction between individuals, dyads, sub-groups and groups.

One does not have to be committed exclusively to the principles of structural analysis in order to make effective use of these structural tools. Individuals' choices are constrained, not absolutely limited, by the others with whom they choose to associate. The picture painted by these structural tools can often be interpreted in different ways. These structural tools and the pictures they paint (or the graphs they draw) would remain meaningless without strong historical and ethnographic research. It is not my intention to explore the many methodological questions about social networks that are raised and, at times, answered by my research. Instead, I use social network analysis as a tool to better understand race relations in the handline fishing industry on South Africa's Western Cape coast.

Figure 21. Commercial Handline Ski-Boat Fishers Returning from a Day at Sea
source: author

The success of a commercial handline skipper depends on more than just his lone ability to find and catch a lot of fish. These skippers operate in dense networks of professional support.

A skipper must be adept at owning and/or controlling the boat, managing finances and personnel, finding and hiring good crew, finding the right buyers with the highest prices, and finding out just where the fish are biting in any particular week. In other words, the skippers are dependent on information sharing networks to improve the likelihood of their success. There are certainly other major constraints on a captain's ability to provide enough work for himself and his crew, the most obvious reasons being the uncertainty of the physical environment (e.g. weather and ocean conditions), the uncertainty of the location of migratory species and the technology available to the skipper. Variations in the individual ability to manage ecological constraints will not be measured here. But even the ability to manage ecological constraints can be aided by a large, dense network of other professionals willing to share their knowledge. For the handline skippers, the availability of crucial technology does not vary significantly from one skipper to another.

One of the most important resources social networks provide is information (Granovetter 1985). Trust and reciprocity are important components when critical information is involved. In the case of handline ski-boat fishing on South Africa's Western Cape coast, skippers rely on each other for critical information that influences all aspects of their work. They call trusted colleagues in their network for information, like if the weather in a particular area is conducive to fishing, what prices hawkers are paying on the open market, what crew they should pick up on the harbor that morning and, most importantly, where the fish are biting. Regardless of the common myth that commercial fishers are rugged individualists throwing caution to the wind, skippers constantly minimize risk to their health and their livelihood through their social networks. They rely on others that do the same type of work they do (Pollnac, Poggie and Vandusen 1995; Pollnac, Poggie and Cabral 1998). Therefore, one of the most important questions among the name generators used in this project was Name Generator 9: "When it comes to information you need that will enable you to catch more fish or get higher prices for your fish, who are the skippers that you contact for important information?" Skippers were asked to limit their responses to those skippers that fit the criteria for this study, i.e., full-time commercial handline ski-boat skippers who traveled between Lambert's Bay and Arniston. This information network forms the core of the names used for analysis of the whole/global network. The names retrieved from the other generators, combined with the skipper name generator, are used in calculations of the ego-network data.

Global Network Representation

Introduction

Once relational data have been collected, it must be related in the form of a data matrix for the purposes of network analysis. A typical anthropological data matrix is a respondent by variable matrix. A respondent by variable matrix is described as rectangular, as the columns and rows are independent from each other. A single rectangular matrix can then be transformed into two square matrices, one describing the columns and the other describing the rows. In this research I am most interested in the respondent-by-respondent matrix, often called the actor-by-actor matrix. Formally known as an adjacency matrix, most techniques in network analysis involve the manipulation of relational data via these square matrices. For this research a list of alters was generated for each skipper, carefully noting which generator was used for generating each name. Characteristics of each alter were then collected so as to make an alter-by-attribute rectangular data matrix for each skipper. For the global network, alter names were replaced with id codes from the list of skippers in the network, where appropriate. The global network statistics were run on the names generated by name generators 1–6 and 8–11. Names derived from Name Generator 7 were omitted for future analysis as this generator was designed to test negative ties. Name Generator 12 was specifically designed to obtain information about a skipper's current crew, regardless of whether they were mentioned in their general friendship or professional networks.

Table 15. Sample Matrix Representing Skipper x Skipper Network

	Skipper 1	Skipper 2	Skipper 3	Skipper 4	Skipper 5	Skipper 6
Skipper 1	X	1	1	1	1	0
Skipper 2	1	X	1	1	1	1
Skipper 3	1	1	X	1	1	0
Skipper 4	1	1	1	X	0	0
Skipper 5	0	1	0	0	X	0
Skipper 6	0	1	0	0	0	X

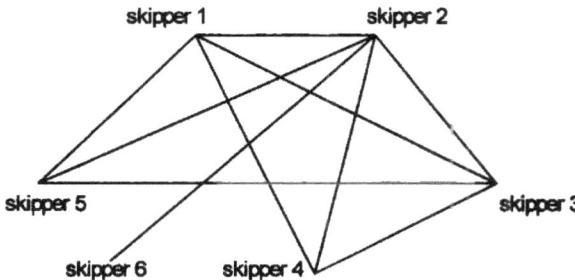

Figure 22. Sociogram for Sample Skipper x Skipper Network

Table 15 and Figure 22 represent a simple example of the more complex network analysis to be discussed later. In this example, skippers 4, 5 and 6 are relatively more peripheral to the network than the others; they have fewer overall connections. Skipper 6, called an outlier, is connected to the network only through skipper 2. Any information that flows through the network, e.g. where the fish are biting, would be less likely to reach the less connected individuals or would reach them slower than the rest. If skipper 6 were the one with the important information, the rest of the network would be dependent on skipper 2 for that information.

Global Network Properties

One of the easier ways to analyze dynamics in the entire network is to display it graphically. Multidimentional scaling (MDS) is one of the techniques appropriate for representing the proximity of actors in a network. "Multidimensional scaling seeks to represent proximities (similarities or dissimilarities) among a set of entities in low-dimensional space so that entities that are more proximate to each other in the input data are closer in the space, and entities that are less proximate to each other are farther apart in space" (Wasserman and Faust 1994:288). The distances between actors should not be taken as physical distance separating actors but as the representation of the distance of each actor in the communications network. MDS can then be used to see who is most central to the group and if there are any major subgroups or outliers.

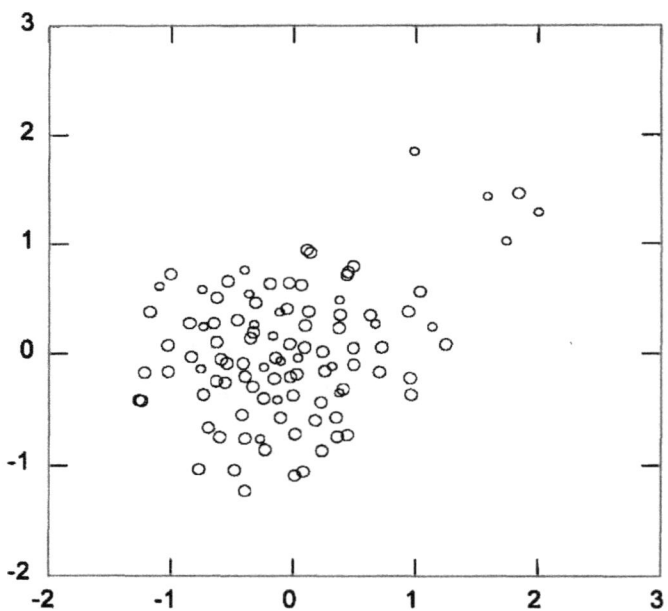

Figure 23. Multi-Dimensional Scaling Scatterplot of Proximity of Skippers in Network
source: SYSTAT (1998) output

Notice that most of the skippers cluster in one big group. Subgroups would be difficult to analyze given just this central group. But the more interesting data to be gleaned from this graph is the five outliers in the northeast quadrant of the graph. Two of the outliers are white, one of whom is a retired skipper who claims not to be connected to anyone in the network. This graph confirms that likely no one else mentioned him in their network either. The other skipper classified as white was an interesting exception to the racial categories. When asked what race he was classified under apartheid, he replied: "Portuguese." Other skippers mentioned the "Portuguese" skipper in my conversations with them, but no one included him in their network. This skipper admitted that most of his network was outside the handline fishing industry; he had a number of relatives who owned fish shops and worked at the management level in other fishing enterprises.

The three coloured skippers identified as outliers by this graph each have an interesting ethnographic explanation for their distance from the group. One of the three was identified by many of the other skippers as a boat full of "skollies" (roughnecks) with a reputation for violence, drugs and theft. One skipper said that when that particular boat was in town, everyone knew it was time to lock up the electronic equipment on the boat and in the bakkies. One of the other two coloured skippers identified as outliers has a boat that he operates for his father's fishing wholesale business. He was adamant that he works with no one else because he trusts no one else. The final coloured skipper identified as an outlier was geographically the most distant from the rest of the group. Admitting that he traveled the West Coast in search of snoek, by looking at his lack of contacts in the industry it is likely that his networks are situated more closely to where he lives. The town he lives in is also well-known for its subsistence and local fisheries, which would support the theory that his contacts are most likely more local.

Cliques

One way of finding cohesive subgroups in a whole network is through the formal analysis of cliques. A clique consists of a subset of actors who are directly connected to each other, and no other actors are adjacent to all of the others in the same clique. "One can think of a clique as a collection of actors all of whom 'choose' each other, and there is no other actor in the group who also 'chooses' and is 'chosen' by all of the members of the clique" (Wasserman and Faust 1998:254). Cliques in a graph may overlap. The same actor or group of actors can belong to more than one clique. However, no clique can be contained within another clique. As used for the purpose of formal network analysis, a clique is a strict mathematical way of defining a cohesive subgroup (see figure 24). For the purposes of this global analysis of the skipper network, the assumption is that the ties between skippers are non-directional. In other words, when one skipper mentioned another, the relationship is assumed to be mutual.

cliques: {1,2,3}, {1,3,5}, {2,3,4,7} and {3,4,5,6}

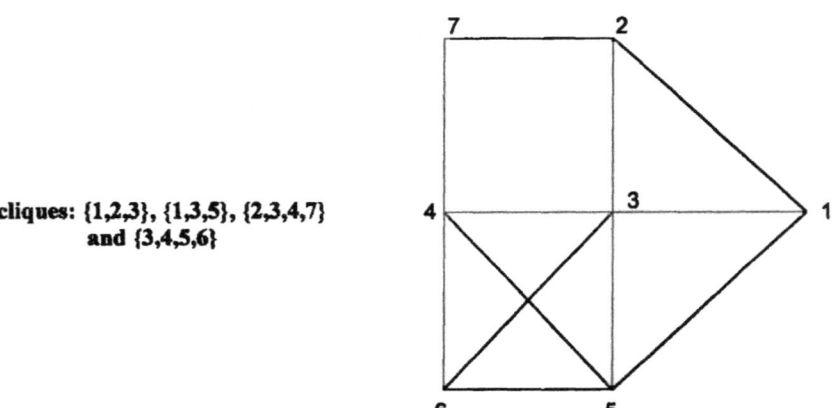

Figure 24. A Graph and Its Cliques

Analysis of the network data was facilitated by UCINET (Borgatti, Everett and Freeman 1999). When analyzing cliques it is important to set the minimum group size that you want to consider a clique. Analyzing a minimum group size of two or three would be ethnographically uninteresting. In a network of 102 people, it is highly likely that most individuals would be in one clique or another at that level, and the patterning would be lost. In the interviews skippers reported that they most often only work with a handful of other skippers. Using their judgement as an ethnographic approximation for group size, I ran the analysis of cliques with a minimum size of four skippers to a group. The following is a list of the sixteen cliques found through a Ucinet procedure (Bron and Kerbosch 1973).

Cliques in the Skipper Network:

Minimum size = 4
16 Cliques found (Skipper ID_W = white; Skipper ID_C = coloured):

1: Skipper 3_W; Skipper 9_W; Skipper 13_W; Skipper 78_W; Skipper 89_W
2: Skipper 9_W; Skipper 13_W; Skipper 43_W; Skipper 78_W; Skipper 89_W
3: Skipper 9_W; Skipper 13_W; Skipper 62_W; Skipper 78_W
4: Skipper 11_C; Skipper 13_W; Skipper 78_W; Skipper 83_C
5: Skipper 13_W; Skipper 35_W; Skipper 62_W; Skipper 78_W
6: Skipper 13_W; Skipper 35_W; Skipper 78_W; Skipper 83_C
7: Skipper 3_W; Skipper 13_W; SKIPPER 72_W; Skipper 78_W
8: Skipper 13_W; SKIPPER 72_W; Skipper 78_W; Skipper 102_W
9: Skipper 8_W; Skipper 13_W; Skipper 32_W; Skipper 101_W
10: Skipper 7_W; Skipper 12_C; Skipper 19_C; Skipper 94_C
11: Skipper 10_W; Skipper 30_W; Skipper 56_W; Skipper 89_W
12: Skipper 12_C; Skipper 19_C; Skipper 42_C; Skipper 94_C
13: Skipper 23_W; Skipper 34_W; SKIPPER 38_W; Skipper 78_W
14: Skipper 23_W; SKIPPER 38_W; Skipper 78_W; Skipper 98_W
15: Skipper 23_W; SKIPPER 38_W; Skipper 98_W; Skipper 99_W
16: Skipper 53_W; Skipper 55_W; Skipper 63_W; Skipper 93_C
Source: UCINET output; Borgatti, Everett and Freeman (1999)

The racial patterning in these subgroups is not surprising. Of the sixteen cliques found in the skipper's network, 81% (13) consists solely or predominantly of white skippers. Only 12.5% of the cliques consisted solely or predominantly of coloured skippers. One of the cliques had an even number of coloured and white skippers. With 70% of the skippers being white, you would expect the groupings to be dominated by white skippers. What is interesting is how the patterning is in part determined by geographic proximity and family ties. A full 87% (14/16) of the cliques has at least two members of the clique who are members of the same family. This confirms information given by the skippers that emphasized the close family relations in the industry. Brothers tended to have networks that were similar. As there are no inter-racial families in the network, the racially exclusive nature of the cliques could also be influenced by the strength of family ties.

Table 16. Single-Link Hierarchical Clustering

```
race    W W W C W W W W W W W W W W W W C W W W W W
        1                                       1 1
        0   1 1 3 3 3 4 5   3 2 3 6 7   7 1 8 8 9 9 0 0
Level   0 8 0 1 0 2 4 8 6 3 5 3 8 2 2 9 8 3 3 9 8 9 1 2
-----   - - - - - - - - - - - - - - - - - - - - - - - -
   8    . . . . . . . . . . . . . . . . XXX . . . . . .
   3    . . . . . . . . . . . XXX . . XXXXX . . . . . .
   2    . . . . . . . . . XXXXXXXXXXXXXXXXXXXXX . . .
   1    . XXXXXXXXXXXXXXXXXXXXXXXXXXXXXXXXXXXXXXXXXXXXXX
   0    XXXXXXXXXXXXXXXXXXXXXXXXXXXXXXXXXXXXXXXXXXXXXX
```
source: UCINET 5 output

The structure of the cliques can be further illuminated by an analysis of the number of times each pair of actors is in the same clique. Based upon this information, UCINET provides a single link hierarchical clustering that allows for a visual analysis of these pairs (Borgatti, Everett and Freeman 1999). Hierarchical clustering partitions actors that are similar to each other when compared to the entire group. Each of the skippers is then placed on the graph, a portion of which is represented in Table 16. I have included only the significant partitions in the table. The hierarchical clustering confirms the importance of family connections in the skipper-by-skipper network. The skippers analyzed as most closely related in the network, or most similar by this hierarchical clustering method (in each case highlighted by bold X's), are two of the four sets of brothers out of the group.

Network Centrality

Skippers in the network vary on how central they are to the network. The most effective work on centrality in social networks has been done by Lin Freeman (1979). There are various perspectives on what constitutes centrality in a network. I have chosen to represent centrality by the comparative use of three different measurements: Degree Centrality, Betweenness Centrality and Closeness Centrality. Marsden reports that "degree based measures (in essence, network size) focus on levels of communication activity; "betweenness" measures stress control or the capacity to interrupt communcation; and "closeness" measures reflect freedom from the control of others" (1990:454).

Degree centrality is the simplest and most intuitive variation of centrality measures. It measures an individual's centrality according to the number of connections that one individual has to others. Central individuals have strong connections to other individuals in the group, while peripheral individuals do not. With this technique, centrality is calculated by measuring the number of alters to which ego is connected.

Table 17. Skippers with the Highest Degree Centrality

ID	Race	Rank	Degree	NrmDegree
13	W	1	20	19.802
78	W	2	20	19.802
89	W	3	17	16.832
98	W	4	14	13.861
95	W	5	13	12.871
14	W	6	12	11.881
48	W	7	12	11.881
62	W	8	12	11.881
93	C	9	12	11.881
101	W	10	12	11.881

Source: UCINET 5 output

For this study, the degree centrality measurement of an individual skipper reveals which skippers have the most amount of contacts in the information sharing network with other skippers. The two skippers with the highest degree centrality are central players in the town with the most popular harbor, Yzerfontein. Many of the skippers rely on information from them to decide if they should risk the cost of travelling the long coastal road to get there for a day's fishing. Third on the list is a skipper who is a central player in the major fisherman's association, the South African Commercial Fisherman's Corporation (SACFC).

Betweenness centrality measures the extent to which a particular point lies between the various other points in the graph. Betweenness centrality acts as a caution against ignoring the intermediary role that actors play in a network; someone may not have the highest number of connections in the network (as measured by degree centrality), but they may connect a larger number of other pairs of actors. "The betweenness of a point measures the extent to which an agent can play the part of a 'broker' or 'gatekeeper' with a potential for control over others" (Scott 1991:89–90).

Table 18. Skippers with the Highest Betweenness Centrality

ID	Race	Rank	Between	nBetween
13	W	1	586.927	11.622
93	C	2	556.045	11.011
95	W	3	513.702	10.172
78	W	4	458.224	9.074
89	W	5	451.227	8.935
98	W	6	421.843	8.353
62	W	7	322.685	6.39
14	W	8	301.667	5.974
85	C	9	294.962	5.841
48	W	10	281.844	5.581

Source: UCINET 5 output

It is interesting to note that the only coloured skipper ranked high in degree centrality is ranked even higher in betweenness centrality. This particular skipper, one of the skippers who lives in suburban Cape Town, is well connected to a number of different subgroups. It is also interesting to note that the top six skippers are each leading skippers by reputation from each of four different regions, Yzerfontein, Cape Town's southern suburbs, the Strand, and the Stompneusbaai/St. Helena regions. This finding continues to support the conclusion that despite the overall mobility of the skippers, skippers from the same region tend to band together for support.

Closeness is a more global measure of centrality that measures a skipper's closeness to members of the network as a whole, not just to his immediate ties. This means that the indirect ties are also taken into account. The assumption for this measure is that an individual is more central if that individual can interact quicker with others. "Actors occupying central locations with respect to *closeness* can be very productive in communicating information to the other actors. If the actors in a set of actors are engaged in problem solving, and the focus is on communication links, efficient solutions occur when one actor has very short communication paths to the others" (Wasserman and Faust 1994:183–184).

Table 19. Skippers Closeness Centrality

ID	Race	Rank	Farness	nCloseness
13	W	1	813	12.423
78	W	2	814	12.408
89	W	3	821	12.302
14	W	4	828	12.198
95	W	5	829	12.183
48	W	6	834	12.11
98	W	7	834	12.11
62	W	8	840	12.024
10	W	9	841	12.01
56	W	10	844	11.967

Source: UCINET 5 output

Skippers with the highest closeness ranking will be more likely to find out important information in the network earlier than others, even when news travels throughout the entire network. In a business where the early skipper catches the fish, early notification is crucial. It is interesting to note that none of the coloured skippers are among skippers with the highest closeness. There are only four coloured skippers ranked in the top 40% in closeness, while over half of the skippers measuring with the lowest 40% in closeness are coloured. While coloured skippers have the reputation for being the better skippers with the most experience, they are being marginalized in the spread of information.

Race and the Structure of Ego Networks

Ego-centered network analysis is the study of the ties that are centered around an individual. "An ego-centered network consists of a focal actor, termed *ego*, and a set of alters who have ties to ego, and measurements on the ties among these alters" (Wasserman and Faust 1994:42). The graphical representation of these networks most approximates a star, with nodes radiating from a central point. Summary properties can be gathered on the actors and the alters and compared. Comparisons can be run on the actors by summarizing the alter data down to an attribute of the skipper. For example, the average number of ties among the skippers interviewed for this study was nineteen for coloured skippers and twenty for white skippers, not a statistically significant difference. But through careful collection of data on the attributes of both skippers and their alters, significant conclusions can be made about the composition of their personal networks as they compare to each other. A significant difference in this study compared to other ego-centered network studies is that subjects were not randomly selected to generalize to some known population. Instead, an entire network was identified and ego network data was collected on the entire network. Collection of the ego-centered network data provided answers and insight for the research questions and hypotheses posed in the methodology section. Analyzing how the composition of networks varied by race provided significant results, the core of which is reported here.

If networks serve as the conduit of information and resources, knowing what social factors affect the structure and content of these networks will reveal the potential and the constraints these social factors place on the transfer of information and resources. One of the key issues for this study has been the effect that race has on the social networks of the skippers studied. The first major question to be answered is: What kinds of individuals are more likely to be involved in social networks of greater racial heterogeneity? In other words, what factors lead an individual to communicate and associate with persons of the same racial category, and what factors lead an individual to communicate and associate with persons of a different category. Taken in the context of the handline fishing industry, the analysis takes the form of a comparison between white and coloured skippers and the similarities and differences in their ego-networks.

Among the skippers of the handline fishing industry on South Africa's Western Cape Coast, the race of the skipper seems to be the strongest determinant of the racial make-up of his social network, both professional and personal. Skippers tend to go to others racially like themselves when they want to share intimate information with friends, when they want to share general information with people that are close to them, and when they want to share important job information with colleagues. Name generators were used to elicit various kinds of networks for each skipper, including one generator for their friendship networks, three generators for their personal networks and seven generators for their professional networks.

I hypothesized in Chapter 2 that education will have no significant effect on the racial heterogeneity of social networks. As it turns out, there is a very strong correlation between race and education (.58). The average formal years of education for coloured skippers, at 8.1 years, is significantly lower than for white skippers, who have an average 11.5 years. The effect that education has on the network can, for the most part, be seen as a proxy for race. The national disparities in the education system between whites and non-whites in South Africa are reflected in the population of handline skippers. There is one notable observation in regard to the influence of education on the social networks of the handline skippers. When attempting to predict the racial make-up of skippers' total networks by including race, the years they had relied on being a handline skipper, the years of experience they had in fishing, their age and their education, race was a highly significant predictor and far more predictive than any other variable. Education remained the only other significant variable, at the .05 level. This means that, after controlling for race, education still had a significant predictive value on the racial make-up of the social network. The higher the level of education, the more likely the skipper was to have whites in their network, regardless of that skipper's race. Since whites have a significantly higher average number years of education, this may simply point to the fact that after you account for race, those with similar levels of education will tend to associate with one another more frequently. However, race proves to be more important than education in determining the racial composition of social networks.

I hypothesized in Chapter 2 that age would have no significant effect on the racial heterogeneity of social networks. In fact, this proves to be the case. There is no significant age difference between coloured and white skippers, with whites averaging around 39.1 years and coloureds averaging around 42.5 years.

The next hypothesis I made in Chapter 2 predicted that skippers with a racially heterogeneous personal network would also have a racially heterogeneous professional network. It turns out that personal networks for both white and coloured skippers are less heterogeneous than their professional networks. The difference turns out to be statistically significant for both coloured and white skippers. Skippers are more likely to turn to same-race alters when personal matters are at stake than when professional information is needed. This difference in the percentages between personal and friendship networks can be explained by the high number of family members that were included in the personal name generators 1 and 2, but were excluded by design from the friendship name generator, number 2. None of the skippers reported family members that were not of the same race they claimed to be; therefore family ties would necessarily increase the homogeneity of the network.

Table 20. Percentage of Same-Race Ties in Skipper's Social Networks

	Friendship	Personal	Professional	Entire Network
Coloured	88%	92%	65%	82%
White	91%	94%	88%	91%

Coloured skippers regularly go outside the skipper network for job-related information. And, according to the interviews, white skippers are doing the same thing. What is more interesting to note is the significant difference in the racial composition of coloured and white professional networks. In Chapter 2 I hypothesized that skippers categorized as coloured will be more likely to have racially heterogeneous professional networks than friendship networks and that there will be no significant difference in the racial composition between the personal and professional networks. White skippers will be less likely to have racially heterogeneous professional networks. Both of these hypotheses turned out to be true. The economic advantages that whites have over coloureds in South Africa make it likely that those with lower socioeconomic status would seek information and resources from those who have been at an advantage. As is clear in the handline ski-boat industry, ownership of the boats is highly skewed in favor of whites. A significantly higher number of the hired skippers are coloured. The access to resources is strongly predicted by race. If the networks that provide access to these resources continue to be strongly skewed by race, access to resources will continue to be highly skewed.

The final hypothesis of the first research question posed in Chapter 2 was that there will be no significant difference in the racial heterogeneity of friendship networks between different racial categories. This has turned out to be the case for these skippers. On average 88% of coloured skipper's closest friends were coloured and 92% of the white skippers friends were white.

It is interesting to note that, in general, coloured skippers identify people in their network closer to themselves than white skippers do. When asked to rate the alters they mentioned on a scale from 1–4 with 1 being "distant," 2 being "less close," 3 being "close" and 4 being "especially close," coloured skippers rated their average tie at 2.5, statistically significantly different from what white skippers rated their average tie. Closeness is also significantly positively correlated with age, meaning that the older the skipper, the closer they were likely to rate members of their social network. Across the board, skippers understandably rated their personal and friendship networks closer than their professional networks.

Table 21. Average Closeness of Ties in Skipper's Social Networks

	Friendship	Personal	Professional	Entire Network
Coloured	3.4	3.6	3.0	2.5
White	3.2	3.4	2.9	2.1

Building on the work done by Ooka and Wellman, it is assumed that people make use of both inter- and intra-racial ties for accessing important job-related information. "The advantages (or disadvantages) of working in an ethnic economy or ethnic niches depend on the resources that particular ethnic groups can mobilize through their co-ethnic networks" (1999:3). Even though the majority of workers in the fishing industry tend to be coloured, for the handline skippers the most important information for their job comes from other skippers. Inter-ethnic ties have been shown to be advantageous, particularly for developing entrepreneurs (Cobas, Aikin and Jardine 1993). Entrepreneurs can increase their opportunities by making use of important ties outside "co-ethnic networks," particularly with persons of higher status ethnic groups.

When beginning this research I wondered to what extent individuals use inter- as opposed to intra-racial ties for accessing important job-related information. I hypothesized that members of historically low status racial groups (i.e., coloureds in this case) would be more likely to use inter-racial than intra-racial ties for obtaining important job information. Conversely, I hypothesized that members of historically high status racial groups (i.e., whites in this case) would be more likely to use intra-racial as opposed to inter-racial ties for obtaining job information. The results of this network study show that both coloured and white skippers use intra-racial ties to a greater extent than they use inter-racial ties for obtaining important job-related information, but coloured do so significantly less. Coloured skippers are more likely to go to whites for job-related information than white skippers are to go to coloured members of their social networks.

When I began this research I also thought that the longer a skipper was in the business, the more likely he would be to use inter-racial ties. There turned out to be no significant relationship between tenure in the fishing industry and the use of inter-racial ties to obtain job-related information.

Following Portes et al (1995) I have proven here that age itself is not a significant determinant of the racial heterogeneity of social networks. Historically disadvantaged racial and ethnic groups in South Africa (e.g. black or coloured) still face systemic racism. For example, systemic racism still affects the education levels of the general population. Persons from disadvantaged groups are more likely to use diverse networks to gain access to the information and resources available through the networks of the advantaged. Conversely, persons from historically advantaged communities (i.e., white) will be more likely to use densely knit, tightly bounded social networks to maintain benefits they already have. Friendship networks are more socially conservative than professional networks and will thus be more homogenous regardless of how ego classifies herself and others.

CHAPTER 9
CONCLUSION

Broader Streams of Influence

I've always found it important to place my research in the context of the important work being done in the field of social history. Much of my work has been influenced by the academic world of social history. My dissertation forms the beginnings of what will potentially be a more developed social history. Although my work is neither as broad in scope nor as ambitious as the works of social historians like Shula Marks, Kaletso Atkins, Iris Berger or Charles van Onselen, my work is in part indebted to their example. In Threads of Solidarity (1992), Berger explored how South African women shaped and were shaped by their work in the factories. She showed how important the relationship was between factory, family and community. She examined what options were available and what limitations were placed on women in the garment industry. Consistently she pointed out the multiplicity of roles and responsibilities required of women as they were expected not only to excel as employees, but also as mothers, as community leaders, as wives, as house-workers, as heads of households and a range of other roles that allowed them to be involved simultaneously at work, at home and in the community. Berger teased out the complex relationship between race, class and gender, and at no place did she collapse the categories or oversimplify the relationship. This work follows her lead by providing the social and historical context for the development of inter-racial relationships in the handline fishing industry. The profound power of socially constructed race relations is all the more evident when the structures and ideas that support that power are explained.

In all of the works scholars of South African labor history have produced, few have attempted to excavate the ideological artifacts that provide flesh and blood to the dry bones of political and economic analysis. My work is intended to contribute to these artifacts in ethnographic fashion. In The Moon is Dead! Now Give us our Money (1993), Kaletso Atkins attempted to unearth the role that cultural differences played in the construction of an African working class in South Africa in the second half of the nineteenth century. Focusing her attention on the notion of an "African work ethic," she traced the development not only of the African working class itself, but also examined the motivations, the attitudes and the beliefs that informed the different perspectives of this working class. I have zoomed the analytical focal length in on the motivations, attitudes and beliefs of the working class in South Africa's commercial fishing industry with a particular aim of understanding how race structures relationships.

Atkins debunked the myth of the "lazy kaffir" and proved that there was indeed a strong work ethic among African workers (1986). In contrast to much of the liberal scholarship that had preceded her, Atkins focused her analytical lens on the common worker, not the African elite. Like Van Onselen in The Seed is Mine (1996), she explored the rhythms of daily life. Atkins described more than a series of events in the lives of individuals or groups. She attempted to describe the social and intellectual milieu behind a range of legislative and social inequalities. I have attempted to do the same in regard to handline fishers. She showed how uninformed biases and prejudices formed the motivating force behind the creation of a negative image of African workers. The core argument of The Moon is Dead is best summarized in her concluding remarks: "Whites created the "lazy Kafirs" by believing them real... Then, after saddling the African with a string of negative misattributes and having thoroughly vilified his actual nature, they set out to refashion—profoundly—*that which never objectively existed in the first place* into what they thought the black man ought to be" (1986:144). My work has shown how the image of the "Cape Coloured fisher" was similarly constructed by persons both within and outside the fishing industry.

Shula Marks explored the complex interrelatedness of individual psychology and a culture bounded social order in Not Either an Experimental Doll (Moya, Palmer and Marks 1985). Here she explored the bond between three South African women from three different social backgrounds. While she depicted each of the three women as strong and independent thinkers, she also showed how their actions were limited by the norms of the greater South African social milieu. Much like the social anthropologists writing in the first half of the twentieth century, Marks emphasized the overarching constraints that social structure places on human agency. While we get a glimpse of the intimate and personal worlds of three South Africa women, Marks is careful to point out how the tentacles of structural inequality reached into the heart of human relationships. For example, even those like Mabel who were considered "friends of the natives," those with liberal sensibilities and generous intentions, could or did do little to improve the situation for blacks at the midpoint of the twentieth century. Rather than lay the blame for the inequities at any of the three women's feet, Marks carefully elaborates on the complex struggles each faced trying to survive in an environment hostile to an educated woman and hostile to interracial relationships that may improve the plight of even one young black girl. The myths of racial difference continue to weigh down the development of inter-racial relationships in South Africa, as was evident from the relationships between the handline skippers. Beliefs about the proper social hierarchy continue to exclude some skippers from communications networks that would greatly increase their opportunities for social mobility.

With painstaking ethnographic detail, Van Onselen retold South Africa's story of dominance and resistance, of paternalism and those who reacted against it through the life of Kas Maine (1996). Much like I have shown to be the case in the commercial fishing industry, he showed how the beginning of the twentieth century was a time of relative freedom of movement and economic activity for non-Whites. The paternalism of colonial rulers and unionists allowed for greater freedom for rural Blacks than did apartheid law; apartheid eroded even the smallest of advantages that could be taken. This can be read in any modern historical work on South Africa.

What makes Van Onselen's treatment of the theme of paternalism so strong is his willingness to examine the complexity of the social and economic relations within and between dominant and subordinate groups. He described paternalism as "part chain, part umbilical cord" (1996:289). This type of paternalism was clearly evident among the commercial handline skippers, as was evidenced by what they said and the way they constructed their social networks. As the power relations continue to shift between different racial groups in South Africa, it will be important to track how these shifts affect how relationships are constructed.

Van Onselen tracked how interracial friendships were formed in the midst of alienation (1996). The relationship between landowner (or manager) and sharecropper was shown to have been one of interdependence. While there is no doubt that the sharecropper received only a small portion of the proceeds, the property owners relied on skilled labor to extract the optimum from the land. Kas was able to sharecrop for the majority of his lifetime, even though it had been illegal since 1913. Van Onselen argued that sharecropping allowed for relationships that transcended their economic contracts. In this sense, sharecropping can be compared to the modern handline fishing industry. "Poor Afrikaners emerged from the comparative seclusion of [their] shared experience far more "Africanised" than their protestations would lead one to believe, while better-off Africans were far more "Afrikanerised" than cultural purists are willing to concede" (1996:7–8). Coloured and white skippers shared the same level of mutual influence. Van Onselen explored the diversity of class relations among Afrikaners as well as among the "Africans," showing varying degrees of interactions between Whites and Blacks at different class levels. I have tried to do the same.

Implications for Marine and Coastal Management

One of the areas of fruitful future research that this research points to is in the area of fisheries management. As the South African government continues to struggle with what it means to equitably redistribute resources, they will need the kind of ethnographically informed research to support the implementation of their redistribution plans. Racial categories can serve as symbols around which political and economic resources can be mobilized. Conversely, ethnic and racial categories can also serve as ways to exclude others from access to resources. Such a misuse of these categories of human difference divided South Africans during more than four decades of apartheid. In his study of the impact of apartheid legislation on Indian workers, Freund noted that, "a striking feature of the industrial economy of Durban is the conjuncture of occupation and ethnicity, of jobs and race" (1995:52). Such racial and ethnic segmentation served to help some carve a political and economic niche for themselves in a hierarchy increasingly defined by race and ethnicity. Slaves and indentured servants from India were initially brought in to work the sugar plantations in Natal but eventually South Africans of Indian descent dominated the food and textile industries in major industrial centers like Durban. "Such segmentation helps to define ethnicity, as well as to be determined by it, in the circumstance of a competitive labour market" (Freund 1995:52). In the Western Cape, the fishing industry has historically been associated with coloured workers. Coloured and white families populate the fishing communities all along the Cape coast. Socialization into the fishing community has largely remained along these racial lines. The levels of access that coloured and white fishers have to the allocated resources in the commercial industry remain determined in large part by racial category.

It will be difficult for the South African government to move beyond the politics of race. "Despite the absence of a government mandate to implement race-based preferences, affirmative action is central to the organizational politics and policy of South Africa's social, economic, and governmental institutions" (Price 1997:145). In the fishing industry, affirmative action or "regstellende aksie" (lit. corrective action) as Mamphele Ramphele (1996) has called it, takes the form of the reallocation of fishing quotas. The "transformation" language that is used by Marine and Coastal management and the ruling party is vague and does not guarantee those with an historic stake in the industry a piece of the new pie.

Robert Price argued that the affirmative action policies in South Africa elevates the

salience of race to levels inconsistent with the non-racial platform established when the ANC

came to power in 1994.

> It is not just the White-Black racial divide whose salience is heightened by affirmative
> action policy, but race consciousness is also elevated among Coloureds and Indians.
> Members of these groups worry that they will be unjustly ignored in the granting of
> preferences and that their opportunities for advancement will shrink as a result of
> preferences granted to Africans (Price 1997:145)

Combine the fear that coloureds will be caught between the economic dominance of

whites and the political power of blacks with the lack of commitment from the government to

reallocate quotas to those historically involved in fishing and it is easy to see why the coloured

fishermen in the handline industry have no hope for significant social mobility.

Coloured fishers fear that they will be lost in the reallocation process. One of the rural

coloured skipper shared his fear of being left out of the new benefits in South Africa:

> I'm coloured, but that was an apartheid name. Coloured means that you were always
> disadvantaged. I don't feel like I'm a citizen of this country, particularly because of how
> we are being denied quotas. Other people feel we are left out too. The country functions
> only between the whites and the blacks. Coloureds in the southern Cape are at a
> particular disadvantage when it comes to quotas. If you look at the list of quota holders,
> you see only white and black businesses.

In a sense, a move toward class-based affirmative action programs would dissipate some

of the motivation for developing race-based institutions and organizations. But in the fishing

industry, the discrimination of apartheid affected coloured fishers more than any other group,

simply because there were more coloureds than any other population group in the fishing

industry.

The government's decision to use the allocation of quotas as the primary means of

redistribution in the fishing industry neglects the needs of the small, entrepreneurial operations

that provide the bedrock economy for rural fishing communities and for large networks of historic

fishing families that have never had access to the industrial sector. Many of the white skippers

came into the ski-boat handline industry with a nest-egg, with a measure of start-up capital from a previous job. Due to historic discrimination and institutional racism, many coloured skippers never had the opportunity to develop that capital base. In addition to the double-bind that coloured skippers feel due to their race, those that are handline ski-boat operators face their own double-bind when it comes to the allocation of quotas. Most of the skippers and owners are independent operators and do not have the infrastructure to manage a quota if it did come their direction. Their operations are small enough to fall under the fiduciary radar of banks and government loan programs, but they are too large to qualify for subsistence permits. As it is, those that are able to subsidize their fishing from other sources of income are the most likely to survive.

There have been some positive steps taken in the past year to assist the small-scale operators. Subsistence permits were allocated to individuals in small, disadvantaged fishing communities on the southern and western Cape coast. The government also funded an extensive sociological survey of coastal communities in an attempt to identify the needs of fishers in those communities (Clark 2000). The Subsistence Fisheries Task Group recommended to Marine and Coastal Management that they create a new category of fishers, a small-scale commercial category, in their management structure that could capture the type of business these handline ski-boat skippers operate (Clark 2000). The creation of such a category, accompanied by access to micro-loans or small business seed money, would legitimize the industry and provide a significant increase in security for hundreds of fishers along the coast.

According to researchers funded by South Africa's Marine and Coastal Management, the South African linefishery is currently a multi-user fishery that exploits more than 200 species. Ninety-five of these 200 contribute to the bulk of catches. The fishery includes significant recreational and commercial sectors. The commercial sector, i.e.,, those boats commercially licensed by MCM, is made up of some 3,000 boats which operate on the continental shelf in depths of 5–100m. The recreational sector includes estuarine anglers who fish from boats or riverbanks, rock-and-surf anglers, and a recreational lineboat sector that operates in an environment and manner similar to the commercial sector. It is estimated that the linefishery, excluding the estuarine component, is estimated to provide employment for more than 13,000 persons and generates a calculable revenue of around R2.2 billion per annum for the coastal provinces. (Verheye 1998:12).

The lack of legal distinction between commercial and recreational line fishermen has caused there to be significant subsidization of effort in the line fishery. MCM has not been able to accurately determine the respective effort and the respective effect on the resource. MCM researchers admit that the handline industry is overcapitalized and are planning to reduce inputs (i.e.,, the number of boats allowed to fish commercially), but they are uncertain how to fairly determine who deserves this access and who does not. MCM has committed to prioritizing access to those with a history of viable commercial activity, but MCM has very limited socio-economic research on which to base this determination. Furthermore, the majority of historically disadvantaged line fishers are rarely able to obtain access to capital that would allow for ownership and have little or no experience at running a small scale fishing business (e.g. financial management, establishing markets, negotiating contracts). Basing new allocations on reported catch history, for example, will inevitably benefit predominantly historically advantaged boat owners (recreational and commercial). The responsibility for fishers to return reliable harvesting statistics has been voluntary. Given the variety of reasons and tendencies to over- or under-report catch statistics, the validity and reliability of this data is highly suspect.

MCM marine biologists have recently determined that most of the line fish stocks are on the verge of commercial collapse (publication pending). The resource (e.g. snoek, yellow tail, Cape salmon, hottentot) enjoys little protection from MCM. Aside from size limits (e.g. 60cm for snoek), the only regulations that apply to line fish species are the commercial quotas that are currently allocated for tuna (albacore) and hake. The attempts by MCM to manage the applicable fisheries to a maximum sustainable yield are sabotaged by the lack of accurate catch statistics. MCM has quality biological statistics on the health of the stocks, but they are forced to rely on very crude and arguably inaccurate catch data from which to judge appropriate adjustments in allocations.

A wide range of communities and families who rely on the line fishing industry or a large part, if not all, of their livelihood find themselves and their futures increasingly uncertain. The relatively small scale of the commercial handline industry may, on the one hand, seem of insignificant economic value on the grand scale and deserving of a low status on MCM's priority list. However, as a small-scale commercial sector the formalization process here may serve as a test case for the implementation of larger fisheries management practices. The high number of communities affected by this industry is not readily evident from the small number of boats involved. The high mobility of these fishers ensures that individuals from virtually every community in the Western Cape are involved. As those in the handline industry tend to be very politically active, a modest commitment from MCM to prioritize this formalization process will be a good investment in social and political capital. If equity and sustainability are truly at the heart of the current management strategy, MCM would be well-advised to carefully consider the socio-economic conditions of those most affected by the strategies put in place.

The handline ski-boat fishers do not even register as a blip on the radar of the Western Cape economy. They provide for less than a percentage of the total income for the fishing industry, and the fishing industry itself provides barely more than one percent of the Western Cape's Gross Domestic Product (MCM 1999). Yet the cultural importance of the handline fishers, their centrality to the identity of the Cape far outweighs their economic importance.

The relatively small scale of the commercial handline industry may, on the one hand, seem of insignificant economic value on the grand scale and deserving of a low status on MCM's priority list. However, as a small-scale commercial industry the formalization process here may serve as a test case for the implementation of larger fisheries management practices. The high number of communities affected by this industry is not readily evident from the small number of boats involved. The high mobility of these fishers ensures that individuals from virtually every community in the Western Cape are involved. As those in the handline industry tend to be very politically active, a modest commitment from MCM to prioritize this formalization process will be a good investment in social and political capital. If equity and sustainability are truly at the heart of the current management strategy, MCM would be well-advised to carefully consider the socio-economic conditions of those most affected by the strategies put in place.

These suggestions are not intended to minimize the importance or value of the recreational line fish industry, but to encourage a clear distinction between those who fish for a living and those who fish for fun. Formalization will take a lot of pressure off MCM and the whole transformation process in the industry while securing a better livelihood for the communities concerned. A formal industry will protect the "sites" or jobs for crew. By eliminating the effects of recreational fish on the market, crews will receive better prices for their catches. Crews will receive long term benefits from more consistent employment. A formal system will simultaneously start protecting the resource through reliable data and encourage more effective management through greater participation at the local level. These factors combined will lead to more content, better protected and well informed fishing communities. Communities will be made to feel that they are part of the transformation process in the industry. Fishers will feel that the government has taken their interests, their livelihoods and their plight seriously.

GLOSSARY

Agtermekaar – neat and complete

Anderkleuriges – persons of other color

Bakkie – known in the U.S. as a pick-up truck

Boer – lit. farmer; used as a nickname for white Afrikaans speaking South Africans

Boertjie – lit. the diminuative for farmer; often used as a nickname for young, white Afrikaner males

Chakkies – The small, wooden boats modeled after the whalers of the early twentieth century.

Gumboots – latex boots worn to keep the feet and ankles dry; commonly used by mine and farm workers as well

Holhangers – lit. those that hang on my ass; derogatory slang term used by fishers to describe those that relied on others to find the fish

Kaffer – derogatory racist slur used to designate a black South African; originally from the Arabic "kafir" meaning non-believer

Laaitjies – lit. little drawers; the partitions in small-scale commercial handline boats that provide for a spot for the fisher to stand and a bin in which to throw the fish.

Langaaner – a fish hawker; oral tradition has it that Langaaner is a derivative of an Indonesian word for fishmonger

Lood – silver spinners handline skippers use as a form of bait for shoaling fish species

Oilskins – latex overalls and jacket combination fishers commonly used to protect against the weather

Paloepa – a term given to a crew member who is bouncing around from boat to boat seeking a permanent site/spot for fishing; also known as a fisherman that has "rubber boots"

Papslange – weaklings; people who don't pull their weight

Piel - lit. penis; fishers used this term to label the person who had caught the least amount of fish on the boat for the day

263

Skollie – roughneck; beatnick

Suiwer Afrikaans – lit. pure Afrikaans; sometimes used to distinguish the Afrikaans taught in schools and universities from colloquial Afrikaans

Tekkies - known in the U.S. as sneakers or tennis shoes

Vingerlappies – lit. finger rags; neoprene tubes sized for each finger, used by handline fishers to protect their fingers from being cut by the lines or the fish

DEMOGRAPHICS and PERSONAL HISTORY:
1. Code Name:

2. Age:

3. Years of education (standard/grade)

4. Before the end of Apartheid, what race were you classified?

5. Neighborhood of residence (zip code of home address or town name)

6. Primary language spoken at home

7. Secondary language(s) spoken at home

8. Married/live-in partner?

9. Do you belong to a church, a mosque or some other religious organization?

9a. How often do you gather with the other members:
1) More than once a week; 2) once a week; 3) a couple times a month; 4) a couple times a year; 5) hardly ever

10. Are you a member of a union? Which ones? For how long?

11. Are you a member of any political party? Which one?

12. Who all lives in your household?

13. You said that you were classified under apartheid as _____. What does this classification mean for you today?

14. Are you the primary breadwinner (the one who makes the most money in the house)?

15. Which other people in the house also bring an income into the home?

16. What percentage of your family's total income do you contribute?

17. What other sources of income do you have besides fishing?

18. What percentage of your total annual income would you say comes from your work on this boat?

ON THE JOB

19. Can you describe for me the typical or the true fisherman?

19a. Why do you do the work you do now, instead of any other work? Why are you a commercial fisherman?

20. How long have you been making a living from fishing?

21. How long have you been a skipper professionally?

22. Do you have any formal Seaman training, like at the Training Centre for Seamen, Wingfield Technical College, Algoa Bay School of Seamanship, navy, etc.? If so, what classes?

23. How long have you worked on this boat?

24. How did you become skipper on this boat? Please outline your work history for me, from when you left school.

25. Who was most responsible for you getting the job on this boat?

26. What other kinds of boats have you worked on? When?

27. What other jobs have you had in the fishing industry in the last two years? What role? When? (factory worker, driver, etc.)

28. Are you a member of any commercial fishing organizations? Which ones? For how long?

29. Do you own the boat?
    29a. If no, whom do you work for now and for how long?
    29b. If yes, do you have any partners? How long have you been partners?

30.

31. Whom do you consider to be your major competition? Why?

32. Name the top five skippers that you know? Why do you classify them as the top skippers? What makes them better?

33. Have you been to any meetings for the commercial fishing industry in the last three years? Which ones?

34. How much of your recreational time outside of work do you spend with other commercial fishers and their families?
1) I spend very little time with other fishers outside of work; 2) I occasionally spend time...; 3) I spend a lot of time...; 4) I spend most of my recreational time with other fishers and their families.

35. Where have you gotten credit or capital for the business when you need it? Owner? Investor? Business loan? Personal loan? Fishing Company? Government? Loans from family/friends? Microcredit (e.g. cooperatives)? Other?_____

36.
37.
38.

39. NETWORKS:

I'd like to get an idea of how people are connected in the fishing industry, how they know each other. I'd like to ask you a number of questions about the people you know. Remember that all names and anything you tell me about them will be kept in the strictest of confidence. I will not tell one person what another says about them. (Of course, if someone else tells me something about you, I also can't tell you that):

1) From time to time, most people discuss important matters with other people, people they trust. The range of important matters varies from person to person across work, leisure, family, politics, whatever. The range of relations varies across work, family, friends and advisors. **If you look back over the last six months, who are the handful of people with whom you discussed matters important to you?**

2) Consider the people with whom you like to spend your free time. **Over the last six months, who are the handful of people you have been with most often for informal social activities such as having a potjie or braai together, having drinks together, going to films, visiting one another's homes, and so on?**

3) **Who would you say are your closest three or four friends?** This may or may not be the people you spend the most time with.

4) **Of all the people working in the commercial fishing industry on the western Cape coast, who are the people who have contributed most to your success in fishing – i.e. your most valuable work contacts?**

5) **Suppose you had a friend who wanted to do what you are for a living. Who are the most important people (that you know personally) you would introduce them to who would give them the best information and advice? Who do they really need to get to know?**

6) Are there any individuals you regard as a mentor, someone who has taken a strong interest in how well you do as a fisherman and has provided you with the opportunity or means to do better?

7) Of all the people you know in the industry, who has made things most difficult for you to do well in what you do? Remember that all names are coded and kept confidential and will not be released from my research except as combined statistics.

8) If you decided to find another job in the commercial fishing industry, who are the people with whom you would most likely discuss and evaluate your job options? These could be people who work with you now, or people from other than where you work now such as friends, family, people who work on other boats or other people in the fishing industry.

9) When it comes to information you need that will enable you to catch more fish or get higher prices for your fish, who are the skippers that you contact for important information (e.g. where the fish are biting, what prices hawkers are paying on the open market, recommendations for new crew members, etc)?

10) If you wanted to have a friendly but business related sit down chat with the head of Marine and Coastal Management, who would be the people you contacted to set it up for you?

11) Look over this list of names. Can you name anyone else whom you would consider as important to you as the people you see on this list?

12) Please list the first names of the crew that currently works with you.

Now I would like to ask you some details about the people you mentioned.
40. NAME INTERPRETERS (use Name Table; APPENDIX D)

sex =   male (0); female (1)
race =   ego's perception of what they would have been categorized under apartheid
reside =   the town/neighborhood they live in (smallest geographical unit known)
lang1 =   primary language spoken at home:
lang2 =   secondary language spoken at home
(f) =   How often do you communicate with this person: 1) Daily; 2) Weekly; 3) Monthly; 4) Less than Monthly

duraton =	How long have you had a relationship with this person?
role =	What does this person do in the fishing industry, if any?
	Factory Ownership (FO); Factory Management (FM); Factory Labour (FL); Boat Owner (BO1 & BO2*); Boat Skipper (BS1 &BS2*); Boat Crew (BC1 & BC2*); Administration Local (AL; ministry; staff); Administration National (AN; ministry; staff); Administration Research (AR) Other (O) <* - 1=own boat; 2=other boat>
family =	How is this person related to you, if at all?
	(spouse, mchild, fchild, hmparent, hfparent, wmparent, wfparent, hsibling, wsibling,, hmparentsib, hfparentsib, wmparentsib, wfparentsib, hgrandparent, wgrandparent, other adult, other child)? (m=male; f=female; h=husband; w=wife; child=under19)
close =	How close do you consider this person to you?
	1) Distant (avoid contact unless it is necessary) ; 2) Less close (Ok to work with, no desire to develop friendship); 3) Close (close, but not one of the closest); 4) Especially close (one of the closest)
religon =	Do any of the members on your list attend the same religious congregation you do?

WOMEN IN FISHING

I'm curious as to why there are so few women who fish for a living.

40a. Can you name any women close to you who are in the commercial fishing industry and what role they serve (boat owner, skipper, crew, buying and selling fish, buying and selling bait, bookkeeping, running errands, etc.; be specific)

40b. Why do you think there are so few women that fish (go to sea) for a living?

40c. What do you think the reaction of the other fishermen would be if a woman wanted to start fishing full time in the same areas they fish?

GEAR:

41. What type of boat and engine(s) do you have?

42. What type of electronic technology do you have on the boat? For which of these do you have formal training?

	A. Tech on Boat?	B. Formal Training?
a. Compass		
b. VHF Radio		
c. HF Radio (29 Mhz)		
d. Cell Phone		
e. Echo Sounder		
f. GPS (plotter)		
g. Satellite		
h. Radar		
i. Other fish finder		
j. Other		

43. Do you or the crew use anything other than handlines to fish on this boat?

ANNUAL ROUND:

44. Please describe your fishing seasons. What type have you done in the past 2 years? When do you do what kind of fishing?

45. Can you A.) rank the species that you caught and sold over the past 12 months, and estimate B.) the percentage of your annual catch and C.) the percentage of your annual income for each species?

A. Rank	B. % of catch	C. % of income

46.

47.

48. Think of all the slips you launched from in the past two years. Can you A.) rank where you have fished commercially in the past two years from the most to the least. B.) Give the percentage of times launched for the top 3. What is C.) the primary and D.) secondary species that you target there? E.) To whom do you most often sell your catch at these various places? F.) Who gives you the best price?

	A. Rank	B. Top 3 % launched	C. Primary species?	D. Secondary species?	E. Sold to?	F. Best Price
a. Lambert's Bay						
b. Eland's Bay						
c. Bergrivier/Laaiplek/Velddrif						
d. St. Helena Bay/Paternoster Sandy Point/Stompneusbaai						
e. Saldanha						
f. Yzerfontein						
g. Cape Town Harbour						
h. Hout Bay						
i. Simonstown						
j. Kalkbaai						
k. Gordon's Bay/Strand						
l. Hermanus/Kleinmond/ Hawston						
m. Gansbaai						
n. Struisbaai/Arniston						
o. Other:						

CREW (According to Captain)

49. What language do you use most often on the boat? Any others?

50. What is the maximum and minimum crew you take with you?

51. Are you responsible for hiring or choosing the crew? If so, how do you decide whom to hire?

52. How would you describe the ideal crew member?

53. How would you describe your current crew?
54.
55. How is the boat (are you) compensated? How are the crew compensated?

Regulations/liscencing
56. How often in the last two years did you return "Voluntary Catch" reports to MCM? (the blue book)

57. What do you think about how the current quota system works?

58. Have you ever owned a quota, or are you part owner/share holder in a company that holds a commercial fishing quota? Which one? For how long? What kind of quota?

59. Do you know personally any of the government officials responsible for regulating the fishing industry? How do you know them?

60. How do you hear about the new fishing regulations put out by the government?

60a. What do you think of the poaching that has been so prominent in the news lately?

Future of Fishing
61. What do you see yourself doing in the next three to five years?

62. What do you think is the future in what you do for a living?

63. Do you want your children to go into commercial fishing for a living? Why/why not?

Job Attachment

64. If you had to do it all over again, would you still become a commercial fisherman?

65. Have you recently seriously considered any other profession? What would that be? Have you made any steps in that direction?

66. Are you planning to stay fishing for a living for the foreseeable future? If not, what are you planning?

Job Satisfaction

67. How do you feel about:

	1.Very Unsatisfied	2.Unsatisfied	3.Neither Satisfied nor Unsatisfied	4.Satisfied	5.Very Satisfied
a. Being a fisherman					
b. Your independence as a fisherman					
c. The respect you receive as a fisherman					
d. Working outdoors					
e. How important your job is to other people					
f. What you earned last year from fishing					
g. Your future as a fisherman					

APPENDIX B
NAME TABLE

Code Name: Place: Date:

Name	Sex	Race	resid	Lang1	Lang2	(f)	durat	Role	Fam	close	Relig

APPENDIX C
RESEARCH ASSISTANT JOB DESCRIPTION AND CONTRACT

Project: The Structural and Cultural Construction of Race in the Handline Fishing Industry on South Africa's Western Cape Coast

Project Director: James F. Gates, B.A.; M.Div.; ABD, University of Florida

I, _____, contract as Research Assistant for the aforementioned project beginning Monday, 5 June 2000 and ending no later than 31 August 2000. I understand that my primary responsibility will be to conduct interviews with skippers of commercial handline ski-boats that work on the western Cape coast. I understand that I will receive training in the interview skills required to assist in the project. This training will include basic interview techniques and an orientation to the theoretical and methodological issues inherent to this project.

I understand that I am being employed as an independent contractor and will be compensated per interview. I have agreed to be paid R120 per interview with a minimum of ____ and a maximum of ____ complete interviews, subject to quality control by the Project Director. I understand that my commitment to the project extends from 5 June 2000 until the target number of interviews has been reached, but not to extend beyond 31 August 2000. I understand that the interviews will be scheduled at my own convenience and that the compensation offered per interview includes travel and subsistence costs. I understand that I will be provided with the necessary stationery and office supplies to complete the interviews.

I understand that the materials used and results obtained from this research are the property of the Project Director. Any use of the materials or results outside the context of this project are by permission of the Project Director only.

By signing this contract, I agree to keep the information I gain from this project in the strictest of confidence. I will not divulge information shared with me by the interviewees or the Project Director to other parties. I understand that I may not share with one interviewee what another has said. I agree to protect the anonymity of the interviewees. Prior to each interview I will read the Informed Consent form and formally request consent from each interviewee for their participation.

Finally, I understand that information from this project may not be used in any way, including publication, without the prior consent of the project director.

Signed: _____   Date: _____

Project Director: _____

APPENDIX D
INFORMED CONSENT

Verbal consent was requested of each person interviewed. No information was recorded without this consent. The following introduction and instructions was given to each person interviewed, along with my business card with contact information:

Identification:
My name is Jamie Gates. I am a Doctoral candidate in the cultural anthropology department at the University of Florida in the United States. I am doing research toward the completion of my Ph.D. (doctorate) in cultural anthropology.

Explanation of Research:
My research is designed to get an understanding the work and social lives of commercial handline fishers and their crew. I am interested in what you do to make a living. I am also interested in the network of acquaintances, friends and family that support you and help make your work possible. I will be asking you a series of questions about your work and about your network of support. My questions should take about an hour and a half of your time.

Privacy:
Anything you tell me about yourself, your work and your network of support will be kept confidential. You will be assigned a code number and any information you give me will be referenced by your code number. I may also create a name for you and use that name instead of a code number. I will create a new name for your boat, since you will be easily identifiable from that name. The information that you and other fishers tell me will be used to draw general conclusions. If I quote from what you have said, I will use the name I have created for you.

Benefits and Risks:
There will be no immediate benefit to you directly for your participation in this study. But, as all information is kept confidential, there are also no anticipated risks for your participation in this study. *You do not have to answer any question you do not wish to answer.* If at any time you wish to withdraw any part of what you have said you may do so by contacting me by the information on my business card (to be handed to each informant, including South African and U.S. campus address and phone so that any participant can reach me later).

If you have further questions or concerns about your rights, I can give you the address of my University's Institutional Review Board (UFIRB office, Box 112250, University of Florida, Gainesville FL 32611-2250).

APENNDIX E
MARINE LIFE MENTIONED IN THIS STUDY

English	Afrikaans	Scientific name
Abalone	Perlemoen	Haliotis Midae
Cape Spiny Lobster	Kaapse Kreef	Jasus lalandii
Cape Salmon	Geelbek	Atractoscion aequidens
Cob	Kob	Argyrosomus spp.
Hottentot	Hottentot	Pachymentopon blonchii
Shad	Elf	Pomatomus saltatrix
Silver Fish	Silwervis	Argyrozona argyrozona
Snoek	Snoek	Thyrsites atun
South African Fur Seal	Suid-Afrikaanse Pelsrob	Arctocephalus pusillus
Yellowtail	Geelstert	Seriola lalandi

REFERENCES CITED

Acheson, James M.
    1981   Anthropology of Fishing. Annual Review of Anthropology 10:275-316.
    1988   The Lobster Gangs of Maine. Hanover, NH: University Press of New England.
    1989   Winds of Change: Women in Northwest Commercial Fishing. Seattle: University of Washington Press.
Acheson, James M., ed.
    1994   Anthropology and Institutional Economics. Lanham, MD: University Press of America.
Acheson, James M., Bonnie J. McCay, Fikret Berkes, and David Feeny
    1990   'The Tragedy of the Commons': Twenty-Two Years Later (Garrett Hardin's book focusing attention on overpopulation. Human Ecology: An Interdisciplinary Journal 18(1):1–19.
Adhikari, Mohamed
    1994   Coloured Identity and the Politics of Coloured Education. International Journal of African Historical Studies 27(1/Winter):101–27.
Agar, Michael
    1996   The Professional Stranger : An Informal Introduction to Ethnography. San Diego: Academic Press.
Agger, Ben
    1992   Cultural Studies as Critical Theory. London: The Falmer Press.
Anderson, Benedict
    1993   Imagined Communities. New York: Verson.
Appadurai, Arjun, ed.
    1986   The Social Life of Things: Commodities in Cultural Perspective. Cambridge: Cambridge University Press.
Armstrong, John
    1996   Achetypal Diasporas. In Ethnicity. J. Hutchinson and A.D. Smith, eds. pp. 120–126. Oxford: Oxford University Press.
Ashmore, Malcolm
    1989   The Reflexive Thesis: Writing Sociology of Scientific Knowledge. Chicago: Chicago University Press.
Atkins, Keletso E.
    1993   The Moon is Dead! Give Us Our Money!: The Cultural Origins of an African Work Ethic, Natal, South Africa, 1843–1900. Portsmouth, NH: Heinemann.
Babbie, Earl
    1990   Survey Research Methods. Belmont, CA: Wadsworth Publishing Company.
Bailey, C.
    1991   Social Relations of Production in Rural Malay Society: Comparative Case Studies of Rice Farming, Rubber Tapping, and Fishing Communities. In Small-Scale Fishery Development: Sociocultural Perspectives. J.J.Poggie and R.B. Pollnac, eds. Kingston, RI: International Center for Marine Resource Development.

Baker, Lee D.
    1998   From Savage to Negro: Anthropology and the Construction of Race, 1896–1954. Berkeley: University of California Press.

Barnes, J. A.
    1951   Marriage in a Changing Society: A Study in Structural Change Among the Fort Jameson Ngoni. Cape Town: Published for the Rhodes-Livingstone Institute by Oxford University Press.
    1969   Graph Theory and Social Networks: A Technical Comment on Connectedness and Connectivity. Sociology 3(2):215–242.
    1972   Social Networks. Reading, MA: Addison-Wesley Pub. Co.

Barth, Fredrik, ed.
    1969   Ethnic Groups and Boundaries. Boston: Little Brown.

Baudrillard, Jean
    1981   For a Critique of the Political Economy of the Sign. St. Louis, MO: Telos Press.

Behar, Ruth
    1993   Translated Woman: Crossing the Border with Esperanza's Story. Boston: Beacon Press.

Bekker, Simon
    1993   Ethnicity in Focus: The South African Case. Pietermaritzberg, South Africa: The Natal Witness Printing and Publishing Company.

Benedict, Ruth
    1934   Patterns of Culture. New York: Houghton Mifflin.
    1945   Race: Science and Politics. New York: Viking Press.

Berger, Iris
    1992   Threads of Solidarity: Women in South African Industry, 1900–1980. Bloomington: Indiana University Press.

Berkes, Fikret
    1985   Fishermen and the "Tragedy of the Commons." Environmental Conservation 12:199–206.

Bernard, H. Russell
    1987   Sponge Fishing and Technological Change in Greece. In Technology and Social Change. H.R.Bernard and P.J. Pelto, eds. pp. 167–206. Prospect Heights, IL: Waveland.
    1994   Methods Belong to All of Us. In Assessing Cultural Anthropology. R. Barofsky, ed. pp. 168–177. New York: McGraw-Hill, Inc.
    1995   Research Methods in Anthropology: Qualitative and Quantitative Approaches. Walnut Creek: AltaMira Press.

Bernard, H. R., P. Killworth, L. Sailer, and D. Kronenfeld
    1985   On the Validity of Retrospective Data. Annual Review of Anthropology 13:495–517.

Bickford-Smith, Vivian
    1995   Ethnic Pride and Racial Prejudice in Victorian Cape Town: Group Identity and Social Practice, 1875–1902. Cambridge: Cambridge University Press.

Bickford-Smith, Vivian, Elizabeth van Heyningen, and Nigel Worden
    1999   Cape Town in the Twentieth Century: An Illustrated Social History. Cape Town: David Philip Publishers.

Boas, Franz
    1932   Anthropology and Modern Life. New York: W. W. Norton & Company, Inc.

Bordieu, Pierre
    1987   In Other Words: Essays Towards a Reflexive Sociology. Matthew Adamson, transl. Stanford, CA: Stanford University Press.

Borgatti, S.P., M.G. Everett, and L.C. Freeman
    1999   Ucinet 5 for Windows: Software for Social Network Analysis. Natick: Analytic
            Technologies.

Bott, Elizabeth
    1971   Family and Social Network. New York: Free Press.

Brodkin, Karen
    1989   Toward a Unified Theory of Class, Race, and Gender. American Ethnologist
            16(3):534–50.
    1998   How Jews Became White Folks and What That Says About Race in America.
            New Brunswick, NJ: Rutgers University Press.

Bron, C. and J. Kerbosch
    1973   Finding All Cliques of an Undirected Graph. Communication of the ACM
            16:575–577.

Brunt, Dave
    1993   The Role of the South African Marine Linefish Management Association. The
            Second South African Marine Linefish Symposium, Durban, 1993, pp. 179–181.
            The Oceanographic Research Institute.

Burke, Timothy
    1996   Lifebuoy Men, Lux Women: Commodification, Consumption, and Cleanliness in
            Modern Zimbabwe. Durham: Duke University Press.

Burt, Ronald S.
    1982   Toward a Structural Theory of Action. New York: Academic Press.
    1984   Networks and the General Social Survey. Social Networks 6:293–339.
    1985   General Social Survey Network Items. Connections 8:1119–123.
    1997   A Note on Social Capital and Network Content. Social Networks 19:355–373.

Carse, Tommy
    1959   Die Blou Dam is hul Oesland. Cape Town: H.A.U.M.

Clark, Barry M.
    2000   Subsistence Fisheries Programme: Research Report. Cape Town: University of
            Cape Town.

Clifford, James and George E. Marcus, eds.
    1986   Writing Culture: The Poetics and Politics of Ethnography. Berkeley: University
            of California Press.

Cobas, Jose A., Mikel Aickin, and Douglas S. Jardine
    1993   Industrial Segmentation, the Ethnic Economy, and Job Mobility: The Case of
            Cuban Exiles in Florida. Quality and Quantity 27:249–270.

Cobas, Jose A. and Ione DeOllos
    1989   Family Ties, Co-Ethnic Bonds, and Ethnic Entrepreneurship. Sociological
            Perspectives 32:403–411.

Cohen, Ronald
    1978   Ethnicity: Problem and Focus in Anthropology. Annual Review of Anthropology
            7:379–403.

Cole, Sally
    1992   Anthropological Lives: The Reflexive Tradition in a Social Science. In Essays on
            Life Writing: From Genre to Critical Practice. M. Kadar, ed. pp. 113–27.
            Toronto: University of Toronto Press.

Collier, Jane Fishburne, Maurice Bloch, and Sylvia Junko Yanagisako
    1987   Gender and Kinship: Essays Toward a Unified Analysis. Stanford, CA: Stanford
            University Press.

Committee to Review Individual Fishing Quotas, National Research Council (U.S.)
- 1999   Sharing the Fish: Toward a National Policy on Individual Fishing Quotas. Washington, DC: National Academy Press.

Constitutional Assembly of the Republic of South Africa
- 1997   The Constitution of the Republic of South Africa, 1996. Annotated Version. Wynberg: Hn Communications.

Crapanzano, Vincent
- 1980   Tuhami, Portrait of a Moroccan. Chicago: University of Chicago Press.

Dalton, George
- 1961   Economic Theory and Primitive Society. American Anthropologist 63:465–470.

Dannhaeuser, Norbet
- 1989   Marketing in Developing Urban Areas. *In* Economic Anthropology. S. Plattner, ed. pp. 222–252. Stanford, CA: Stanford University Press.

Davis, D.L. and J. Nadel-Klein
- 1992   Gender, Culture, and the Sea: Contemporary Theoretical Approaches. Society and Natural Resources 5:135–148.

De Jongh, Michael
- 1995   Social Networks and Mobility, Resources and Strategies: The Peripatetics of the South African Karoo. pp. 18. Cape Town: University of Cape Town African Studies Centre.

Degenne, Alain, and Michel Forse
- 1999   Introducing Social Networks. A. Borges, transl. London: Sage Publications.

Denzin, Norman K. and Yvonna S. Lincoln
- 1994   Handbook of Qualitative Research. Thousand Oaks: Sage Publications.

Department of Environmental Affairs and Tourism
- 1998   Marine Living Resources Act. Cape Town, South Africa.
- 1999   Investigation and Management Findings of an Internal Audit of the Chief Director: MCM. Cape Town: Marine and Coastal Management.

Derrida, Jacques
- 1972   Structure, Sign and Play in the Discourse of the Human Sciences. *In* The Structuralist Controversy: The Languages of Criticism and the Sciences of Man. R. Macksey and E. Donato, eds. pp. 247–64. Baltimore: Johns Hopkins University Press.
- 1978   Writing and Difference. Alan Bass, transl. Chicago: Chicago University Press.

Dickens, David R. and Andrea Fontana
- 1994   Postmodernism and Social Inquiry. New York: Guilford Press.

Drake, S.C.
- 1980   Anthropology and the Black Experience. Black Scholar 11(7):2–31.
- 1987   Black Folk Here and There: An Essay in History and Anthropology. Los Angeles: Center for Afro-American Studies, University of California.

Du Bois, W. E. B.
- 1993   The Souls of Black Folk. New York: Knopf.

Du Pre, Roy Howard
- 1994   Separate But Unequal: The 'Coloured' People of South Africa, a Political History. Johannesburg: Jonathan Ball Publishers.

Du Toit, Brian M.
    1995a   Boer Settlers in the Southwest. El Paso: Texas Western Press.
    1995b   Colonial Boer: An Afrikaner Settlement in Chubut, Argentina. Lewiston: E. Mellen Press.
    1995c   Regional Conflict Resolution and the New South Africa. *In* Journal of Third World Studies.
    1998   The Boers in East Africa: Ethnicity and Identity. Westport, CN.: Bergin & Garvey.

Dubow, Saul
    1995   Illicit Union: Scientific Racism in Modern South Africa. Cambridge: Cambridge University Press.

Durkheim, E.
    1933   On the Division of Labor in Society. New York: McMillan.

Durrenberger, E. Paul
    1992   It's All Politics: South Alabama's Seafood Industry. Chicago: University of Illinois Press.
    1993   The Skipper Effect and Folk Models of the Skipper Effect Among Mississippi Shrimpers. Human Organization 52(2):194–202.

Durrenberger, E.P. and G. Palsson
    1985   Peasants, Entrepreneurs, and Companies: The Evolution of Icelandic Fishing. Ethnos 1–2:103–122.

Dwyer, Kevin and Faqir Muhammad
    1982   Moroccan Dialogues: Anthropology in Question. Baltimore: Johns Hopkins University Press.

Eacker, Susan A.
    1994   Mullet, Mangoes and Midwives: Gender and Community in a West Coast Florida Fishing Village. PhD Dissertation, Miami University, Ohio.

Eigelaar, Johnnie
    1999   As die Skipper op die Voorstewe Staan. Cape Town: Nasionale Boekdrukkery.

Eller, Jack and Reed Coughlan
    1993   The Poverty of Primordialism: The Demystification of Ethnic Attachments. Ethnic and Racial Studies 16:2–23.

Emerson, Robert M., Rachel I. Fretz, and Linda L. Shaw
    1995   Writing Ethnographic Fieldnotes. Chicago: Chicago University Press.

Emirbayer, Mustafa and Jeff Goodwin
    1994   Network Analysis, Culture, and the Problem of Agency. American Journal of Sociology 99(6 May):1411–1454.

Erickson, Thomas
    1993   Ethnicity and Nationalism. London: Pluto Press.

Evans-Pritchard, E. E.
    1940   The Nuer. Oxford: Clarendon Press.
    1951   Social Anthropology. New York: Free Press.

February, V.A.
    1981   Mind Your Colour: The Coloured Stereotype in South African Literature. Boston: Kegan Paul International Ltd.

Finley, Moses
    1996   The Ancient Greeks and their Nation. *In* Ethnicity. J. Hutchinson and A.D. Smith, eds. pp. 111–115. Oxford: Oxford University Press.

Firth, Raymond, ed.
    1970   Themes in Economic Anthropology. London: Tavistock.

Fisher, Claude S.
    1982   To Dwell Among Friends: Personal Networks in Town and City. Chicago: University of Chicago Press.

Food and Allied Worker's Union
    1997   A Response to the Fisheries White Paper. Cape Town: Labour Research Service, Sea Fisheries Development Project.
    2000   Press Release: FAWU Protest Action Against Corruption in the Fishing Industry. S. Claassen and B. Stemmet, eds. pp. 1–2. Cape Town: Food and Allied Workers Union, Western Cape Region.

Foucault, Michel
    1980a A Foucault Reader. New York: Pantheon Books.
    1980b Power/Knowledge: Selected Interviews and Other Writings, 1972–1977. Colin Gordon, Leo Marshall, John Mephem, and Kate Soper, transl. New York: Pantheon Books.

Fox-Genovese, Elizabeth
    1991   Feminism Without Illusions: A Critique of Individualism. Chapel Hill: University of North Carolina Press.

Franck, Bruce and Frank Robb
    1975   Fishermen of the Cape. Cape Town: Longman Penguin Southern Africa.

Frankenberg, Ruth
    1993   White Women, Race Matters: The Social Construction of Whiteness. Minneapolis: University of Minnesota Press.

Fraser, Nancy
    1989   Unruly Practices: Power, Discourse, and Gender in Contemporary Social Theory. Minneapolis: University of Minnesota Press.

Fredrickson, George
    1981   White Supremacy: A Comparative Study in American and South African History. New York: Oxford University Press.
    1995   Black Liberation: A Comparative History of Black Ideologies in the United States and South Africa. New York: Oxford University Press.

Freedberg, Jean
    1987   Changing Political Identity of the "Coloured" People of South Africa: A Political History, 1652–1982. Dissertation Abstracts International 48–09(A):2441, University of California.

Freeman, L.C.
    1979   Centrality in Social Networks: Conceptual Clarification. Social Networks 1:215–39.

Freeman, L.C. and A.K. Romney
    1987   Words, Deeds and Social Structure: A Preliminary Study of the Reliability of Informants. Human Organization 46:330–34.

Freeman, L.C., A.K. Romney, and S.C. Freeman
    1987   Cognitive Structure and Informant Accuracy. American Anthropologist 89:310–325.

Freund, Bill
    1995   Insiders and Outsiders: The Indian Working Class of Durban, 1910–1990. Portsmouth, NH: Heinemann.

Friedman, Milton
    1953   Essays in Positive Economics. Chicago: Chicago University Press.

Friedman, Milton
    1962   Capitalism and Freedom. Chicago: University of Chicago Press.

Garrity-Blake, Barbara J.
    1994   The Fish Factory: Work and Meaning for Black and White Fishermen of the American Menhaden Industry. Knoxville: University of Tennessee Press.

Gates, James F.
    1999   Book Review, Coloured Ethnicity and Identity: A Case Study in the Former Coloured Areas in the Western Cape/South Africa. *In* Transforming Anthropology. I. McClaurin, ed.

Geertz, Clifford
    1973   Thick Descriptions: Toward an Interpretive Theory of Culture. *In* The Interpretation of Cultures. C. Geertz, ed. pp. 1–32. New York: Basic Books.
    1988   Works and Lives: The Anthropologist as Author. Stanford, CA: Stanford University Press.
    1994   The Uses of Diversity. *In* Assessing Cultural Anthropology. R. Barofsky, ed. pp. 454–66. New York: McGraw-Hill, Inc.

Gladwin, Christina
    1989   On the Division of Labor Between Economics and Economic Anthropology. *In* Economic Anthropology. S. Plattner, ed. pp. 397–428. Stanford: Stanford University Press.

Godelier, Maurice
    1986   The Mental and the Material. London: Verso.

Goldin, Ian
    1987   Making Race: The Politics and Economics of Coloured Identity in South Africa. New York: Longman, Inc.

Gordon, Edmund Tayloe
    1998   Disparate Diasporas: Identity and Politics in an African Nicaraguan Community. Austin, TX: University of Texas Press Austin Institute of Latin American Studies.

Granovetter, Mark
    1973   The Strength of Weak Ties. American Journal of Sociology 78:1360–80.
    1974   Getting a Job: A Study of Contacts and Careers. Cambridge, MA: Harvard University Press.
    1982   The Strength of Weak Ties: A Network Theory Revisited. *In* Social Structure and Network Analysis. P. Marsden and N. Lin, eds. pp. 105–130. Beverly Hills, CA: Sage.
    1985   Economic Action and Social Structure: The Problem of Embeddedness. American Journal of Sociology 91:481–510.

Green, Ben
    1985   Finest Kind: A Celebration of a Florida Fishing Village. Macon, GA: Mercer University Press.

Gregory, Steven and Roger Sanjek
    1994   Race. New Brunswick, NJ: Rutgers University Press.

Griffiths, Marc
    2000   Life History of South African Snoek *Thyrsites atun* (Pisces: Gempylidae): A Pelagic Predator of the Benguela Ecosystem. *unpublished* .

Guastella, Lisa
    1997   Outboard Motors. SA Commercial Marine March-May:16–17.

Gump, James
    1994   The Dust Rose Like Smoke: The Subjugation of the Zulu and the Sioux. Lincoln: Nebraska University Press.

Habermas, Jurgen
    1987   The Theory of Communicative Action. Volume 2. Boston: Beacon Press.

Halter, Marilyn
    1993   Between Race and Ethnicity: Cape Verdean American Immigrants, 1860–1965. Urbana: University of Illinois Press.
Hammer, M.
    1984   Explorations into the Meaning of Social Network Interview Data. Social Networks 6:341–71.
Hardin, Garrett
    1968   Tragedy of the Commons. Science 162:1243–48.
Harris, Marvin
    1964   Patterns of Race in the Americas. New York: Walker.
    1968   The Rise of Anthropological Theory: A History of Theories of Culture. New York: Crowell.
    1979   Cultural Materialism: The Struggle for a Science of Culture. New York: Random House.
    1993   Culture, People, Nature: An Introduction to General Anthropology. New York: Harper Collins College Publishers.
Harrison, F.V.
    1995   The Persistent Power of a Race in the Cultural and Political Economy of Racism. Annual Review of Anthropology 24:47–74.
Hauck, Maria
    1999   Regulating Marine Resources in South Africa: The Case of the Abalone Fishery. *In* Environmental Justice and the Legal Process. J. Glazewski and G. Bradfield, eds. pp. 211–28. Cape Town: Juta.
Hauck, Maria and Renee Hector
    2000   An Analysis of Operation Neptune: Government's Response to Marine Poaching. Cape Town: Institute of Criminology, University of Cape Town.
Hechter, Michael
    1986   A Rational Choice Approach to Race and Ethnic Relations. *In* Theories of Race and Ethnic Relations. pp. 115–39. Cambridge: Cambridge University Press.
Hersoug, B
    1998   Fishing in a Sea of Sharks: Reconstruction and Development in the South African Fishing Industry. Transformations 35:77–102.
Horowitz, Donald
    1985   Ethnic Groups in Conflict. Berkeley: University of California Press.
Hutchinson, John and Anthony D. Smith
    1996   Ethnicity. Oxford: Oxford University Press.
Hutton, T. and S.J. Lamberth
    1997   Opportunities for Co-management: The Application of a Research Framework to a Case Study from South Africa. *In* Co-Management in Africa. pp. 205–232.
Iggulden, Jill
    1982   Kalk Bay: A Ray of Light. Odyssey 6(2):13–18.
Ignatiev, Noel
    1995   How the Irish Became White. New York: Routledge.
Isaacs, Moeniba
    1998   Conflict or Co-Operation? Attitudes Towards the New Fisheries Policy in Three Fishing Communities in Cape Town. Research Report, University of the Western Cape.
James, Wilmot and Daria Caliguire, ed.
    1996   Now that We are Free: Coloured Communities in a Democratic South Africa. London: Lynne Rienner Publishers.

James, Wilmot G. and Mary Simons, ed.
    1991   Class, Caste, and Color: A Social and Economic History of the South African Western Cape. New Brunswick, NJ: Transaction Publishers.

Jiobu, Robert M.
    1990   Ethnicity and Inequality. Albany: State University of New York Press.

Johnson, Irvin, ed.
    1964   South African Fish and Fishing: How Fish are Caught in the Waters around Southern Africa, How Fish are Preserved, Transported and Processed, How the Fishing Industry is Organized. Cape Town: Irvin and Johnson Limited.

Johnson, Jeffrey C.
    1994   Anthropological Contributions to the Study of Social Networks: A Review. *In* Advances in Social Network Analysis: Research in the Social and Behavioral Sciences. S. Wasserman and J. Galaskiewicz, eds. pp. 113–51. London: Sage Publications.

Johnson, Jeffrey C. and David C. Griffith
    1995   Promoting Sportfishing Development in Puerto Rico: Travelagents' Perceptions of the Caribbean. Human Organization 54:95–104.

Johnstone, Andy
    2000   Towards the Restructuring of the Fishing Industry in South Africa. Cape Town: Artisanal Fisher's Association.

Junger, Sebastian
    1997   The Perfect Storm: A True Story of Men Against the Sea. New York: Norton.

Keegan, Tim
    1996   Colonial South Africa and the Origins of the Racial Order. Charlottesville: University of Virginia Press.

Keynes, John Maynard
    1936   The General Theory of Employment, Interest and Money. New York: Harcourt, Brace and World.

Kirk, Jerome and Marc L. Miller
    1986   Reliability and Validity in Qualitative Research. Volume 1. Beverly Hills: Sage Publications.

Kleinschmidt, Horst
    2000   Draft Discussion Document for the Fisheries Management Plan To Improve the Process of Allocating Fishing Rights. Cape Town: Department of Environmental Affairs and Tourism.

Kochen, M., ed.
    1989   The Small World. Norwood, NJ: Ablex Publishing Corporation.

Kottak, Conrad and Elizabeth Colson
    1994   Multilevel Linkages: Longitudinal and Comparative Studies. *In* Assessing Cultural Anthropology. R. Barofsky, ed. pp. 396–412. New York: McGraw-Hill.

Kuhn, Thomas S.
    1970   The Structure of Scientific Revolutions. Chicago: University of Chicago Press.

Kuznar, Lawrence A.
    1997   Reclaiming a Scientific Anthropology. Walnut Creek, CA: AltaMira Press.

Latourette, Kenneth Scott
    1975   A History of Christianity. New York: Harper & Row.

Lees, Robin
    1969   Fishing For Fortunes: The Story of the Fishing Industry in South Africa and the Men Who Made It. Cape Town: Purnell.

Leffler, A., R.S. Krannich, and D.L. Gillespie
    1986   Contact, Support and Friction: Three Faces of Networks in Community Life.
            Sociological Perspectives 29:337–55.
Levi-Strauss, Claude
    1963   Structural Anthropology. C. Jacobson, transl. New York: Basic Books.
Lewis, Gavin
    1987   Between the Wire and the Wall: A History of South African 'Coloured' Politics.
            New York: St. Martin's Press.
Light, Ivan and Edna Bonacich
    1988   Immigrant Entrepreneurs: Koreans in Los Angeles 1965–1982. Berkeley:
            University of California Press.
Lin, Nan and Mary Dumin
    1986   Access to Jobs through Social Ties. Social Networks 8:365–385.
Lindsay, B.
    1997   Toward Conceptual, Policy, and Programmatic Frameworks of Affirmative
            Action in South African Universities. Journal of Negro Education 66(4):522–
            538.
Lindsay, Lois A.
    1999   Environmental Perceptions of Fishery Resource Users at Struis Bay. South
            Africa, University of Guelph.
Lipuma, E. and S. K. Meltzoff
    1997   The Crosscurrents of Ethnicity and Class in the Construction of Public Policy.
            American Ethnologist 24(1):114–131.
Locke, John
    1894 [1690]   An Essay Concerning Human Understanding. Oxford: Clarendon Press.
Lowie, Robert Harry
    1920   Primitive Society. New York: Boni and Liveright.
Lyotard, Jean-Francois
    1984   The Postmodern Condition: A Report on Knowledge. Geoff Benningston and
            Brian Massumi, transl. Minneapolis: University of Minneapolis Press.
Mamdani, Mahmood
    1996   Citizen and Subject: Contemporary Africa and the Legacy of Late Colonialism.
            Cape Town: David Philip.
Mandela, Nelson
    1996   Citizens of a Single Rainbow Nation. In Now that We Are Free: Coloured
            Communities in a Democratic South Africa. W. James and D. Caliguire, eds. pp.
            6–8. London: Lynne Reinner Press.
Mannheim, Karl
    1936   Ideology and Utopia. New York: Harcourt, Brace.
Mara, Joe
    1973   A Fisherman's Tale: Fifty Years of Angling along the Natal Coast. Durban:
            Angler Publications and Promotions.
Marais, J.S.
    1939   The Cape Coloured People, 1652–1937. London: Longmans Green and Co.
Marcus, George
    1986   Afterword: Ethnographic Writing and Anthropological Careers. In Rereading
            Cultural Anthropology. G. Marcus, ed. Durham, NC: Duke University Press.
    1994   After the Critique of Ethnography: Faith, Hope and Charity, But the Greatest of
            These is Charity. In Assessing Cultural Anthropology. R. Barofsky, ed. pp. 40–
            53. New York: McGraw-Hill.

Marine and Coastal Management
    1997   White Paper: A Marine Fisheries Policy for South Africa. Cape Town: Department of Environmental Affairs and Tourism.
    1999   Application for Commercial Fishing Rights. Cape Town, South Africa.

Marks, Shula
    1994   Divided Sisterhood: Race, Class, and Gender in the South African Nursing Profession. New York: St. Martin's Press.

Marsden, P.V.
    1990   Network Data and Management. Annual Review of Sociology 16:435–63.

Marsden, P.V. and K.E. Campbell
    1984   Measuring Tie Strength. Social Forces 63:482–501.

Marx, Anthony W.
    1998   Making Race and Nation: A Comparison of South Africa, The United States, and Brazil. New York: Cambridge University Press.

Mathew, Sebastian
    1997   Fisheries Policy: Straddling the Colour Barrier. Brussels: International Collective in Support of Fish Workers.

Matthiessen, Peter
    1988   Men's Lives: The Surfmen and Baymen of the South Fork. New York: Vintage Books.

Mauss, Marcel
    1954 [1924]   The Gift. I. Cunnison, transl. New York: Free Press.

McCay, Bonnie J. and James M. Acheson, eds.
    1987   The Question of the Commons: The Culture and Ecology of Communal Resources. Tucson: University of Arizona Press.

McClaurin, Irma
    1996   Women of Belize: Gender and Change in Central America. New Brunswick, NJ: Rutgers University Press.

McNeill, William H.
    1996   Ethnicity in History. Oxford: Oxford University Press.

Mead, Margaret
    1928   Coming of Age in Samoa. New York: Morrow.
    1949   Male and Female. New York: Morrow.

Miller, Marc L. and John Van Maanen
    1979   Boats Don't Fish, People Do: Some Ethnographhic Notes on the Federal Management of Fisheries in Glouster. Human Organization 38(4):377–85.

Mitchell, J.C.
    1969   Social Networks in Urban Situation. Manchester: Manchester University Press.

Montagu, Ashley
    1974   Race: Man's Most Dangerous Myth: The Fallacy of Race. New York: Oxford University Press.

Morgan, Lewis Henry
    1963 [1877]   Ancient Society. New York: Meridan Books.

Morris, Donald R.
    1992   South Africa: The Politics of Racial Terminology. Political Communication 9(2/April-June):111.

Moya, Lily Patience, Mabel Palmer, and Shula Marks
    1987   Not Either an Experimental Doll: The Separate Worlds of Three South African Women. London: Women's Press.

290

Mukhopadhyay, Carol C. and Yolanda T. Moses
    1997   Reestablishing Race in Anthropological Discourse. American Anthropologist
            99(3):517–33.
Nadel-Klein, Jane and Dona Lee Davis
    1988   To Work and to Weep: Women in Fishing Economies. St. John's: Institute of
            Social and Economic Research Memorial University of Newfoundland.
Naidoo, Ashley D., ed.
    1999   Marine and Coastal Management Research Highlights 1998–1999. Volume 8.
            Cape Town: Department of Environmental Affairs and Tourism.
Narotsky, Susana
    1997   New Directions in Economic Anthropology. Chicago: Pluto Press.
O'Conner, M.I.
    1990   Women's Networks and the Social Needs of Mexican Immigrants. Urban
            Anthropology 19:81–92.
Okamura, J.Y.
    1981   Situational Ethnicity. Ethnic and Racial Studies 4:452–63.
Olson, Mancur
    1965   The Logic of Collective Action. Cambridge, MA: Harvard University Press.
Ooka, Emi and Barry Wellman
    1999   Does Social Capital Pay Off More Within or Between Ethnic Groups: Analyzing
            Job Searchers in Five Toronto Ethnic Groups. December 1999.
Oostindie, Gert and H. Hoetink
    1996   Ethnicity in the Caribbean: Essays in Honor of Harry Hoetink. London:
            Macmillan Caribbean.
Ostrom, Elinor
    1990   Governing the Commons: The Evolution of Institutions for Collective Action.
            New York: Cambridge University Press.
Palsson, Gisli
    1991   Coastal Economies, Cultural Accounts: Human Ecology and Icelandic Discourse.
            New York: Manchester University Press.
Penny, Andrew
    1993   The National Marine Linefish System. The Second South African Marine
            Linefish Symposium, Durban. pp. 68–72. The Oceanographic Research Institute.
Petersen, Sydney Vernon
    1945   As die Son Ondergaan. S.l.: Maskew Miller.
Philander, Peter John
    1963   Vuurklip, Bekroonde Digbundel, Letterkundige Wedstryd Rereël. Kaapstad:
            Nasionale Boekhandel.
    1965   Die Bruin Kokon. Stellenbosch: Kosmo-Uitgewery.
    1978   Konka. Johannesburg: Perskor.
Pickel, Birgit
    1997   Coloured Ethnicity and Identity: A Case Study in the Former Coloured Areas in
            the Western Cape, South Africa. Hamburg, Germany: University of Hamburg.
Plattner, Stuart, ed.
    1989   Economic Anthropology. Stanford: Stanford University Press.
Podolny, J.M. and J.N. Baron
    1997   Relationships and Resources: Social Networks and Mobility in the Workplace.
            Amrican Sociological Review 62(5):673–94.
Polanyi, Karl
    1957   Trade and Market in the Early Empires: Economies in History and Theory.
            Glencoe, IL: Free Press.

Pollnac, R.B. and J.J. Poggie
    1991   Small-Scale Fishery Development: Sociocultural Perspectives. *In* Small-Scale
          Fishery Development: Sociocultural Perspectives. J.J. Poggie .and R.B. Pollnac,
          eds. Kingston, RI: International Center for Marine Resource Development.

Pollnac, R. B., J. J. Poggie, and S. L. Cabral
    1998   Thresholds of Danger: Perceived Risk in a New England Fishery. Human
          Organization 57(1):53–59.

Pollnac, R. B., J. J. Poggie, and C. Vandusen
    1995   Cultural-Adaptation to Danger and the Safety of Commercial Oceanic
          Fishermen. Human Organization 54(2):153–59.

Portes, Alejandro, ed.
    1995   Economic Sociology of Immigrants: Essays on Networks, Ethnicity and
          Entrepreneurship. New York: Russell Sage Foundation.

Price, Robert
    1997   Race and Reconciliation in the New South Africa. Politics and Society 25:149–
          79.

Pulfrich, A. and C.L. Griffiths
    1988   The Fishery for Hottentot *Pachymetopon blochii* in the South-Western Cape.
          South African Journal of Marine Science 7:227–41.

Rabinow, Paul
    1986   Representations are Social Facts: Modernity and Post-modernity in
          Anthropology. *In* Rereading Cultural Anthropology. G. Marcus, ed. pp. 234–61.
          Durham, NC: Duke University Press.

Radcliffe-Brown, A. R.
    1922   The Andaman Islanders: A Study in Social Anthropology (Anthony Wilkin
          studentship research, 1906). Cambridge: The University Press.
    1952   Structure and Function in Primitive Society. London: Oxford University Press.
    1958   Method in Social Anthropology. Chicago: University of Chicago Press.

Ram, Kalpa
    1991   Mukkuvar Women: Gender, Hegemony, and Capitalist Transformation of a
          South Indian Fishing Community. London: Zed Books.

Ramphele, Mamphela
    1996   Treading the Thorny Path to Equity. *In* Now that We Are Free: Coloured
          Communities in a Democratic South Africa. W. James and D. Caliguire, eds. pp.
          83–92. London: Lynne Reinner Publishers.

Rappaport, Roy A.
    1984   Pigs for the Ancestors: Ritual in the Ecology of a New Guinea People. New
          Haven: Yale University Press.

Ricoeur, Paul
    1971   The Model of the Text: Meaningful Action Considered as Text. Social Research
          38:529–62.

Ridd, Rosemary, Helen Callaway, and University of Oxford. Women's Studies Committee
    1987   Women and Political Conflict: Portraits of Struggle in Times of Crisis. New
          York: New York University Press.

Robben, Antonius Cornelis Maria
    1986   Sons of the Sea Goddess: An Interpretive Study of Brazilian Fishermen: Thesis
          (Ph.D. in Anthropology). Berkeley, University of California.

Roediger, David R.
    1991   The Wages of Whiteness: Race and the Making of the American Working Class.
          London: Verso.

Roelofse, Anton and James F. Gates
      2000   Interview with Anton Roelofse, director of the Marine Investments branch of
              Business Partners (formerly the Small Business Development Corporation).
Romanucci-Ross, Lola
      1995   Matrices of an Italian Identity. *In* Ethnic Identity: Creation, Conflict and
              Accommodation. L. Ross-Romanucci and G.A. De Vos, eds. pp. 73–96. Walnut
              Creek, CA: AltaMira Press.
Romanucci-Ross, Lola and George A. De Vos
      1995   Ethnic Identity: Creation, Conflict, and Accommodation. Walnut Creek, CA:
              AltaMira Press.
Rook, K.S.
      1984   The Negative Side of Social Interaction: Impact on Psychological Well-Being.
              Journal of Personality and Social Psychology 46:1097–108.
Roosen, Eugeen
      1989   Creating Ethnicity: The Process of Ethnogenesis. London: Sage.
Rousseau, Jean Jacques
      1964   The First and Second Discourses. Roger D. Masters and Judith R. Masters, transl.
              Volume 1. New York: St. Martin's Press.
Sacks, Boris and Bella Silverman
      1993   Before Memories Grow Dim: The Story of a Family Business. Cape Town:
              National Book Printers.
Sanders, Jimmy and Victor Nee
      1996   Immigrant Self-Employment: The Family as Social Capital and the Value of
              Human Capital. American Sociological Review 61:231–49.
Sanjek, R.
      1971   Brazilian Racial Terms: Some Aspects of Meaning and Learning. American
              Anthropologist 73:1126–143.
Sauer, W.H.H., A.J. Penney, C. Erasmus, B.Q. Mann, S.L. Brouwer, S. J. Lamberth, and T.J.
Stewart
      1997   An Evaluation of Attitudes and Responses to Monitoring and Management
              Measures for the South African Boat-Based Linefishery. South African Journal
              of Marine Science 18:147–63.
Scheper-Hughes, Nancy
      1987   Child Survival: Anthropological Perspectives on the Treatment and Maltreatment
              of Children. Boston: D. Reidel.
      1995   The Primacy of the Ethical: Propositions for a Militant Anthropology. Current
              Anthropology 36(3):409–20.
Schneider, Harold K.
      1974   Economic Man: The Anthropology of Economics. New York: Free Press.
Schutte, De Wet
      1993   A Study of the Development Potential of Selected Fishing Communities on the
              West and South Coasts. Cape Town: Human Sciences Research Council.
Scott, John
      1991   Social Network Analysis: A Handbook. London: Sage Publications Ltd.
Small, Adam
      1960   Die Eerste Steen? Kaapstad: Haum.
      1962   Kitaar My Kruis. Kaapstad: Pretoria.
      1965   Kanna Hy Kô Hystoe: 'N Drama. Kaapstad: Tafelberg.
      1971   A Brown Afrikaner Speaks: A Coloured Poet and Philosopher Looks Ahead.
              Pasadena: Munger Africana Library.

Smith, Adam
    1905   The Wealth of Nations. New York: P.F. Collier & Sons.

Smith, Court
    1991   Patterns of Wealth Concentration. Human Organization 50(1):50–60.

Smith, Court and Suzanna S. Hanna
    1993   Occupation and Community as Determinants of Fishing Behaviors. Human Organization 52(3):299–303.

Smith, M. Estellie
    1977   Those Who Live from the Sea: A Study in Maritime Anthropology. St. Paul: West Publishing Co.

    1989   The Informal Economy. *In* Economic Anthropology. S. Plattner, ed. pp. 292–317. Stanford, CA: Stanford University Press.

Smith, Suzanna and Michael Jepson
    1993   Big Fish, Little Fish: Politics and Power in the Regulation of Florida's Marine Resources. Social Problems 40:39–49.

Smith, Suzanna, Michael Jepson, and Gary Lee
    1993   Rethinking the Environment as Gendered Space. Annual Meeting of the Rural Sociological Society, Orlando, FL. *unpublished.*

South Africa Committee of Inquiry into Fishermen's Community Trusts
    1994   Report of the Committee of Inquiry into Fishermen's Community Trusts. Cape Town: The Ministry of Environment Affairs and Tourism.

Spencer, Herbert
    1873   The Study of Sociology. New York: D. Appleton.

Statistics Council, Minister of Finance
    1996   The People of South Africa: Population Census, 1996. South Africa.

Stibbe, George and Iain Moss
    1998   A Traditional Way of Life: The Story of the Kalk Bay Fishermen. Cape Town: National Book Printers.

Stuttaford, M., ed.
    1996   Fishing Industries Handbook: South Africa, Namibia and Mozambique. Volume 24. Stellenbosch: Marine Information cc.

    1998   Fishing Industries Handbook: South Africa, Namibia and Mozambique. Volume 26. Stellenbosch: Marine Information cc.

    1999   Fishing Industry Handbook: South Africa, Namibia and Mozambique. Volume 27. Cape Town: Exbury Publications.

Subsistence Fisheries Task Group
    2000   Draft Recommendations for Subsistence Fisheries Management in South Africa. Cape Town: Subsistence Fisheries Task Group.

Suggot, Mungo
    1997   The Bizarre World of Apartheid's Mad Scientists. *In* Mail and Guardian. pp. A1,6. Johannesburg.

Taylor, Mark C.
    1984   Erring: A Postmodern Theology. Chicago: University of Chicago Press.

Thompson, Leonard
    1949   The Cape Coloured Franchise. *In* South African Institute of Race Relations, New Africa Pamphlet No. 20. Cape Town: Peninsula Press Ltd.

    1995   A History of South Africa. New Haven: Yale University Press.

Thompson, P.
    1985   Women in Fishing: The Roots of Power Between the Sexes. Comparative Studies in Society and History 27:3–32.

Tredgold, Arderne
    1965   Village of the Sea: The Story of Hermanus. Cape Town: Human & Rousseau.
    1985   Bay Between the Mountains. Cape Town: Human & Rousseau.
Turner, J.W.
    1991   A Trojan Horse?: The Impact of Commercial Fishing on Melanesian Societies, a
            Case From Papua New Guinea. *In* Small-scale Fishery Development:
            Sociocultural Perspectives. J.J. Poggie and R.B. Pollnac, eds. Kingston, RI:
            International Center for Marine Resource Development.
Uchendu, Victor C.
    1995   The Dilemma of Ethnicity and Polity Primacy in Black Africa. *In* Ethnic Identity:
            Creation, Conflict and Accommodation. L. Romanucci-Ross and G.A. De Vos,
            eds. pp. 125–35. Walnut Creek, CA: AltaMira Press.
Vail, LeRoy
    1993   The Creation of Tribalism in South Africa. Claremont: David Philip.
Van den Berghe, Pierre L.
    1978   Race and Racism: A Comparative Perspective. New York: Wiley.
Van der Elst, Rudy
    1981   A Guide to the Common Sea Fishes of Southern Africa. Cape Town: C. Struik
            Publishers.
Van der Ross, R.E.
    1979   Myths and Attitudes: An Inside Look at the Coloured People. Cape Town:
            Tafelbert Publishers Ltd.
Van Onselen, Charles
    1996   The Seed is Mine: The Life of Kas Maine, a South African Sharecropper, 1894–
            1985. New York: Hill and Wang.
Van Sittert, Lance
    1992   Labour, Captial and the State in the St. Helena Bay Fisheries c. 1856–1956.
            Ph.D. Dissertation, University of Cape Town. *unpublished.*
Van Tonder, Deon
    1993   Boycotts, Unrest, and the Western Areas Removal Scheme, 1949–1952. Journal
            of Urban History 20(1/November):19–54.
Venter, A.L.J.
    1974   Coloured: A Profile of Two Million South Africans. Cape Town: Human &
            Rousseau.
Verheye, Hans M., ed.
    1998   Sea Fisheries Research Institute Research Highlights 1997–1998. Volume 7.
            Cape Town: Department of Environmental Affairs and Tourism.
Wade, Peter
    1995   Blackness and Race Mixture: The Dynamics of Racial Identity in Colombia.
            Baltimore: Johns Hopkins University Press.
Walker, Michael
    1999   Coastal Memories: Muizenberg, St. James, and Kalk Bay 1870–1920. Cape
            Town: Michael Walker.
Wallerstein, Immanuel
    1974   The Modern World System. New York: Academic Press.
    1979   The Capitalist World-Economy: Essays. Cambridge: Cambridge University
            Press.
Walsh, A.C. and J. Simonelli
    1986   Migrant Women in the Field: The Functions of Social Networks. Human
            Organization 45:43–52.

Warman, George, ed.
  1999   Fishing Industry Handbook, South Africa, Namibia and Mocambique: The
          Authoritative Work of Reference for the Fishing Industry. Volume 27. Cape
          Town: Exbury Publications.

Wasserman, Stanley and Katherine Faust
  1994   Social Network Analysis: Methods and Applications. New York: Oxford
          University Press.

Weber, Max
  1968   Economy and Society: An Outline of Interpretive Sociology. 3 vols. Roth,
          Guenther, Wittich, Claus, transl. New York: Bedminster Press.

Wegener, Bernd
  1991   Job Mobility and Social Ties: Social Resources, Prior Job and Status Attainment.
          American Sociological Review 56(1):60–72.

Whisson, M. G.
  1971   The Coloured People. *In* South Africa's Minorities. P. Randall, ed. pp. 46–77.
          The Study Project on Christianity in Apartheid Society. Vol. 2. Johannesburg:
          SPRO-CAS.

Wilcox, S. and J.R. Udry
  1986   Autism and Accuracy in Adolescent Perceptions of Friend's Sexual Attitudes and
          Behavior. Journal of Applied Social Psychology 4:361–74.

Wilk, Richard R.
  1996   Economies and Cultures: Foundations of Economic Anthropology. Boulder, CO:
          Westview Press.

Wissler, Clark
  1922   The American Indian: An Introduction to the Anthropology of the New World.
          New York: Oxford University Press.

Wolf, E.R.
  1982   Europe and the People Without History. Berkeley: University of California Press.
  1994   Facing Power: Old Insights, New Questions. *In* Assessing Cultural
          Anthropology. R. Barofsky, ed. pp. 218–28. New York: McGraw-Hill, Inc.

Worden, Nigel and Clifton Crais
  1994   Breaking the Chains: Slavery and Its Legacy in the Nineteenth-Century Cape
          Colony. Johannesburg: Witwatersrand University Press.

Yelvington, Kevin A.
  1993   Trinidad Ethnicity. London: Macmillan Caribbean.
  1995   Producing Power: Ethnicity, Gender, and Class in a Caribbean Workplace.
          Philadelphia: Temple University Press.

Young, Crawford
  1994   The African Colonial State in Comparative Perspective. New Haven: Yale
          University Press.

Young, Robert
  1995   Colonial Desire: Hybridity in Theory, Culture and Race. London: Routledge.

Zerner, C.
  1991   Sharing the Catch in Mandar: Changes in an Indonesian Raft Fishery (1970–
          1989). *In* Small-Scale Fishery Development: Sociocultural Perspectives. J.J.
          Poggie and R.B. Pollnac, eds. Kingston, RI: International Center for Marine
          Resource Development.

Zimmer, Catherine and Howard E. Aldrich
  1987   Resource Mobilization through Ethnic Networks: Kinship and Friendship Ties of
          Shopkeepers in England. Sociological Perspectives 30:422–55.

BIOGRAPHICAL SKETCH

James F. Gates, known to friends and family as Jamie, was born in Boston, Massachusetts on the 26th of January, 1971. Born on a college campus, the first few years of his life were spent accompanying his parents as his father pursued his formal education. He grew up as the son of a preacher man. He was in part raised by the Church of the Nazarene, a denomination that is known for ministering to those from the other side of the railroad tracks. In 1979 the Gates left their small Alloway, New Jersey congregation to take an assignment as missionaries among the Ndebele of South Africa. Except for the 1983–84 US academic year, Jamie attended South African public schools, first in the predominantly Afrikaans-speaking farming town of Groblersdal in the province then known as the Transvaal. His parents' choice not to send their kids to English-speaking boarding schools meant that he and his sister, Heather, quickly enculturated, becoming the only "Yanks" in the area to speak Afrikaans as well as any other grade-schoolers. In 1986 the family moved to Johannesburg's West Rand, to Roodepoort. Jamie finished his high school years at the English-speaking West Ridge High School.

With roots in a deeply religious family, Jamie returned to the city of his birth to pursue his Bachelor's degree at Eastern Nazarene College (ENC), double-majoring in Psychology and Relgion. His senior thesis was entitled "The Intersection of Psychology and Theology" and involved a theoretical exploration of themes commonly explored in both disciplines. Jamie attended ENC from 1988–1992. On June 13, 1992 Jamie was married to Michelle L. Krebs of York, Pennsylvania.

Jamie continued his education at Nazarene Theological Seminary (NTS) in Kansas City, Missouri. Graduating with a Master's of Divinity, Honors Program, he majored in Theology and

Social Philosophy. His Master's Thesis was entitled "The Role of Women in the Oscillating Migrant Labor System of Southern Africa." He attended NTS from 1992–1995.

On March 13, 1996 Jamie and Michelle welcomed their first child, Charisa Elieson, into their lives. She was born while Jamie and Michelle were living in Kansas City preparing for Graduate School. On November 13, 1997 Jamie and Michelle welcomed Anthony Charles into their lives. Charisa and Anthony provided most of the healthy distractions and comic relief necessary for maintaining sanity during graduate school.

In 1996 Jamie was awarded the Pew Younger Scholar's Fellowship, a three-year full graduate stipend portable to any of the top schools in his chosen discipline. Jamie chose to pursue his Ph.D. in cultural anthropology at the University of Florida (UF). He attended UF from 1996–2001.

I certify that I have read this study and that in my opinion it conforms to acceptable standards of scholarly presentation and is fully adequate, in scope and quality, as a dissertation for the degree of Doctor of Philosophy.

Brian M. du Toit, Chair
Professor of Anthropology

I certify that I have read this study and that in my opinion it conforms to acceptable standards of scholarly presentation and is fully adequate, in scope and quality, as a dissertation for the degree of Doctor of Philosophy.

R. Hunt Davis
Professor of History

I certify that I have read this study and that in my opinion it conforms to acceptable standards of scholarly presentation and is fully adequate, in scope and quality, as a dissertation for the degree of Doctor of Philosophy.

Anthony Oliver-Smith
Professor of Anthropology

I certify that I have read this study and that in my opinion it conforms to acceptable standards of scholarly presentation and is fully adequate, in scope and quality, as a dissertation for the degree of Doctor of Philosophy.

Suzanna Smith
Professor of Sociology

This dissertation was submitted to the Graduate Faculty of the Department of Anthropology in the College of Liberal Arts and Sciences and to the Graduate School and was accepted as partial fulfillment of the requirements for the degree of Doctor of Philosophy

May 2001

Dean, Graduate School

LD
1780
20 _ol_

.6259

UNIVERSITY OF FLORIDA

3 1262 08556 6486

LD
1780
20 01

.6259

UNIVERSITY OF FLORIDA

3 1262 08556 6486

CPSIA information can be obtained
at www.ICGtesting.com
Printed in the USA
BVHW011433100619
550611BV00002B/303/P